MW01098219

MONTH-BY-MONTH GARDENING

PRAIRIE & PLAINS STATES

Quarto is the authority on a wide range of topics.

Quarto educates, entertains and enriches the lives of
our readers—enthusiasts and lovers of hands-on living.

www.quartoknows.com

© 2016 Quarto Publishing Group USA Inc.

First published in 2016 by Cool Springs Press, an imprint of Quarto Publishing Group USA Inc., 400 First
Avenue North, Suite 400, Minneapolis, MN 55401 USA. Telephone: (612) 344-8100 Fax: (612) 344-8692

quartoknows.com
Visit our blogs at quartoknows.com

Cool Springs Press titles are also available at discounts in bulk quantity for industrial or sales-promotional use.
For details contact the Special Sales Manager at Quarto Publishing Group USA Inc., 400 First Avenue North,
Suite 400, Minneapolis, MN 55401 USA.

Library of Congress Cataloging-in-Publication Data

Barash, Cathy Wilkinson, 1949- author.
    Prairie & plains states month-by-month gardening : what to do each month to have a beautiful garden
        all year / Cathy Wilkinson Barash.
    Minneapolis, MN : Cool Springs Press, 2016.
    Includes index.
    ISBN: 978-1-59186-649-7 (pb)
    1. Gardening--United States. I. Prairie and plains states month by month gardening.
    SB453 .B355 2016
    635.0973--dc23
                        2015040352

    LC record available at http://lccn.loc.gov/2015040352

Acquiring Editor: Billie Brownell
Project Manager: Sherry Anisi
Art Director: Brad Springer
Layout: S. E. Anglin

Printed in China

10 9 8 7 6 5 4 3 2 1

MONTH-BY-MONTH GARDENING

PRAIRIE & PLAINS STATES

**What to Do Each Month to Have
a Beautiful Garden All Year**

CATHY WILKINSON BARASH

COOL
SPRINGS
PRESS
Home and Garden Experts™

MINNEAPOLIS, MINNESOTA

Dedication

This book is dedicated to my mother and father, May and Fritz Wilkinson, who instilled in me from a very young age the love of gardening, a respect for all life, the appreciation of the beauty that surrounds us, and the pleasure that comes from enjoying the fruits of the harvest—both ornamental and edible. I only wish they were here to see the gardener and person I am now and will continue to become.

To my aunt, Toodie (Wilkinson Walt) Powell, who lived and gardened in southern California (Zone 10b) her entire life until 2013 when, at age 87, she remarried and moved to the mountains of western North Carolina (Zone 6a). She is enthusiastically learning to garden in an entirely different climate ("There's nothing but gray and brown in winter!")—and shoveling snow too. What an inspiration! I am looking forward to a family reunion to celebrate her ninetieth birthday in 2016.

And to Rizz Arthur Dean, for whom I created my first month-by-month gardening calendar: the eighteen years I lived in a wing of her house and gardened on her property were full of creativity and wonder. Thank you, Rizz, for your kind generosity and gentle spirit.

Acknowledgments

There are so many people who have helped me—not only on this book in particular but also on the road of lifelong gardening that led to it. Thank you, all.

The Garden Writers Association (GWA)—as a group and individual members—for all the friendships, contacts, and knowledge everyone generously and unflaggingly continues to share.

My gratitude to the gardeners (who I define as anyone who puts hands in the soil and grows things—no training needed) I've met throughout the prairie and plains states. They generously showed me their gardens, taught me how to adapt and garden in this region, introduced me to a whole new world of plants, and shared their experiences and knowledge, which, in turn, have fed and enriched me tremendously.

Special thanks to Susan Howell, Danielle Heltzel, and the Monday Meditation Group (Pat Deaton, Penny Forest, Lynda and David Haupert, and Pam Kvitne), who helped me keep body and mind together. Without them, I could not have finished this book.

My deepest thanks to Billie Brownell for giving me the opportunity to write this book, continuing and expanding on what I learned writing *Month-by-Month Gardening in the Prairie Lands* 12 years ago. I am doubly grateful to have Billie as my editor. Her eagle-eye, insight, compassion, and guidance—not to mention excellent editing— have been stellar.

Last, but not least, I am eternally grateful for my constant companions, who inspire laughter, demand attention, and provide love and purrs—Tiarella, Bogart, and Pause.

Contents

Introduction

For 18 years I was a caretaker on a 14-acre "estate" on Long Island, New York. Fortunately, much of the land was woodland. In addition, there was a 1,200-foot-long beach, yet there was still enough to keep me busy. Surveying the property after my first two years, I realized that my timing for various activities had been off—not to mention the things I forgot to do. The first year I had an excuse; I was new, just getting the feel of all that was there and what needed to be done—and the best time to do it. The second year, I remembered some of the tasks I had overlooked the previous year and forgot about some of the ones I had done. I jotted down notes of things to do and tasks forgotten, but it was a mass of scraps of paper.

I had to get organized. I got a large, blank (no specific year) month-by-month calendar and started entering the various tasks I needed to do—week by week. Some were not date dependent but relied on the weather for timing. I entered those in the approximate time—in a different color ink. Other jobs repeated and some went through the entire growing season; they too were marked in yet another color. I went through each scrap of paper, entering the activity on the calendar. When I was done, my desk was a lot neater, and I didn't have to worry about my cat playing in the memo scraps, losing some vital task.

As I went through the gardening season, I tweaked some of the dates, added and deleted various tasks. By the third winter, I was ready to make what I thought was my "ultimate updated garden calendar." When I moved from Des Moines, Iowa, that calendar was in my carry-on luggage.

GARDEN REALITY

The reality of gardening in most of the prairie and plains states is that the outdoor growing season is compressed into about five months—if you're lucky (except for the gardeners in Zones 7 and 8, who have a bonus month). Mid- to late spring is the busiest time of year for gardeners: repairing winter damage, waking up the garden, amending soil, digging new beds, planting, mulching, pruning . . . the tasks go on. It is so easy to get caught up with one activity that another one inadvertently falls by the wayside. So although it may slack off outdoors from mid-fall to early spring, that's the time to recoup your energy, get organized, and plan for the next growing season. This book is your key to doing just that—and more.

Since I had moved from Zone 7 to Zone 5, acid to alkaline soil, rich loam to rich clay, a lot of the information in my calendar didn't apply. Yet I found that if I moved everything listed on the calendar ahead by one month, I was close to the target dates for central Iowa. How I wish I had a book like this when I started working on the Long Island estate. It would have saved me an immense amount of time and eliminated two years' worth of aggravation. That garden would have been in tip-top shape from the beginning.

This book is so superior to my first gardening calendar. Rather than having to look at small handwriting on a wall calendar and decipher the color codes, it's quick and easy to turn to the month to see what should be done. It is so helpful to turn to each of the task lists—Plan, Plant, Care, Water, Fertilize, and Problem-Solve—and then look at the plant type—Annuals & Biennials, Bulbs, Edibles, Lawns, Perennials & Ornamental Grasses, Trees & Shrubs, and Vines & Groundcovers—to see exactly what needs to be done. If it has been raining for a week, you don't have to look at the Water section, but you'll want to know what you should be fertilizing. For me, a big advantage of this book is that the to-do list provides the information for the month, rather than an entry on a single day, making it much easier to visualize what you need to do.

Although in some months the when-to and to-do lists may be long, it actually seems like you're

Winters may be long, but they allow time for planning what you want to do in the upcoming months.

doing less garden work as it's easier with similar tasks grouped together—Plant, Fertilize, Water, and so on. In addition, this organization simplifies journaling.

WEATHER CONDITIONS

Before I was transplanted to Iowa 18 years ago, I had been warned about the winters—a month or more with no sun, endless days when the mercury climbs *up to* -20 degrees Fahrenheit. So I was ready to meet winter head-on. However, not a single soul mentioned that the summers are often unbearably hot and humid (yet can be dry with meager rain except for "severe weather" in this land of tornadoes and hailstorms). Nor was there a single whisper about the wind. Yet these are the basic elements you have to deal with in creating any garden in the prairie and plains states. As challenging as it may be, when it all comes together, the reward seems even sweeter. Take a long drive through the countryside, and you'll see the splendid and varied gardens that people have successfully created. I'd bet that those charming, small, front-yard gardens on farms are not mollycoddled.

This is a region of extremes. As people say, "If you don't like the weather, wait and it will change within the hour." Winter can mean the first snow in October before the trees have shed their leaves, ice storms, blizzards, and temperatures in the -30s. Or it could be so balmy that you're cutting roses to grace the Christmas table or dry and windy so that plants desiccate.

Spring is a tease—a few warm days so the buds on early-blooming trees and shrubs swell, followed by a 60-degree drop in temperature. This can be a season of drought or floods; if the winter was dry and spring rains are heavy, water doesn't have a chance to seep into the ground. Suddenly, it seems that everything explodes into bloom at once—lilacs and daffodils, redbuds and tulips, forsythia and violets—a veritable phantasmagoria of flowers. The edibles burst forth—asparagus and lettuce, arugula and morels.

Severe weather marks the transition of spring into summer, bringing formidable storms that may be accompanied by lightning, hail, torrential rains, and maybe even tornados. It can also be a time of flooding. Summer, too, is capricious—days when the temperature and humidity flirt with three-digit readings interspersed with gorgeous blue sky days, low humidity, and temperatures in the 70s.

Fall can be frustratingly short or delightfully long. Some years it seems that summer segues right into winter. In other years, the first frost may be early, followed by an extended Indian summer. Relish each day, as the respite ends too soon, and the bleakness of winter descends.

It's amazing that plants can acclimate themselves to such a barrage of diverse weather conditions, yet many do. In our ever-changeable climate, it pays to be tough: either it grows or it doesn't. And if it doesn't, it becomes compost.

One of the first gardening tenets I learned as a child was not to bemoan a dead plant. Unless it's diseased, any garden casualty goes on the compost pile where it will decompose over time, transforming into rich compost—gardener's gold. In turn, the compost is added to the soil, feeding it so that new plants can be well nourished. It's all part of the circle of life. Since moving to Iowa, I've made a lot of compost, which in turn has made my clay soil much richer and more aerated with better drainage.

SOIL CONDITIONS

Although some people use the words soil and dirt interchangeably, to my way of thinking, soil is what is in the garden—the nourishing medium into which we put our plants. Soil is living matter; a

■ Top: *Sandy soil does not hold together when you squeeze it and water runs right through it.* Center: *Clay soil compresses, holding its shape when squeezed, not allowing moisture to get through.* Bottom: *Loam is ideal—a mix of sand, clay, and silt that holds together lightly but easily breaks apart when squeezed.*

variety of biological, chemical, and physical forces are constantly at work. You may be surprised to know that soil has five major components: air; living organisms (from microscopic bacteria, fungi, and bacteria to earthworms and insects—both good and bad); humus (organic material in varying states of decay); water; and inorganic particles of minerals and rocks.

Dirt, on the other hand, is the result of working a day in the garden. It's what's smeared on my face and ground in under my nails; it's in every corrugation of my sneakers, leaving muddy tracks on the carpet. It shows up so well on the back of my pants, where I habitually wipe my hands, or on the sides of my waist, a reminder of my pose of great concentration. Whatever you want to call it—soil or dirt—you want to know what you have to start with.

Determining your soil type can be high tech (expensive) or low tech (dirt cheap). A simple test done right in the garden will get you off to a good start. Gently squeeze a small amount of soil in your hand, and then rub it between your fingers.

Sandy soil is comprised of the largest particles, does not stay together when squeezed, and is gritty to the touch. Sandy soil is easy to work. It also drains very well—almost too well. Water moves quickly and easily through sandy soil, draining off most of the nutrients.

Clay (sometimes called heavy soil) absorbs and holds a tremendous amount of moisture. Its particles are so fine that it holds its shape when compressed. However, the fine texture of clay soil does not let air or moisture move through it.

Silt is midway in particle size between sand and clay, with a smooth texture. Silt can be squeezed together but does not remain compacted, even when it's dry.

The ideal garden soil is **loam**—a mixture of the three types. Rub it between your fingers and it breaks up into smaller particles. Loam holds moisture well and encourages the biological activity necessary for healthy, living soil.

KNOWING YOUR SOIL'S pH IS KEY

No discussion of soil is complete without talking about pH, which is a measurement of alkalinity and acidity, ranging from 0 (most acid) to 14 (most alkaline), with 7.0 as neutral. If the soil pH is not right for a particular plant, it cannot get the nutrients it needs from the soil. There are simple kits for home pH testing. Your local Cooperative Extension Service offers pH testing for a small fee, as do some nurseries and garden centers. Knowing the pH of the soil and the requirement of the plants leads

to the next step—changing the soil pH. Add elemental sulfur (applied according to package directions) to make the soil more acidic or granular limestone to make the soil more alkaline (sweet).

In many regions within the prairie and plains states, the soil is rich and dark as can be because what is now land was the bed of a great inland sea millions of years ago. The soil is generally on the alkaline side, with a pH of about 7.5, varying from rich loam to clay, with some rocky and even sandy areas. In general, our soil is rich.

HARDINESS ZONES

The USDA Hardiness Zone Map, a publication of the United States Department of Agriculture, originally came out more than 40 years ago. After many years of studying the records of winter temperatures (collected from agricultural colleges and Cooperative Extension reports), the original map was compiled. It consisted of ten hardiness zones, based on the lowest *average* winter temperatures; the difference between one zone and the next is 10 degrees. The lower the zone number, the chillier the winter lows. The map was a remarkable tool for farmers and gardeners alike. For example, with a quick glance at the map, I could see that Des Moines was on the cusp of Zones 4 and 5, which would have an average minimum temperature between -30 and -20 degrees Fahrenheit. Zone 3 was 10 degrees chillier—between -30 to -40 Faherenheit, while Zone 5 seemed almost balmy at -10 to -20 degrees.

Plant growers caught on, as did books about plants and gardening; suddenly, there was much less trial and error involved in growing plants. In 1990, the map was revised. In general, the demarcations were the same, with the northern half of both Iowa and Nebraska in Zone 4 and the southern sections in Zone 5. However, they divided each zone, calling them A and B, so the increments between each of these was only 5 degrees.

In 2012, the USDA issued a new map based on data collected from 1986 to 2005, and it expanded to 13 zones (to include Hawaii and Puerto Rico). What is remarkable to me is how within that time, the average minimum temperatures have risen. Most of Iowa is now Zone 5, with only small patches of Zone 4 dotted in the northern regions.

All the other states featured in this book have warmed too. The new map is interactive: go online, enter your zip code, and get local information at www.planthardiness.ars.usda.gov/PHZMWeb/#. Turn to page 19 to see the state maps.

In addition to knowing your hardiness zone, before you plant it is helpful to know the **last frost date**. That is the date in spring *after which it is unlikely* that the temperature will go below 32 degrees Fahrenheit. The **first frost date** is the date in fall *before which it is unlikely* that the temperature will dip below freezing. Go to www.davesgarden.com/guides/freeze-frost-dates/#b for the best interactive feature. Enter your zip code and it will give you the first and last frost dates, including the probability for hard freeze and light frost (24 versus 32 degrees Fahrenheit).

MICROCLIMATES

Knowing what will grow well for you is just a matter of looking up your hardiness zone, right? Nope. No doubt you've noticed that some areas of your yard and garden are warmer than others—against or near a south-facing wall, protected by the hardscape or large stones. There are also cooler spots—the north-facing side of the house, exposed and open areas, as well as low-lying spaces. These are *microclimates*.

Employ microclimates to your advantage. For example, if a plant is questionably hardy in your zone, site it in one of the warmer places. Conversely, if you live in Zone 8 Oklahoma, and the plant you want to grow is hardy to Zone 7, place it where it will be kept cooler by shade or breezes. When considering the microclimate, take into account the soil type and drainage before you plant. It is one thing to have a plant merely survive; you want your plants to thrive!

PLANNING YOUR GARDEN

After learning what type of soil you have to work with, it's time to make a major decision—one that will determine what direction your garden will take. The choices are: live with the soil you have and grow plants that thrive in that environment, or amend the soil to meet the particular needs of the

plants. Or, you could do a little of each, making your all-over landscape more varied—plants that survive boggy conditions where it is clayey, succulents and cacti (prickly pear cactus, *Opuntia humifusa*, is extremely hardy) where it's driest, and plantings in loam for the rest of the garden.

A big part of the planning process is research. To learn what will grow well for you, visit friends and neighbors—see what's growing in their yards. If you see something that catches your eye, ask about the plant. Take pictures with your smartphone and keep a pocket-sized notebook to take down notes (or keep those in your phone too). Not only will your friends and neighbors be impressed, you'll remember and do what they suggest.

When seeking advice and ideas, your nearest botanical garden or arboretum is a great resource. Plan to make a day of it. Bring along your smartphone or camera to take some pictures or

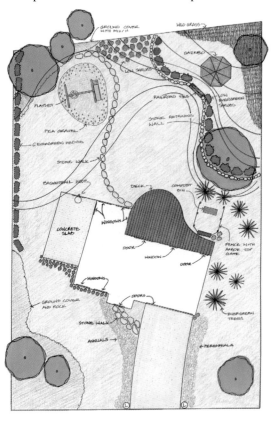

■ *A site map identifies existing plantings, buildings, and other elements on your property. Make changes to it as needed.*

videos to refresh your memory later. And by all means, go with someone else—to share the beauty and to have another set of eyes to see things you may overlook. Go on garden tours in your locale to get some inspiration and fresh ideas.

Your local Cooperative Extension Service (despite budget cuts) is *the* local authority about what you can grow successfully within your hardiness zone, offering lots of free information, pamphlets, and guidance. It may also offer soil testing and a lab where you can bring in samples of plant problems.

SITE AND SOIL PREPARATION

Soil is the major source of food and water for any plant. Taking the time to choose the proper location (and knowing what your plant requires) is well worth it. The highest quality, most expensive plant, if grown in the wrong soil conditions will die. Conversely, a so-so plant put in ideal growing conditions will, with some TLC, probably thrive. For a majority of plants, the qualities that will help them flourish are good drainage, plenty of humus, and an abundance of nutrients available to the plant.

Good soil contains a large amount of organic matter, an abundance of nutrients that are available to the plant, and has good drainage. Most soils benefit from the addition of organic matter. Turn the soil with a pitchfork or spade, and break up any large clods. Add at least 10 to 15 pounds of compost or well-rotted manure and 2 pounds of rock phosphate (ground up rocks) per 100 square feet. It may be easier, especially if you are putting in a few plants, to simply amend each hole with a couple of handfuls of compost and a half-cup of rock phosphate as you go.

COMPOSTING

I am a strong believer in composting—it saves hauling heavy garbage bags and cuts down on the landfills. I am constantly mixing compost into my soil, which is on the clayey side. Good compost is full of all those wonderful microorganisms that help get the nutrients—vitamins, minerals, and organic matter—from the soil to the plant through the plant's rootlets. Some gardeners call compost "black gold"—it certainly pulls its weight. I *always* amend my soil with compost before I plant. The exception is when I'm planting trees and shrubs, which grow better in unamended soil.

■ *A plastic compost bin like this holds the material, allows for air circulation, and lets rain in.*

■ *Mix green (lawn clippings, garden prunings, and non-animal kitchen waste) and brown (shredded leaves, black-and-white newspaper, and computer printouts) matter to make compost.*

■ *Add a layer of garden soil for microbes that help break down the green and brown matter into compost. Water lightly.*

■ *Turning the compost pile helps speed up the process but is not necessary.*

Composting can be as simple or as complex as you wish. You don't have to follow complicated recipes or spend a lot of money on a fancy tumbling composter. Organic matter rots all on its own. When you compost, you're just organizing the material a bit for more efficient decomposition.

Put the compost bin in a sunny spot and add several inches of soil (the good stuff with lots of worms and microorganisms to get the pile "started"). As you pull up small weeds (if in flower or seed, throw in the trash to avoid growing more weeds from the compost), toss them into the compost. Add healthy garden cuttings—less than ½-inch diameter (larger items take too long to break down; make a brush pile for them); shredded leaves; grass clippings (less than 1 inch of clippings at a time or they can compact and become slimy, preventing water and air from permeating the pile); and all of the non-animal kitchen garbage—vegetable peels, leftover cooked vegetables, coffee grounds, eggshells (the exception to the animal rule), moldy fruit left in the crisper—you get the idea. Also add shredded newsprint (black and white only). When you first get the pile going, water it lightly. After that, rain should supply ample moisture. If the pile dries out, the process slows down. Once you have the compost going, you'll feel less guilty about throwing food out when it's eventually going to enrich your soil. With two bins, you can start the second when the first pile is filled. By the time the second bin is filled, the material in the first will have broken down into black gold. No turning, no muss, no fuss.

SOIL AMENDMENTS

Most soils are not perfect, rich, dark, friable loam. They can benefit from the addition of various materials—organic or inorganic. When you have your soil tested by a lab, you get a breakdown of the nutrients in the soil—with suggestions to correct any deficiencies or excesses. The various amendments affect clay and sandy soils differently. The following list shows what to use for each situation. Be sure to mix the amendments thoroughly into the soil.

CLAY SOIL
- To loosen it, add compost, well-rotted manure, leaf mold, or gypsum dust.
- To improve aeration, add humus, Canadian sphagnum peat moss, or builder's sand (use in combination with one of the organic materials).
- To feed the soil, add compost or leaf mold.

SANDY SOIL
- For more texture and volume, add compost, well-rotted manure, leaf mold, ground bark, or sawdust.
- To aid in water retention, add Canadian sphagnum peat moss, humus, or water-retentive polymer crystals.
- To feed the soil, add compost, humus, well-rotted manure, or leaf mold.

SELECTING PLANTS

If you want only one or two plants of a particular annual, biennial, or perennial, you are best off buying plants locally. They are available in a range of container sizes. A 4- or 6-cell pack is the smallest. Each cell is about a 1-inch square. You can find individual young plants in 3-, 4-, or 6-inch pots or larger. Full-sized plants in a variety of containers, especially hanging baskets, are also available. Obviously, the larger the container, the higher the price. However, if you want instant gratification and need to fill in a hole in the garden, by all means go for the larger pot.

■ *Always choose healthy-looking plants. Avoid plants like this that are rotting.*

Choose the best plant. When selecting plants, look at the bottom of the container for roots coming out through the holes. Avoid these, as they are probably rootbound and likely to be stressed. Although it is tempting to buy a plant in full bloom, choose plants with buds and lots of leaves.

While purchasing the plants, get a container of transplant/starter solution—it's invaluable when planting or transplanting. It consists mainly of vitamins in solution that stimulate root growth. I use it whenever I am planting or transplanting; it can even bring new life to half-dead plants rescued from the sale bin at the end of the season.

PLANTING

The ideal time to plant or transplant is on a cloudy day or late in the afternoon when bright sunlight won't stress the plant. When you are ready to plant, mix up a batch of transplant solution (following label instructions) in a bucket or container deep enough to set the plant in to soak up solution. The amount of solution depends on how many plants you are planting. Allow at least 1½ cups per small plant, 3 cups for 6-inch pots and larger.

■ *If the plant is growing in a peat pot, tear off the pot to just below the soil line.*

■ *Pinch or cut off all the flowers so the plant's energy can go into producing a strong and healthy root system.*

Dig a hole the size and depth of the container. Remove any flowers and buds from the plant. At this time, you want to stimulate root growth; flowers will take away energy from the roots. Dip the container in the transplant solution for about one minute. Gently remove the plant from its pot. If it is rootbound (little visible soil, roots wrapped around each other or coming out of the bottom of the pot), cut the lower ½-inch of roots off, and gently loosen the roots. Set the plant in the hole so that soil level from the pot is even with the soil level of the surrounding soil. You may need to add or remove soil from the hole. Gently firm the plant and surrounding soil with your hands. Water the soil thoroughly with transplant solution.

Despite all good intentions, you may find that the plant is happier moved to a drier or moister, richer or poorer site. Do not be too quick to give up on a plant. The mere act of putting it in the ground is a shock, as it has been moved from one environment to another.

MULCHING AND COMPOST

Mulch is almost as valuable as compost. It keeps the soil temperature more constant, helps retain water, and most of all it keeps weeds out. It's surprising how few gardeners in the prairie and plains states use mulch. Yet, people continue to complain about weeds.

Good mulching (at least 2 inches thick) solves weed problems almost completely. A few noxious weeds may grow up through the mulch, but not many. Plan your garden so there aren't large bare spots between plants so that weed seeds won't have the space or light to germinate.

An organic mulch eventually breaks down, adding humus to the soil, improving soil structure, and providing nutrients. As the lower layer of mulch becomes part of the soil, add a new layer, usually once a year. Mulch in spring, before weeds get a chance to establish themselves.

The material you use is a personal, aesthetic choice. Some mulches have a more formal look while others are more natural. Some are free, while others are pricey—especially for a large area. Options include grass clippings, straw, cocoa hulls, peanut hulls, buckwheat hulls, pine needles, wood chips, wood shavings, sawdust, twice-shredded bark, pine bark nuggets, chopped leaves, well-rotted manure, and ground corn cobs.

■ *Twice-shredded bark makes ideal mulch for trees, shrubs, and woody perennials.*

■ *Gravel (pictured), turkey grit, or sand are the best mulches for succulent plants and Mediterranean herbs such as rosemary, lavender, and thyme.*

■ *Pine straw makes a good mulch for plants that like acidic soil; it slightly lowers the soil's pH as it breaks down.*

In spring, add a layer of compost around your plants, which will feed the soil. Cover the compost with an organic mulch, such as wood chips, twice-shredded bark, grass clippings (no more than 1 inch at a time), or shredded leaves. Each spring renew the mulch, much of which will have broken down into compost itself. If you continue this process, you will have healthy soil, which then grows healthy plants, which in turn are less susceptible to pests and diseases.

Mediterranean herbs, such as thyme, rosemary, lavender, and oregano, don't tolerate wet soil. This also applies to most silver- or gray-leafed plants. They benefit from a mulch that lets water pass through

■ *Potted plants benefit from the proper mulch too. Sand works well for rosemary (pictured) and other Mediterranean herbs.*

quickly—such as sand, turkey grit, gravel, bluestone, pebbles, or river rock. The deciding factors are the size of the plant and your aesthetic taste. The most unique mulch I've seen was potshards—bits of broken terracotta pots—surrounding a large shrub. Not only was it unusual to look at, it kept critters away—and people as well.

LIGHT

Knowing how much light a plant requires is essential for successful gardening. Plant labels indicate the amount of light a plant needs, so it's important to define the terms. **Full sun** is more than six hours a day (including midday); **part sun** is four to six hours (including midday); **part shade** is three to five hours of indirect sun—morning or afternoon. **Shade** is less than three hours of sun. However, you cannot grow plants in complete darkness.

Look at the plant for a clue that you may be doing something wrong. A plant that is leaning toward the sun needs to be moved to where it gets more light. Sun-lovers will have more vivid colors with more light. Conversely, some shade-lovers will wilt in the heat of the day, and colors may fade.

■ *Straw is a utilitarian mulch for vegetable gardens—not much to look at but it's inexpensive, controls weeds, and conserves moisture.*

WATER

All living things—plant or animal—need water. If you live in an area with drought and watering your garden is prohibited or limited, this is not the time to start planting anything new, with the possible exception of cacti and succulents. Right after planting is the crucial time to nurture a plant, giving it the attention and water it needs to develop properly. Once established, a plant with a well-developed root system will be able to fend for itself.

Drip irrigation is the most efficient way to water since the water is released at ground level, where the roots are. It minimizes water loss through evaporation. And by keeping the leaves dry, many fungal diseases can be avoided. You can purchase a kit and make your own custom system, complete with emitters, supply lines, and timers. Systems, whether complicated or simple, are worth the trouble for areas where the soil is not frequently turned and replanted. Another method of watering is to use "leaky" (soaker) hoses. They are made of a material through which water can slowly seep at ground level, near the root zone.

■ *Drip irrigation sends water directly to the roots of plants. New plants can go on either side of the tube.*

Consider getting a rain barrel to collect rain water. Or get several and link them together. Some people are installing underground water storage tanks to keep them going in dry summers. Every little bit of water you can save helps.

FERTILIZE

Test your soil—in different areas throughout your property—and fertilize according to the recommendations from the test.

After planting perennials, trees, or shrubs, do not fertilize until the next spring. If you amended the

■ *Placing a rain barrel on a stand allows you to easily fill a watering can from its spigot.*

soil to suit the plant, it will get ample nutrition. Some annuals and vegetables are heavy feeders. Remember that they need enough energy to grow, flower, fruit, and set seed—all in one growing season.

There are three ways to feed a plant. The first is to feed the soil. If there's plenty of organic matter mixed into the soil (a layer of compost and/or mulch will break down, adding nutrients), many plants don't require supplemental feeding. For those that need more than the soil has to give, you can provide nourishment from two different points of entry: the roots or the leaves.

The second method is traditional fertilizing, which entails spreading powder or granules on the soil, lightly working it into the top layer, and watering well to carry the nutrients down into the soil where the roots draw in the needed nutriments. It *is* possible to add too much fertilizer—especially around a shallow-rooted plant—and burn the roots.

Some traditional fertilizers skip right to the chase: mix the plant food with water and pour the liquid into the soil around the plant. It's as easy as can be, but make sure the dilutions you make are appropriate for the plant you're feeding. Don't use a lawn fertilizer on your roses, cabbage, or mums—and vice versa. Avoid those fertilizers that come in a container that screws onto your hose. The dilutions that come out of the sprayers are not consistent, varying with water pressure and the amount of fertilizer in the container. If there is some left over, what do you do with it?

The third is my preferred method—foliar feeding. Plants can absorb nutrients through their leaves. Fish and kelp emulsions are the most widely used foliar feeds, although teas—compost and manure—are gaining in popularity. Note that the dilutions may change for different plants. Spray diluted foliar food on the leaves—top and bottom—all up and down the stems. Feed early to midday, or you risk a wet plant after the sun goes down, which is a personal invitation for fungus and disease. Never spray if the temperature is above 80 degrees. You'll find more specifics, such as how often to feed, in the "Fertilize" section of each chapter (month).

However you decide to fertilize, be sure to follow the package instructions carefully, When it comes to fertilizers, more is *not* better. Note whether the fertilizer is recommended for the type of plant you are planning to spray. Some aren't recommended for use on edibles. You'll see some "complete" fertilizers advertised, especially for roses and lawns. They may also contain an insecticide, herbicide, and/or pesticide. These are systemics; the plant takes it up through its roots and the entire plant becomes poisonous to its enemies.

PRUNE

For most people, pruning is *the* scariest task in the garden. The fear of cutting off too much and/or killing the plant is very strong. They approach a plant with trepidation. Pruning is one aspect in gardening in which using the proper tool is essential, as is the timing; using the wrong tool or pruning at the wrong time can do more harm to a plant than cutting a bit long or short.

Yet plants benefit from pruning; indeed, some must be pruned to perform well in a cultivated garden. There are three major reasons for pruning: removing dead, diseased, or broken branches; shaping the plant; and stimulating new growth. When you prune, try to keep the natural shape of the plant; no lollipop trees or meatball shrubs, *please*.

A simple rule of thumb for pruning: when in doubt, prune flowering trees and shrubs right after they finish blooming. This works for plants that set their flowers for next year soon after they bloom—you won't be cutting off next

year's flowers. See the Appendix (page 192) for detailed information.

PEST MANAGEMENT

Despite your best efforts, pests may sometimes invade your garden. They come in all shapes and sizes, from the smallest insects to shrub-crunching pests like deer. It's worth spending a half hour once or twice a week doing a garden inspection in order to prevent a minor pest problem from becoming a full-fledged infestation. Stroll around the garden with a cup of tea (iced if it's a very warm day) and look at each plant—tops and bottoms of leaves, stems, flowers, and fruit. It's a productive way to relax in the garden! Many pests can either be handpicked (drop them into a zippered plastic bag) or drowned with a strong stream of water from the hose.

■ *Milky spore is available as a ready-to-mix powder. It controls Japanese beetles, attacking them at the grub (larval) stage.*

TYPES OF PEST CONTROLS
Physical
- Handpicking
- Water spray
- Pinching/pruning
- Traps/lures

Biological
- Predators: birds, ladybugs, green lacewings, predatory mites, soldier bugs, spiders, ants, bats
- Parasitoids: tiny wasps, predatory nematodes
- Pathogens: *Bacillus thuringiensis* (Bt), milky spore disease, fungi
- Genetic modification: built-in Bt, nitrogen-fixing bacteria, resistance to weed killers, hybridization

Chemical
- Mineral: fungicides: sulfur, copper, baking soda, diatomaceous earth (DE)
- Soaps: fatty acids
- Oils: heavy (dormant) oil; light (superior, horticultural) oil
- Botanical poisons: sabadilla, garlic, hot pepper, Neem oil

INTRODUCTION

The only garden that is pest proof is painted concrete. In the real world, planting a diversity of plants usually results in fewer problems than a monoculture (only one type of plant). Including one or two plants that persist through winter (a small tree or shrub, or a dwarf evergreen) offers praying mantis a safe haven for depositing their egg cases. Praying mantis are "good bugs" that eat a prodigious number of aphids, whiteflies, and garden pests.

If you have or suspect a pest or disease problem, it is vital to identify it accurately. Call your local Cooperative Extension Service; it is likely to have a telephone hotline and/or a place to bring plants and pests for identification.

When possible, avoid using any chemicals in the garden. Even the "organic" ones, unless pest-specific, impact all the creatures living in your garden, both good and bad. Being in harmony with your garden and nature is the ideal. Although complete harmony may be a challenge to achieve, the closer you come to it, the better you, your garden, and—in the big picture—the Earth will be. That is what it is all about.

It is reassuring to realize that all green, growing things—whether trees, shrubs, vines, flowers, or vegetables—want to live. None of them comes into your garden with the intention of expiring at the earliest possible opportunity. Nor do they wish to succumb to dreaded diseases, infestations of pests, lack of water, excess of heat or cold, or the depredations of voles, rabbits, or deer. They would rather not be dug up by a cat or trampled and broken by a dog. They propose—indeed prefer—to establish, thrive, flourish, and fruit. With knowledge and care—and this book—you can make this happen.

HOW TO USE THIS BOOK

As a gardener, your responsibility is to cherish and protect the plants you invite into your garden. To fulfill this promise, choose the right plants for the right places. Take into account the right amount and type of light, ample water, and suitable soil for each plant. In addition, it is your duty to fend off predators, whether they are insects, deer, or diseases. This book is your guide to doing this.

Its relatively compact size allows you to start out in one of two ways, depending on the amount of time you have and when you acquire the book. If you have the time or get the book in winter when there are fewer garden tasks, read it completely. This will give you an idea of what's coming in the months ahead. Or you can simply jump in and open it to the current month and get started.

Each month has the same tasks: Plan, Plant, Care, Water, Fertilize, and Problem-Solve. To make it easy to follow, each task lists the different plant types: Annuals & Biennials, Bulbs, Edibles, Lawns, Perennials & Ornamental Grasses, and Trees & Shrubs. That's what makes it so helpful. If, for example, you're *not* growing edibles or don't have a lawn, you can just skip over those parts of each task. By the same token, if you decide to add a plant type, you can jump in that month and know what you should be doing. If the plant type is not listed under a particular task, that means there is nothing to do that month.

I included two different sidebars. The "Here's How To" has step-by-step directions. These range from planting, transplanting, and overwintering specific types of plants to sharpening tools, winterizing various types of equipment, and making a hinged trellis. "Successful Gardening" is tip oriented, including topics from organizing tools, dos and don'ts for bulbs, sharing the bounty, and dealing with thatch, to several recipes for homemade pest and disease controls.

Tracking what has been completed and what still demands attention is straightforward. I write in my books, so I'd make a small check mark next to each task as it is finished. By using a different color ink each year, it's easy to chart accomplishments for several years. (I like the look of different ink colors.)

Please don't let all this talk about tasks overwhelm you. No one says that you must do *everything* on the lists. Armed with this book—and its companion *Prairie & Plains States Getting Started Garden Guide*—you are on the road to a successful garden.

Happy gardening!

USDA PLANT HARDINESS ZONE MAPS

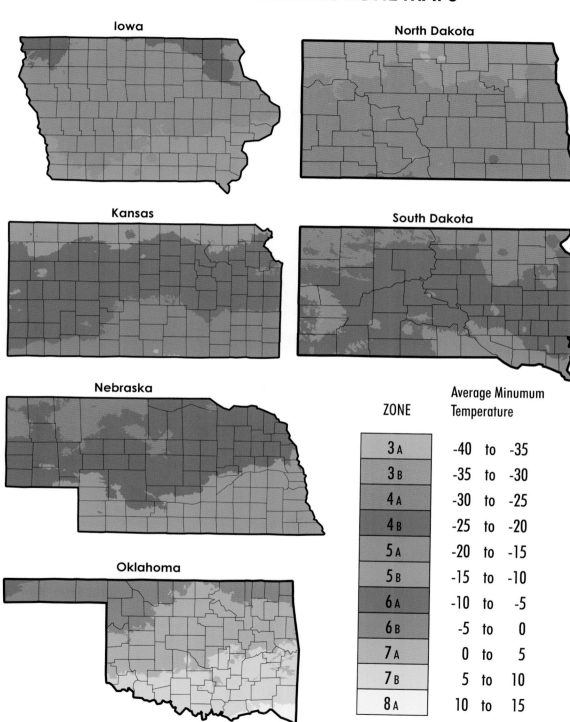

ZONE	Average Minumum Temperature		
3 A	-40	to	-35
3 B	-35	to	-30
4 A	-30	to	-25
4 B	-25	to	-20
5 A	-20	to	-15
5 B	-15	to	-10
6 A	-10	to	-5
6 B	-5	to	0
7 A	0	to	5
7 B	5	to	10
8 A	10	to	15

USDA Plant Hardiness Zone Map, 2012. Agricultural Research Service, U.S. Department of Agriculture. Accessed from http://planthardiness.ars.usda.gov/PHZMWeb/.

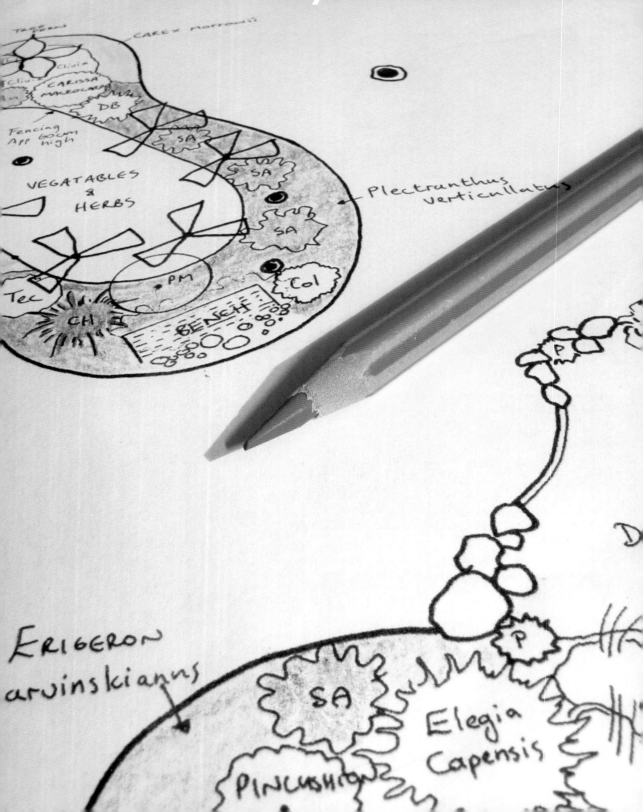

This is a time for thought rather than action as far as the garden is concerned. Planning is this month's keyword. The weather outside may be frightful, but nothing is so delightful as curling up by a fire with the myriad catalogs you receive.

While online catalogs are convenient—and ecologically greener—flipping through printed catalogs, marking pages, and cutting out pictures of your "most wanted" makes choosing plants more fun. Before ordering, go through what you have. Gather your seeds and decide which you'll use. Give unwanted seeds to friends or participate in a seed swap (Seed Swap Day is the last Saturday in January). Go through the catalogs, marking them in your favorite way. Develop a wish list of seeds and plants well suited to *your* growing conditions.

Make a master list to keep track of everything you order (seeds, plants, tools, books, and anything plant-related) to avoid accidentally ordering the same thing more than once.

Review your garden journal, photos, and videos of last year's gardens *before* planning any changes. Do you want to expand existing gardens or add new planting areas? That may *increase* the time you have to spend on maintenance. *Decrease* the time by selecting low-maintenance plants, mulching, sharing the workload with another person, or reducing the planting area. Consider cutting down the size of a single-plant-type garden (annual, perennial, herb, shrub, and so forth) or converting it to a mixed plant area. Integrate beautiful edibles with your ornamentals. Sketch the proposed changes—in general terms, not plant specific. You can add plant names later. Put the drawing aside for a few days and then review your changes.

To get inspired, help plan changes, and work off some holiday excesses, get out and walk around your property and neighborhood. Visit local parks and botanical gardens. Go to home and garden shows as well as flower shows this winter—well worth the price of admission for all the ideas you'll get. Take lots of pictures.

It's cold, the ground may be covered with snow, and the planting season is months away. Do some stretching exercises to keep your gardening muscles limber.

PLAN

ANNUALS & BIENNIALS

Order any seeds that you plan on starting indoors. It will be time to start them soon.

BULBS

Start browsing through catalogs for summer-blooming bulbs, such as cannas, dahlias, calla lilies, lilies (Oriental and Asiatic), tuberous begonias, and gladiolas, that you know you want. There are always new varieties. Look through heirloom bulbs for ones that have stood the test of time. Check the Internet for reputable companies that sell bulbs; you may find some bargains or markdowns. It's likely that you'll fall in love with some bulbs new to you like pineapple lily, galtonia, Chinese summer ground orchid, and triplet lily. Treat yourself and order them—you deserve it. Remember to order enough to pot some up in outdoor containers too.

■ *Buy pre-chilled hyacinths to force in hyacinth glasses. Wrap the base with aluminum foil to prevent algae growth in the water.*

Force some hyacinths. Hyacinth glasses, shaped like hourglasses, are used to force hyacinths in water without soil. A single bulb sits on the top part of the glass, with the bottom of the bulb just above the water that fills the bottom of the glass. This unique method of forcing allows you to see and appreciate the root system of the bulb. Smaller glasses for single crocus and large glasses for amaryllis are available.

EDIBLES

The holidays are over, and tighter clothes signal that it is time to start eating healthy. What better way to do this than to grow your own vegetables, fruit, and herbs? Order any seeds that you'll need to start indoors.

Look around for areas to add some fruit trees, a row of raspberries, or a patch of strawberries. You do not need a lot of space, just some sunlight and creative planning. If you have lost a tree or shrub, or if one is not performing well, replace it with an edible fruit tree.

Think beyond green-leafed plants for color interest. Some herbs have variegated forms—a green leaf edged or spotted with cream or white. Pineapple mint has lovely cream-and-green variegated leaves. Bronze fennel is prized for its graceful bronzy foliage, which looks like ponytails when it starts to come out in spring. Other interesting plants with purple- and bronze-colored leaves include basils, cabbage, lettuce, orach, perilla, and sage.

LAWNS

Consider your options if lawn care was too demanding last year. Reduce the size of the lawn and replace it with a low-maintenance or more productive alternative (you can grow $750 of vegetables in 100 square feet—a 5×20-foot area reclaimed from lawn). Or hire a lawn care professional to do all the work. Perhaps just having someone else mow would ease the burden (look to local youngsters who want to supplement their allowance using your mower).

The amount of upkeep a lawn needs depends on the level of quality you want, as well as the lawn's purpose. A golf course–quality lawn requires much

SUCCESSFUL GARDENING: PLANTING CHART FOR VEGETABLES

This planting chart provides all the information needed on when and how to plant as well as how long it will be before you can harvest. It is indispensible for planning and tracking the edibles you're growing in your garden.

Name	Grow From	Planting Time/ Start Indoors	Spacing (inches between plants/rows)	Days to Harvest
Asparagus	crowns	ESP	18 to 24/36 to 48	3 years first planting
Beans, bush	seeds	MSP, ALF, ESU	2 to 3/24	50 to 70
Beans, lima	seeds	ALF	4 to 6/24	65 to 90
Beans, pole	seeds	ALF	4 to 6/24	45 to 65
Beets	seeds	ESP, SP, MSP, ALF	2 to 3/12 to 18	60 to 110
Broccoli	plants	ESP, ESU	18 to 24/24 to 30	60 to 80
Cabbage	plants	ESP, SP, ESU	18 to 24/20 to 28	60 to 100
Carrots	seeds	ESP, SP, ALF, ESU	2 to 3/12 to 18	60 to 100
Cauliflower	plants	ESP, ESU	18 to 24/24 to 30	60 to 80
Chinese cabbage	plants	MSU	12 to 18/20 to 24	80 to 100
Corn, sweet	seeds	MSP, ALF, ESU	8 to 12/30 to 36	65 to 110
Cucumber	seeds	ALF, ESU	15 to 18/48 to 60	50 to 80
Eggplant	plants	ALF	18/24 to 30	75 to 85
Endive	seeds	ESP, MSU	2 to 4/6	65 to 85
Kale	seeds	ESP, MSU	4/12 to 18	60 to 70
Kohlrabi	seeds	ESP, SP, MSP	4 to 6/15 to 24	50 to 60
Lettuce (leaf)	seeds	ESP, SP, MSP	6/6 to 15	40 to 60
Melon	seeds	ALF	18 to 24/48 to 60	90 to 120
Mustard	seeds	ESP, SP, MSP, MSU	4/12 to 18	40 to 60
Onion	seeds	ESP, SP, MSP	2 to 3/12 to 15	100 to 140
Onion	sets	ESP, SP	2 to 3/12 to 15	90 to 100
Parsley	seeds	ESP, SP, MSP	4/12 to 18	80 to 100
Peas	seeds	ESP, SP	1 to 2/6 to 12	45 to 90
Peppers	plants	ALF	8/24 to 30	70 to 75
Potatoes	eyed pieces	ESP, SP, MSP	12/24 to 36	140 to 150
Pumpkins	seeds in hills	ALF	4/60 to 72	90 to 120
Radishes	seeds	ESP, SP, MSU	1 to 2/6 to 12	21 to 60
Rhubarb	crowns	ESP	36 to 72/36 to 60	1 year
Spinach	seeds	ESP, SP, MSU	3/12 to 18	50 to 70
Summer squash	seeds	ALF	4/24 to 30	60 to 75
Swiss chard	plants	ESP, SP	6 to 8/15 to 18	60 to 75
Tomatoes	plants	ALF	24 to 36/24 to 48	70 to 100
Turnips	seeds	ESU, MSU	18 to 24/18 to 24	60 to 90
Watermelon	seeds	ALF	60 to 84/60 to 84	90 to 130
Winter squash	seeds in hills	ALF	4/60 to 72	90 to 120

KEY
ESP – Early spring or whenever you can work the ground and it is not too wet; SP – Ten to fourteen days after ESP; MSP – Twenty to twenty-four days after ESP; ALF – After the danger of frost has passed; ESU – Early summer (late June, early July) plantings of slow-growing autumn plants; MSU – Midsummer (mid to late July) plantings of fast-growing autumn plants

HERE'S HOW

TO SELECT THE RIGHT GRASS

Putting the right plant in the right place applies to lawns as well as to other garden plants. Cool-season grasses are the best choice for our area. These grasses provide some of the first and last glimpses of green in our climate.

Kentucky bluegrass: Favored for its fine texture (thin leaves) and a good green color, it's best suited for sunny locations.

Fine fescues: These look similar to Kentucky bluegrass but are more shade- and drought-tolerant and are often mixed with bluegrass.

Turf-type perennial ryegrass: It is quick to germinate, so is blended with other grass seeds to provide quick cover until the others germinate. It is a major component of most grass seed mixes.

Tall fescue: It has wide leaves, grows in full sun to part shade (even in dry soil), and is the choice for high-use areas.

■ *Look for Kentucky bluegrass in grass mixes for full sun. Its fine texture adds to the diversity of the blend.*

■ *Tall fescue is an all-purpose grass that does well in sun and part shade. It also tolerates high traffic.*

more care than a lower-quality lawn that has other low-growing greens in it such as clover and even crabgrass in summer. A heavily trafficked lawn where children play needs more care than one that is mostly for show and is rarely stepped on. How you use your lawn and the quality level you desire determine its care.

High-quality lawns with dense weed-free grass need the most fertilization (four or five times a year) and pesticides. A less-than-perfect lawn may only need one feeding in fall and no pesticides. Consider overseeding with white clover. It is a pretty plant with white flowers in early summer that attract pollinators. Clover fixes nitrogen in the soil, feeding the lawn naturally. And who doesn't enjoy searching for four-leaf clovers? No matter what kind of lawn you want, proper care and

properly timed management are key to keeping it healthy and beautiful.

PERENNIALS & ORNAMENTAL GRASSES

Look for areas to convert to perennial gardens as well as locations for adding a few new plants. See "Successful Gardening: Planning a New Garden" (page 36) for tips on creating great gardens.

As you enjoy the winter beauty of ornamental grasses, note which ones perform best. Consider incorporating them in other areas of your landscape and trying new grasses. Add them to your wish list.

ROSES

Need new plants? Check out roses online, thumb through catalogs, and get out magazine clippings from last summer. Resist the allure of the photographs (especially colorful in the bleakness of winter) and look at the hardiness ratings first. If the rose is in your hardiness zone, or better yet, one zone colder, then you can look at the pretty photos and add it to your wish list.

TREES & SHRUBS

As you walk around your property, look for places that trees and shrubs would enhance. They can provide screening, seasonal interest, shade, and act as windbreaks. Select spaces large enough to accommodate a fully grown plant. Don't overlook evergreens for their form and year-round interest.

■ *Early in the season, the new red leaves of Japanese maples may be covered with hoarfrost—a fleeting but beautiful sight.*

Look for trees and shrubs with colorful bark, persistent fruit, or attractive form for winter interest. Consider crabapples and hollies for their decorative fruit and bird attraction. Cherries, snakebark maple (*Acer pensylvanicum*), and red twig dogwood (*Cornus alba*) have interesting bark that is eye catching. Japanese maples are unsurpassed for their evocative form, enhanced with snow on the branches.

Consider dwarf varieties. However, remember that a dwarf is relative to the size of the species; for example, a dwarf evergreen may reach 15 feet tall versus the species at 50 feet.

See how others are using trees and shrubs to add year-round interest. Some botanical gardens sponsor winter walks with local experts. Evaluate the form, color, and fruit of individual plants. Consider how it can help improve your existing landscape. Start a wish list, including ultimate size, form, and soil and sun preferences.

Start a list of pruning that needs to be done.

VINES & GROUNDCOVERS

Look for places around your property that would benefit from vertical interest. A vine-covered arbor or obelisk can brighten up, shade, or screen problem areas.

Consider adding a trellis alongside your home. Vine-covered structures can brighten the outside of your house, soften the feel, and anchor your home in the landscape. Unfortunately, they also get in the way of house painting and other routine chores. See "Here's How To Make a Hinged Trellis" (page 44) for directions on building a hinged trellis that *can* get out of the way.

Identify areas where groundcovers can be used to unify a planting bed, mask surface roots of large trees, or fill a bare area where grass will not grow.

Lawn and garden shows can give you ideas on how to incorporate these plants into your landscape. Many landscape companies build elaborate displays featuring vine-covered structures and beds filled with groundcovers.

PLANT

ALL

Although it is too early to plant outside, it is never too early to prepare for the season ahead.

ANNUALS & BIENNIALS

Start pansies at the end of the month to have large transplants ready for your early spring garden.

EDIBLES

See "Here's How To Start an Indoor Salad Garden" on page 27.

PERENNIALS & ORNAMENTAL GRASSES

Read seed packets for information on pretreating, timing, and planting. Some seeds need to be stratified (treated with cold) for weeks, soaked in

HERE'S HOW

TO MAKE A SEED-STARTING SYSTEM

Prepare a light setup for indoor seed starting. Select an area away from outdoor drafts and indoor blasts of heat that has a nearby power source and ample room (think vertical too) for all the plants you want to grow. Purchase a seed-starting system from a garden supply company, home-improvement store, or build your own:

1. You'll need cool fluorescent lights, a light fixture to hold them, and a system for keeping the lights 6 inches above the tops of the seedlings. An electrical timer isn't necessary, but it makes life easier.

2. Mount the light fixtures on shelves, create tabletop supports for the lights, or design a stand-alone system. Note that a pulley system allows the lights to be raised and lowered as needed over the growing seedlings.

3. Paint the shelving white or use a reflective surface to increase the light the young seedlings receive.

■ *Starting plants from seed doesn't require a lot of space when you have a simple seed-starting rack, complete with fluorescent lights.*

Once the light system is in place, you are ready to start planting seeds. Read the seed packets for the correct timing. Most seeds need warm temperatures for germination and light as soon as they sprout. Many gardeners germinate seeds in a warm location and then move the seedlings under lights after sprouting. Others use bottom heat or a warm location along with the lights to germinate seeds and grow seedlings. (See "Here's How To Start Seeds Indoors" on page 41 for details on seed starting.) You can use this system for any seeds, not just for annuals.

tepid water overnight, or scarified (scratching the seed coat) prior to planting.

CARE

ALL

In preparation for the planting season, be sure you have the basic tools you will be using; everyone has his/her preferences. If you haven't sharpened and oiled them, it's not too late. Tools include: hand pruners (secateurs), loppers, garden fork, hoe, rake, shovel, spade, and trowel. You'll also want a 5-gallon bucket, heavy garden gloves, and a waterproof tarp.

It is important to use the right pruning tool for the size of the stem, branch, or cane. Invest in a good pair of hand pruners (also called pruning shears or secateurs) that are comfortable for your hand. High-end pruners come in sizes to fit delicate or burly hands. Curved-blade bypass pruners (in photo on the next page) cut cleaner than straight-blade, anvil-type pruners. Hand pruners work well on branches up to ½-inch diameter. For branches up to 1-inch diameter, use long-handled loppers. A fine-toothed saw like a Japanese handsaw is best for larger branches. Wear gloves to protect your hands.

ANNUALS & BIENNIALS

Check on dormant geraniums overwintering in cool, dark locations. Pot them up if they begin to grow and move them to a sunny, warm spot with your other overwintering annuals.

Hand pruners

Pruning saw

Loppers

■ *A good pair of bypass hand pruners (secateurs) more than pays for itself as it won't need to be replaced. Loppers with ratchet action make it easier to cut larger branches without needing a lot of strength. A folding Japanese pruning saw is handy. When folded, it can fit in a back pocket.*

HERE'S HOW

TO START AN INDOOR SALAD GARDEN

You can start eating from this windowsill salad garden within three weeks. For the container, use a window box liner with drainage holes. Place a lipped tray underneath to catch water.

1. Lightly moisten soilless seed-starting mix and fill the window box liner to within ¾ inch from the top.

2. In a bowl, mix several varieties of lettuce seeds (leaf types, not heading types) with other greens, such as arugula, corn salad, kale, mâche, mizuna, and mustard—your choice. You now have your own mesclun mix.

3. Sprinkle the seed mix over the soil so that the seeds are about ½ inch apart.

4. Cover the seeds with a thin layer of moist seed-starting mix. Gently press your palms on the soil to ensure that the seeds make

■ *Grow salad greens on a windowsill in a window box or in a seed flat next to a bright window. Cut greens and they will regrow.*

contact with the soil. Cover the top of the container with plastic wrap, creating a greenhouse. Set in a warm place—out of direct sunlight.

5. Lift the plastic and check seeds daily. If moisture is clinging to the plastic, gently tap it off onto the soil. If the top of the soil is dry, water by spraying with a mister. Put the plastic back on.

6. When seedlings emerge, gradually (over a few days), bring the container into bright light/sunlight. Do not let the soil dry out.

7. As everything grows, it will get crowded. Thin the plants using small scissors (manicure scissors work well). Use the "gourmet baby greens" in salads. As the plants grow and more seedlings emerge, thin again. Be sure to leave a variety of plants to grow and mature.

8. Once the leaves are 2 to 3 inches high, begin the harvest. Take one or two outer leaves from each plant—or as many as you need—for salad. Because you are continually removing leaves from the outside of the plants, they will keep producing new leaves at their center.

HERE'S HOW

TO SHARPEN TOOLS

■ *Taking the time to keep digging tools, such as a hoe, sharp makes working with them much easier—readily slicing into the soil.*

Take advantage of this downtime to prepare your tools for the growing season. Sharp hoes, shovels, spades, and trowels make digging and planting easier and less tiring. Clean and sharpen them if you didn't do it in fall.

1. Knock off any soil with a wire brush.
2. Remove rust by rubbing with steel wool or medium-grit sandpaper.
3. Sharpen the edges with a metal file.
4. Rub in a few drops of sewing machine oil to help prevent rust.

Overwintered annuals, such as begonias, coleus, geraniums, and impatiens, tend to get leggy. Pinching the stems back to just above a set of healthy leaves encourages branching and stronger stems.

BULBS

If you forced any double-nose bulbs (a large bulb, usually a daffodil, with two small bulbs on the side), the baby bulbs will likely bloom after the mother bulb. Be patient and give them time.

EDIBLES

Check winter mulches on strawberries. Replace any that were dislodged in bad weather. Can't see the mulch for the snow? That's great. Snow is the best insulation available. No snow and no mulch?

Cover the plants with straw or evergreen branches to protect the overwintering flower buds and prevent frost heaving.

■ *Many herbs, including lavender, basil, chives, rosemary, mint, and savory, grow happily all winter on a south-facing windowsill.*

If your indoor herbs are becoming potbound, repot them in fresh soil in a container no more than 2 inches wider than the one they are in.

■ *Annuals overwintering indoors, such as this coleus, get leggy when they get less sunlight. Pinching them encourages bushier plants and removes flowering stems.*

Harvest indoor herbs and hardy outdoor herbs like thyme and sage, taking only as much as you need each time.

LAWNS

Salt and deicers spread on drives, sidewalks, and walkways, get on adjacent lawns, and can harm them. Cut down on the amount of salt or deicer you use by first shoveling the driveway, sidewalk, and other surfaces to remove as much snow and ice as possible. Or switch to a non-salt deicer, such as magnesium chloride or calcium acetate, which causes less damage to the lawn and plantings. For traction only, non-clumping kitty litter or turkey grit works well.

PERENNIALS & ORNAMENTAL GRASSES

Winter mulch helps protect perennials from fluctuating temperatures. Apply winter mulch *after* the ground freezes. Some years the ground freezes by Thanksgiving, while other years it does not freeze until January. The goal is to prevent soil temperature changes caused by winter thaws and refreezes—not to keep the soil warm. Nature provides the best mulch—snow. Hardy ornamental grasses don't need winter mulch; they are still an attraction in the garden.

Recycle your holiday tree and evergreen decorations by converting them into windbreaks and mulch. Keep a few cut branches handy to use in case of a winter thaw when nature's mulch disappears.

ROSES

Walk around the garden every once in a while, especially after a heavy snow or ice storm. Tie a piece of brightly colored yarn or ribbon on any plants that need attention. Later, you can go back and deal with them—cut off broken canes, tie up canes that are blowing in the wind, or add more mulch around the plant.

TREES & SHRUBS

Brushing or shaking off *frozen* snow from branches can be more damaging—they are easily broken—than letting the snow melt on it own. For shrubs that didn't get winter protection, jot a note on your calendar to do it in October or November. List all winter protection (including tying evergreens,

shielding plants from salt and wind, and watering in well before the ground freezes) you want to complete before the snow arrives.

Cut back any winter-damaged branches as you find them. Don't worry about pruning techniques; just make cuts behind the breaks.

■ *Midwinter is the perfect time to cut branches of early flowering trees and shrubs, such as this cherry, to force into bloom inside.*

Want a preview of spring indoors? Cut some branches of early-bloomers, such as crabapples, forsythia, cherries, star magnolia, and pussy willow, to force into bloom. Once inside, cut the branches at an angle and place them in a bucket of water in a cool (60 degrees Fahrenheit), brightly lit location. Mist the branches several times a day until the stems start to bloom. Use flowering stems in arrangements with other flowers or by themselves. Prolong the bloom by storing the flowering stems in a cooler spot (40 degrees Fahrenheit) at night.

VINES & GROUNDCOVERS

Take a walk through your property and see how the vines and groundcovers are surviving winter. Note plants that are subject to snow loads and salt. Check how plants are faring with the winter sun (reflective light from snow as well). Evaluate these plants in spring. You may need to move sensitive plants.

Check that arbors, trellises, and other supports are well mounted. Secure them against strong winter winds that could dislodge them and damage the vines or nearby plantings.

Observe how winter sun and winds are affecting plants. Both can be drying to evergreen groundcovers and vines. Create a windbreak and shade for pachysandra, English ivy, and other sensitive plants with your Christmas tree. Make a note to move, shelter, or create a more permanent solution.

WATER

ALL

If the temperature remains above freezing and there has been little or no snow, give the outdoor plants (including ones in planters) a good drink of water. Water slowly at ground level, allowing the moisture to seep into the soil.

Check any plants in aboveground planters stored in your unheated garage or porch. Water thoroughly whenever the soil thaws and dries—until water runs out through the bottom of the container.

ANNUALS & BIENNIALS

Adjust your watering schedule of annuals overwintered as houseplants (begonias, coleus, geraniums, impatiens, and others) to match their individual needs. Shorter days, less light, and low indoor humidity of winter change plants' needs. Water the soil thoroughly and wait until it is slightly dry before watering again.

BULBS

Keep the refrigerated potted bulbs you are forcing lightly moist. Do not overwater or mildew can form on the cold soil.

■ *Nothing says spring like a grouping of bulbs forced indoors, such as these hyacinths, crocus, and daffodils.*

EDIBLES

If you have forced-air heat, the humidity is lower than your plants like. Set pots of herbs (except for Mediterranean ones, such as thyme, rosemary, oregano, and sage) on a shallow tray filled with pebbles. Add water to the tray—not quite to the top of the pebbles. If the water level is higher, the plants would sit partially in water and would become waterlogged.

VINES & GROUNDCOVERS

Water tender vines that were moved indoors for winter. Water thoroughly until the excess runs out the bottom. Pour out any water that collects in the saucer. Wait until the top few inches of soil are dry before watering again.

FERTILIZE

ALL

Nothing planted outdoors needs to be fertilized now.

When using *any* fertilizer, always follow all package instructions for directions about proper application, frequency, concentration, and mixing/dilution.

ANNUALS & BIENNIALS

Do not be over-anxious to fertilize impatiens, geraniums, and other annuals growing indoors. Feed only those plants that have stunted growth, yellow leaves, or other signs of nutrient deficiencies with half-strength fertilizer.

BULBS

Forced bulbs do not need feeding unless you want to plant them in the garden come spring. In that case, use half-strength liquid fertilizer every few weeks. If the bulbs are tight in their container after flowering, pot them up in a container that is 2 inches larger. Bulbs forced in water have spent all their energy blooming; add them to the compost pile.

VINES & GROUNDCOVERS

Monitor the health and growth of tender vines growing indoors. The low light and low humidity is tough on these plants. Adding fertilizer just adds to their stress. Only fertilize actively growing plants with pale or stunted growth, using half-strength solution of any fertilizer for flowering houseplants.

PROBLEM-SOLVE

ALL

As you walk around your property, make note of any areas that are flooded or iced over. Enter this location in your garden journal and mark it on your landscape plan. These areas are likely to be problematic come spring; plants may die over winter. The fix may be as easy as moving a downspout or sump pump discharge. Consider amending soil in the area, raising the soil level, moving the plants, or replanting the space as a bog or rain garden.

Look for signs of voles (or meadow mice), including 2-inch-wide runways just below the surface of lawns and gnawed bark on trees, shrubs, or woody perennials. These rodents, which resemble small black mice, scurry under the snow, burrow in the roots of trees and shrubs, and are notorious for chewing the roots of Siberian iris and hostas. They can decimate a hosta garden in a single winter. If

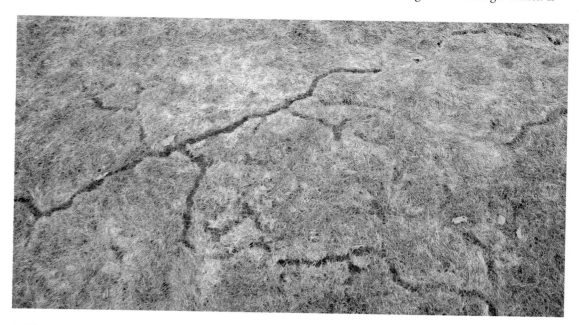

■ *Vole activity in the lawn in winter is evidenced by raised furrows showing the path of their runs.*

possible, remove snow from around the base of trees, shrubs, and woody perennials. A zealous cat or two can also help with vole control. See May Problem-Solve, All (page 93) for information on managing these critters.

Keep an eye out for signs of other animals, including tracks, droppings, and most important, any damage. Look for any breaks in fences and repair them. If rabbit fencing becomes buried in snow, add enough hardware cloth to raise the fence 4 feet above the snow to keep bunnies from snacking as they sit on the snow.

Reapply rabbit and deer repellents to outdoor plants as needed.

Check the label and follow instructions for mixing and applying pesticides, insecticides, repellents, or any other chemicals.

ANNUALS & BIENNIALS

Monitor plants for fungus gnats, mites, aphids, scale, and whiteflies. Fungus gnats do not hurt the plants, but are a nuisance, feeding on the organic matter in the soil like dead plant roots and peat moss. Often mistaken for fruit flies, they flit throughout the house. Keeping the soil slightly drier than normal will reduce the population.

Aphids, mites, and whiteflies suck plant juices, causing leaves to yellow and brown. Signs of infestation are poor growth and a clear sticky substance (honeydew) on the leaves. Several minutes in a strong shower (cover the soil with aluminum foil) in water that is slightly cool to the touch can wash off the offenders. For good measure, repot the plant in a clean pot and new soil just in case any insects were in the soil.

Insecticidal soap can control aphids and mites. Spray the upper and lower surface of leaves and stems. Repeat once a week until these pests are under control. You can buy ready-to-spray (expensive) or concentrated insecticidal soap (less expensive) or make your own (cheap). See "Here's How To Make Insecticidal Soap" on the next page.

Whiteflies can also stress and stunt plants. These insects multiply quickly and are harder to control. Try trapping whiteflies with commercial yellow

■ *Use sticky yellow traps to lure fungus gnats and whiteflies.*

TO MAKE INSECTICIDAL SOAP

Concentrate: Mix equal parts vegetable oil and Ivory dish liquid. Shake well to mix. Cap and store in a cool, dry place.

Working Solution: Mix 1 to 2 teaspoons concentrate in 1 cup of water or mix ¼ to ½ cup concentrate in 1 gallon of water.

Spray affected plants, making sure to spray all surfaces. Outdoors, spray early in the day, once the dew has dried. Never spray if the temperature will be above 80 degrees Fahrenheit.

sticky traps, which are available locally. Or make your own using yellow cardboard and Tanglefoot™, a sticky pine resin—even cooking or motor oil will work. Whiteflies, attracted by the yellow color, get stuck and die. Although this won't get rid of all the whiteflies, it reduces the populations enough to minimize stress to plants. Whiteflies are difficult to control with pesticides. It's safer for you, your children, and pets not to use pesticides indoors.

Neem oil is an organic control for aphids, mites, and whiteflies. Spray the solution on the tops and bottoms of leaves and stems. Some plants can be killed by Neem oil, especially if it is applied heavily. Before spraying the entire plant, test a leaf or two and wait twenty-four hours to check to see if the leaf has any damage. If there is no damage, then the plant will not be harmed by the Neem oil. Apply the oil only in indirect light or in the evening to prevent it from burning foliage and to give it time to seep into the plant.

BULBS

Check on the chilling bulbs that you are forcing. Keep an eye out for dryness, mold, or mildew on the soil.

EDIBLES

Look for any signs of insects on indoor herbs. Read the Annuals & Biennials section (page 32) for more information on these pests and controlling them.

LAWNS

Make note of any areas where snow and ice remain longer than on the rest of the lawn. They will be susceptible to snow mold, which is a gray or pink fungus covering matted areas of the lawn in spring.

ROSES

Insect identification books make good winter reading, and they'll give you a heads up on the good and bad bugs come spring.

TREES & SHRUBS

Keep an eye out for gypsy and tussock moth egg masses, which appear like tan blotches on tree trunks. Scrape them into a plastic bag and throw the bag in the garbage. Eastern tent caterpillar eggs resemble a mud smear on branches and can be easily pruned out. Discard the infested branches; don't put them in the compost.

VINES & GROUNDCOVERS

Wintercreeper, junipers, and other low-growing evergreens make great winter housing and food for rabbits and voles. Apply repellent to high-risk plantings. Repeat when necessary.

SUCCESSFUL GARDENING: WORMS EAT GARBAGE

In winter, the action in a compost pile slows down tremendously. Unlike other times of the year, when it can keep up with whatever you add, the pile just grows and is frozen and immovable. An alternative is indoor vermiculture—raising worms, using a pound of red wigglers and a three-tiered worm bin (or make one yourself from a plastic storage bin with air/drainage holes punched in the sides and bottom). It does not smell, and it's amazing how much worms can eat and turn into castings in a few days. A bonus is that they happily eat the colored pages of the newspaper and all the slick magazines you don't compost. Use the castings to topdress indoor plants for a slow feed.

February

It amazes me that every year when the January thaw arrives—even if it is February—people panic at the sight of bare soil or flowers and leaves emerging in the garden. They run around like Chicken Little convinced that the sky is falling. Not to worry: the earliest spring bulbs such as species crocus and snowdrops (pictured left) grow low to the ground, even generating enough heat to melt snow around them. They are tough. Snow or cold weather won't bother the early risers.

Are you content eating one type of tomato all season when there are hundreds of varieties? Look beyond modern hybrids to heirloom varieties, the seeds of which have been passed down in families for generations. They vary in color from white to pink, yellow, orange, every shade of red, green, brown, and almost black. Look for bicolors and striped tomatoes too. You'll find tomatoes ranging in size from pop-in-the-mouth marbles to giant beefsteaks weighing well over a pound. There is great variety (in seeds) in many other edibles—and flowers too. Try something new—but old—this year.

Continue reviewing your garden journal and images or videos of last year's garden. Make rough sketches of the areas you want to change. With these in hand, go over your seed/plant wish list realistically, taking into account your time and budget. Then edit it. Hang on to the original to use for gift suggestions or if any items you order are sold out. Order seeds, plants, and bulbs as soon as possible, especially those you need to start indoors. Ask friends if they want to share an order. This is a great way to get the benefits of quantity discounts without having to order more plants or bulbs than fit into your landscape. Gather your planting materials while waiting for your order to arrive.

Attend garden lectures and workshops for ideas on designing and landscaping with low-maintenance plants—vines, groundcovers, perennials, and ornamental grasses. Visit the library and check out landscape books and read magazines for inspiration on how to incorporate them into your gardens.

PLAN

ALL

Purchase sterile seed-starting mix. These mixes increase success by retaining moisture, providing good drainage, and allowing plants to start disease-free.

■ *Have plenty of plant labels and a pencil or permanent marker on hand to mark plant names when you are planting or transplanting.*

Gather and clean planting containers. Use flats and pots purchased at garden centers or recycled from last year's garden. Disinfect used pots in a solution of 1 part bleach to 9 parts water. Or gather emptied yogurt containers or used paper coffee cups for seed starting. Rinse these containers and punch holes in the bottom.

Buy or make plant labels to label flats and pots with the name of the seeds you are growing. Recycle Popsicle sticks, plastic spoons, or similar items into labels. Cut plastic ½- or 1-gallon jugs into strips; they are long enough to write plant name, planting date, and other information. Use a pencil or permanent marker when labeling.

Create a seeding chart to record plant names, starting dates, and other important data. Put it in your garden journal, notebook, or computer file to save this valuable information for next year. Consider investing in a journal if you do not already own one. For some, a loose-leaf notebook works well, as it's easy to take a sheet out when you need it or to add another one. Others prefer doing it all on their computer, tablet, or phone. There are plenty of apps to choose from.

SUCCESSFUL GARDENING: PLANNING A NEW GARDEN

Follow these tips for creating a great garden that will thrive:

- Choose a location that has good drainage (see "Here's How To Test Soil Drainage" on page 65 for details) and gets enough sunlight (see Introduction, page 15, for information on sunlight) for the plants you want to grow.
- Site planting beds in front of hedges, walls, walkways, or buildings. Or create an island bed within a lawn area.
- Make sure you can reach all parts of the garden for maintenance. Consider adding steppingstones or a path for easier access.
- Use a mixture of bulbs, perennials, shrubs, and small trees to take advantage of all planting and vertical space.
- Plan for year-round interest. Use a variety of plants that bloom at different times. Look to leaves and fruit for fall color. Berries and bark can be colorful in winter. Form makes plants like yucca stand out in winter.
- Create dramatic impact by massing annuals, biennials, bulbs, perennials, and ornamental grasses in drifts or in large clusters. These large sweeps of color are impressive from a distance.
- Go online to find new and unusual plants. You can also discover plants and combinations on Pinterest.

There are several ways to keep garden records—on a computer, in a notebook, or in a journal especially made for gardeners.

ANNUALS & BIENNIALS

Finish assembling the light setup and seed-starting area. See "Here's How To Make a Seed-Starting System" (page 26) for ideas on creating your own system.

BULBS

A greater variety of summer-blooming bulbs are available through online and mail-order sources than at most local nurseries, garden centers, or home-improvement stores. Plan your garden and order your bulbs as soon as you get your catalogs.

Lilies are easy-to-grow, hardy, summer-blooming bulbs. 'Enchantment' is a classic with its long-lasting, vivid orange blooms.

See January Plan (page 22) for more detail. Don't worry about having to store them; bulbs will be shipped at the appropriate time for planting.

Lilies are unique among summer-blooming bulbs, as you can plant them in spring or fall. There are so many species and hybrids to choose from—Easter lilies to tiger lilies, fragrant Oriental lilies to Turk's cap lilies. So, if you didn't plant lilies last fall, you can always plant them after the soil warms this spring. If the lilies you want aren't available online now, make a list for buying them locally in spring or ordering for fall planting.

EDIBLES

Potted dwarf citrus will grow and fruit in our region. Keep it in a cool, sunny location during winter, move it outside in summer, and you can pick homegrown citrus and enjoy its juicy sweetness. Look at online and mail-order sources for these plants. They will be shipped when the weather warms up.

When you are planning what herbs and vegetables you want to grow, take into account their preferred growing season—cool or warm weather. This information is invaluable, especially if you plan to jumpstart the season by sowing seeds indoors. If you grow plants out of season, they will be stressed, not grow well, yield a poor harvest (if any), or just die. (see "Successful Gardening: Planting Chart for Vegetables" on page 23)

Cool-weather vegetables include Asian greens, beets, broccoli, Brussels sprouts, cabbage, kale, leeks, lettuce, onions, peas, potatoes, spinach, and turnips. They are relatively hardy, tolerating temperatures down to 28 degrees Fahrenheit. Traditionally, they are spring crops; you can start the seeds indoors six to eight weeks before outdoor planting. Many of these tough plants also make excellent fall crops. Some, such as Brussels sprouts and kale, even taste better after a frost.

Warm-weather vegetables thrive when night temperatures range from 60 to 65 degrees Fahrenheit with daytime temperatures in the 75 to 85 degree range. These plants can be particular; the seeds will not even germinate if the soil temperature is below 50 degrees; ideal sprouting temperature is 60 degrees. Plant seeds indoors four to six weeks before the last frost for a jumpstart or seed directly in the ground when the soil has warmed up. These herbs and vegetables include: all annual herbs, beans, corn, cucumbers, eggplant, melons, okra, peppers, squash, sweet potatoes, tomatillos, and tomatoes.

Most herbs and vegetables require at least six hours of sun a day to reach their potential. Fortunately, there are a few exceptions. Sweet woodruff wilts in full sun and is happy in part shade. Many cool-weather plants will grow where trees are deciduous; the plants are up and growing well before the trees start to leaf out. Lettuces and greens will grow in partial shade. In summer, they benefit from the shady coolness; it is 15 degrees cooler than in the sun.

There are a wealth of herb plants you probably have never tried. Most people are more enthusiastic about experimenting with new flavors and colors when they have grown the plant themselves. Just look online and at mail-order catalogs at the myriad herbs, including cilantro, summer savory, salad burnet, and pineapple sage. Make your wish list and get your orders in soon. Plants will be sent at the right time for planting.

LAWNS

Walk around your property and note lawn areas that are flooded or iced over. Plan on filling low spots in spring to reduce future drainage problems. Also note areas bordering sidewalks and driveways where salt or deicers are spread. These treatments may affect the lawn and require serious watering in spring to wash the salts from the soil and prevent permanent damage to grass and nearby plantings.

If you plan to make any planting beds bigger or create new ones, you can use the sod you cut out to repair problem areas in the lawn. Look at the upcoming season. Plan ahead as you'll need plenty of time to cut the sod and plant it where it's needed (having prepared that area) within a day or two after it has been cut.

PERENNIALS & ORNAMENTAL GRASSES

Continue to review photos and videos of last year's landscape. Start sketching areas that you might want to turn into perennial gardens. Once you have a plan, you can make your wish list and start ordering plants and seeds.

ROSES

As you review last year's garden, consider removing any roses that didn't do well or seemed to be a magnet for pests or diseases and replacing them with resistant varieties. Check with your local Cooperative Extension Service for the best roses for your area. Sometimes it is easier to plan when you can visualize it. If you photographed the garden last summer, look at the images, and, if possible, literally "x" out plants that died or you want to move or discard. Photoshop them out if you're computer savvy.

Place your orders for roses by the middle of the month to be assured of getting the varieties you want. To be safe, make a list of alternates in case any roses are sold out. Most companies ship at the proper planting time (a few weeks before the last frost date). To be safe, clearly note on the order form the week that you want to receive *bare-root* plants. Mark it on your calendar so you don't schedule an out-of-town trip without having someone to rescue your roses from a cold and snowy front stoop.

Climbers bloom best on horizontal canes. To get the best show, consider training one or more along a fence, across a broad arbor, on a wide pergola, or splayed out on a fan lattice.

■ *Allow pooled water to dissipate before filling in low areas in the lawn, to make them level with surrounding soil.*

HERE'S HOW

TO DESIGN FOR LOWER MAINTENANCE

Try a few of these design ideas to make maintenance easier:

- Choose the right perennials for your growing conditions. A healthy plant looks more attractive, flowers longer, and needs less care.
- Start small and expand your garden as time allows. It is better to end the season wanting more than to be overwhelmed with weeds and work in August.
- Consider using fewer types of plants but more of each. A garden with 10 different types of perennials is easier to maintain than one with 30. In spring, you'll only have to differentiate weeds from 10 plant types.
- Include native plants like ornamental grasses (big bluestem, little bluestem, switchgrass, and prairie dropseed), purple coneflower, tickseed, black-eyed Susan, false sunflower, compass plant, cardinal flower, yucca, and Joe-pye weed. Most are drought tolerant.
- Plan for year-round interest by interplanting spring-, summer-, and fall-blooming perennials in your gardens. Include ones that provide winter interest and food for wildlife. Add rudbeckias, coneflowers, and other plants that have attractive seedpods. Ornamental grasses look great year-round.
- Think about the foliage as well as flowers. Some plants, such as coral bells, have attractive foliage all season. Others, such as poppies and bleeding heart, fade away in midsummer. Don't overlook fall color. A number of perennials, including willow blue star, evening primrose, and some sedums, have colorful fall foliage.

■ *A handsome, well-mulched bed like this with perennials, ornamental grasses, and a large shrub doesn't need much maintenance.*

TREES & SHRUBS

A tree is a long-term investment. It may start relatively small, but over time will grow and prosper. Shrubs are shorter term, but still an investment. Trees and shrubs not only add beauty to the landscape, they are utilitarian. Plant evergreens on the north side of the house as a windbreak to shelter it from cold winter winds. Plant trees and shrubs on the east and west side to shade the house in summer and keep it cool. Although it might seem logical to plant them on the south side, they would block out much-needed sun that helps warm the home in winter. Throughout the property, use trees and shrubs to hide unsightly views (even the compost pile) and frame beautiful ones.

Look for trees and shrubs with multi-season interest—spring or summer flowers (they attract pollinators and beneficial insects), handsome or colorful foliage, edible fruit or berries, fall color, and even winter interest (bark or form).

Planting season is still at least a month or more away. Start contacting local nurseries as well as mail-order and online sources for information on plant availability.

See "Successful Gardening: Choosing the Type of Tree or Shrub to Buy" on page 40.

SUCCESSFUL GARDENING: CHOOSING THE TYPE OF TREE OR SHRUB TO BUY

■ *Trees and shrubs are available in three forms: (from left to right) bare root, container grown, or balled and burlapped (B&B).*

Trees and shrubs can be purchased as bare-root, balled-and-burlapped, or container-grown plants. Each type has its advantages and disadvantages.

Bare-root plants, which are the least expensive, are generally available from online and mail-order sources. They come with no soil and need to be planted as soon as possible (or heel them in); unfortunately, some don't survive.

Balled-and-burlapped (B&B) plants are available locally. Nurseries dig them—with a large rootball—in late autumn after the leaves fall or in early spring before the plants leaf out. Although choice is limited, you can find large, even full-grown, plants if you are willing to pay the price, and have an instant landscape that will last for many years.

Container-grown plants, also available locally throughout the growing season, have spent most of their lives in pots. Their root system is smaller (sometimes they are rootbound) making them more manageable than B&B plants. Moderately priced, they will thrive with proper care.

Once you decide on the plant, consider how much money you want to spend. Larger, more expensive plants (over 3 inches in diameter) stay the same size for several years as they adjust to their new locations. Smaller, more affordable ones adapt faster to transplanting and often outgrow their larger counterparts. Keep your overall garden budget in mind as you make these decisions. Look at catalogs and online sources for prices of bare-root plants; make your wish list and order now for late winter/ early spring planting.

PLANT

ALL
See "Here's How To Start Seeds Indoors" on page 41.

ANNUALS & BIENNIALS
Check the planting dates on the seed packets and in catalogs. Sow seeds according to the label directions. February is the time to start many of the spring-blooming and long-season annuals.

Start impatiens, petunias, pansies, wax begonias, and coleus in early to mid-February. Mix small seeds with sand and shake them out using a saltshaker. This helps you spread the seeds more evenly over the soil surface. Sow ageratum, lobelia, and love-in-a-mist seeds in mid- to late-February.

EDIBLES
For a continuing harvest of salad greens, plant another window box like the one described in "Here's How To Start an Inside Salad Garden" on page 27. Mix in a few Johnny jump-up or pansy seeds. Their edible flowers will add a subtle hint of minty flavor to salads or desserts.

PERENNIALS & ORNAMENTAL GRASSES
Start perennials from seed indoors following the directions in "Here's How To Start Seeds Indoors" on page 41. Some perennial seeds, including maiden pinks, rose campion, and gaura, can take up to a month to germinate. Check seed packets for specific information on starting times and seed treatment requirements. Grow seedlings under lights for stronger and stouter plants. See "Here's

How to Make a Seed-Starting System" on page 26 for detailed instructions.

CARE

ANNUALS & BIENNIALS

Continue monitoring the dormant annuals that you're storing in the basement. Repot any that start to grow with fresh potting mix and move them to a sunny window. Water the soil thoroughly whenever the top inch starts to dry.

Check annuals that are growing indoors as houseplants. Pinch or cut back the stems that are elongating as they stretch for the light. From these stems, you can start new plants. See "Here's How To Start New Plants From Cuttings" on page 42.

BULBS

Check forced bulbs in cold storage for signs of growth. Take them out when sprouts are about an inch high.

Remove any spent flowers from forced bulbs that are in bloom.

EDIBLES

Renew mulches on herbs and other potted edibles growing indoors.

HERE'S HOW

TO START SEEDS INDOORS

Seeds can be started two ways. Sow them in a flat and then transplant young seedlings into individual containers, or sow one to two seeds directly in individual pots. Read the seed packets for information on germination time, depth, and light requirements. To start seeds:

1. Fill flats or containers with lightly moistened sterile seed-starting mix. Sprinkle fine seeds on the soil surface. For larger seeds, use a chopstick or pencil to make a planting hole and plant the seed at recommended depth. Cover lightly with more mix, and press your palm down gently so the seed makes contact with the soil.
2. Water lightly with a fine mist. Avoid a strong stream of water that can dislodge the seeds. Cover the container with plastic wrap to conserve moisture.

Peat pellets, which you soak in water until they expand, are an alternative to starting seeds in pots or flats.

3. Keep the soil warm and moist to ensure germination. Use a heating cable or place the flat in a warm location (top of refrigerator, heating ducts, or other warm place). Check daily and water often enough to keep the soil surface moist, but not wet.
4. As soon as the seedlings appear, remove the plastic and move the flat to your seed-starting system (see "Here's How To Make a Seed-Starting System" on page 26 for more information) or a sunny window. Adjust lights so they are 6 inches above the plants; keep them on for sixteen hours a day. Lighting them longer isn't beneficial; it just raises your electric bill.
5. Transplant seedlings growing in flats as soon as they form two sets of leaves. Seed leaves (the first to appear) are nondescript and small. The next to appear are true leaves, indicating that it is time to transplant.

Record seed-starting results in your journal and document them with pictures. This information will make next season even more successful. **Remember**: The directions on the back of the seed packets supersede anything—at least as far as planting goes.

HERE'S HOW

TO START NEW PLANTS FROM CUTTINGS

When you pinch back plants, you can use these cuttings to make more plants.

1. Start with a 4- to 6-inch-long stem.
2. Remove the lowest two sets of leaves and dip the bare stem in rooting hormone. This material contains hormones to encourage rooting and a fungicide to prevent rot.

■ *A mix of sterile potting soil and vermiculite keeps cuttings lightly moist longer than vermiculite alone.*

3. Place cuttings in moist vermiculite, perlite, or well-drained sterile potting mix. Keep the mix lightly moist. Within several weeks, roots will form. You can tell if it's rooted when you gently tug on it and it stays in the medium.
4. Transplant rooted cuttings into a small container of potting mix. Water frequently enough to keep the soil slightly moist but not wet.

Unless you are growing your plants directly under a fluorescent or grow light, give each pot a quarter turn so the stems stay straight and the plant isn't reaching for the sun.

Enjoy your fresh herbs and salad greens—so much tastier and more nutritious than anything from the supermarket.

LAWNS

Beat the spring rush and take your lawnmower in to the shop to have a professional sharpen the blades and give the engine a check-up.

Continue the shoveling regimen described in January Care (page 29) to prevent damage from salt and deicers.

PERENNIALS & ORNAMENTAL GRASSES

Transplant seedlings from flats into individual containers as soon as the first set of true leaves appears (these are the second set of leaves). Adjust your watering schedule to fit plant needs. Continue to keep the soil lightly moist but not wet.

■ *Cut back ornamental grasses in late winter to early spring before new growth begins.*

Check winter mulch if the snow has disappeared. You can always add mulch after snow melts. Remember, the goal is to keep the soil temperature consistent and avoid February thaws.

Monitor plantings for frost heaving caused by the freezing and thawing of unmulched gardens. The fluctuating temperatures cause the soil to shift and often push shallow-rooted perennials right out of the ground. Gently press these back into the soil as soon as they are discovered. Make a note to mulch these areas next fall after the ground freezes.

Be patient. Wait for the worst of winter to pass before cleaning out the garden. Many borderline-hardy perennials survive better when the stems are left standing. Snow and the standing plant stems provide extra winter protection to the roots.

ROSES

If you use Styrofoam or plastic cones to protect your roses, keep an eye on the weather. On those suddenly balmy days when you go outside in a light jacket, think of the roses that are steaming in their impenetrable, airless prisons. Remove the brick or whatever you use to weight it down and let the plant breathe. Remember to close it in the afternoon before the light begins to fade.

Canes can break from the wind whipping them. Secure these and prune off any broken part of the cane.

TREES & SHRUBS

Deciduous trees and shrubs are dormant and bare, so you can readily see what needs to be pruned and what you're doing. Start pruning trees and summer-

■ *Climbing roses need support, such as a trellis. Allow space between it and the wall so air can circulate.*

and fall-blooming shrubs now. You can prune them until they start to leaf out. Don't prune spring-blooming shrubs or you'll cut off the flowerbuds. Wait until they finish blooming. See Appendix (page 192) for detailed pruning directions.

VINES & GROUNDCOVERS

Monitor any tropical vines you are overwintering indoors. Remove and discard dead leaves. Prune off wayward and dead branches, cutting them back above a healthy leaf or where it joins another branch. If any don't look healthy (but are insect- and disease-free), increase the light and humidity around failing plants. Move them in front of an unobstructed south-facing window. Add artificial light if needed. Hang fluorescent lights above or aim spotlight-type fluorescent lights up into the foliage.

Buy or build the support structure for new or existing vertical plantings. If possible, install it before you plant so you don't damage tender roots and young stems. The structure should be strong enough to support the weight of the vine while providing a means for the plant to attach itself and climb.

See "Here's How To Make a Hinged Trellis" on page 44.

WATER

ANNUALS, BIENNIALS & EDIBLES

Check seeded flats and seedlings every day. Keep the soil moist until the seeds germinate. Once germinated, continue to check seedlings daily. Water often enough to keep the soil lightly moist but not wet. Overwatering can cause root rot and seedling failure. Allowing the soil to dry out stresses seedlings, resulting in poor growth or even seedling death.

ANNUALS & BIENNIALS

Continue watering annuals you are overwintering indoors. Water thoroughly until the excess runs out the bottom. Allow the top inch of soil to dry before watering again.

BULBS

Monitor bulbs that are still in the cold stage of forcing. The soil should be just lightly moist.

HERE'S HOW

TO MAKE A HINGED TRELLIS

A hinged trellis provides a lovely and strong support, while allowing easy access to the outside of your house. Use pressure-treated wood.

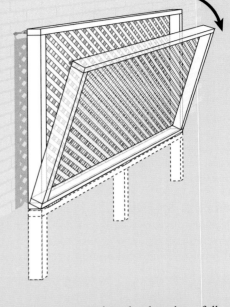

1. Select lattice or other attractive material suited for climbing vines. Cut it to the size and shape you want. Mount it on 2 x 4s.
2. Cut three 18- to 24-inch-long legs of 2 x 2s, 2 x 4s, or 4 x 4s, depending on the size of the trellis and mature size and weight of the vine (the heavier the vine, the sturdier the legs need to be). Mount the legs to a 2 x 4 that is the same size as the bottom of the trellis. Use hinges to attach this to the trellis.
3. Sink the legs into the soil about 6 to 8 inches from the house with the hinged portion about an inch above the soil. Attach eyebolts to the building and corresponding hooks to the top of the trellis. Secure the trellis to the building using the hooks and eyebolts.
4. Grow perennial vines next to the trellis. Tie the vines to the trellis until they attach by their own means.
5. Whenever you need access to that part of the house to paint or repair, simply unhook and carefully bend the vine-laden trellis away from the wall.

Water amaryllis, paperwhites, and any other bulbs you are forcing indoors. Maintain the water level in hyacinth glasses and soilless paperwhite plantings.

EDIBLES

Continue the watering regimen described in January Water (page 30).

PERENNIALS & ORNAMENTAL GRASSES

Check perennial seedlings daily. Keep the soil lightly moist, but not wet. Insufficient water can stunt and kill seedlings while excess moisture can cause rot.

ROSES

If the temperature stays well above freezing for several days, thawing the ground, and there has been little or no snow throughout winter, water.

TREES & SHRUBS

Check container plants overwintering outdoors and in the garage. Water whenever the soil is frost-free and dry. Water enough so that the excess runs out the bottom.

VINES & GROUNDCOVERS

Keep watering vines growing indoors for winter. Water so that excess water runs out the drainage hole. Empty any water from the saucer.

Increase the humidity around a plant by grouping it with other plants. As one plant loses moisture (transpires), those around it benefit. Or place pebbles in the saucer below the pot and keep water at a level just below the bottom of the pot. As the water evaporates, it increases the humidity around the plant where it is needed.

■ *During winter, place pebbles in the saucer and add water to keep plants humidified in the dry indoor climate.*

FERTILIZE

ALL

Do not fertilize outdoor plants or lawns. The fertilizer will just sit on the soil (or snow) and then wash off when it rains or snow melts. This runoff pollutes our waterways.

When using any fertilizer, always follow all package instructions for proper application, frequency, concentration, and mixing/dilution.

ANNUALS & BIENNIALS

Fertilize seedlings once they have sprouted and are actively growing. Use a diluted solution of foliar plant food or a complete water-soluble fertilizer every other week.

BULBS

When a bud or leaf emerges from the amaryllis bulbs you are forcing, begin weekly feedings with half-strength liquid fertilizer.

EDIBLES

Give herbs (except Mediterranean ones), greens, and any other culinary plants growing indoors a foliar feeding. As the emulsions smell a bit briny, you may want to do this in a room where the plants can remain overnight. Bring them back to their proper homes the next day.

PERENNIALS & ORNAMENTAL GRASSES

Fertilize young seedlings with a dilute solution of a complete fertilizer every other week. Or foliar feed with a dilution of fish emulsion or liquid kelp.

VINES & GROUNDCOVERS

Fertilize nutrient-deficient tropical vines you are overwintering indoors. Look for pale leaves and stunted growth. Use a diluted solution of any flowering houseplant fertilizer.

Do not fertilize plants that are showing signs of stress from low light and humidity. Stressed plants lose leaves and have little, if any, new growth. Correct the problem before fertilizing. Adding nutrients to stressed plants can injure them.

■ *Stay ahead of any insect problems. Use a hand lens and keep an insect reference book nearby to identify what you find.*

PROBLEM-SOLVE

ALL

Check seedlings for sudden wilting and stems rotting at the soil, usually caused by damping off. Remove any diseased seedlings as soon as they appear. Prevent damping off by using sterile seed-starting mix and clean containers. Apply a fungicide or a solution of Neem oil as a soil drench on infected plantings. Make sure the product is labeled to control damping off on the type of seedlings you are growing.

Look under leaves and along stems of indoor plants for signs of mites, aphids, and whiteflies. Get out the hand lens and check for speckling, honeydew (a clear sticky substance aphids secrete), and the insects themselves. For complete information on controlling these pests, see January Problem-Solve, Annuals & Biennials (page 32).

Check the label before mixing and applying any pesticide, insecticide, herbicide, repellent, or any other chemical.

Ignore fungus gnats. These pests don't harm plants. Decrease populations by keeping potting mix slightly drier than normal.

If you notice little fruit flies flying around any indoor plant—they seem to come free with bananas—swatting does no good. Instead, put about an inch of sugar water in a clear jar. Top it with a funnel. If you don't have a funnel, fashion one from a coffee filter or a folded piece of paper. Cut a ½-inch hole at the base and set the paper funnel on the jar (so part of the funnel extends down into the jar). The insects, attracted by the sugar water, can easily fly down the funnel to drink. However, they can't get back out. When the sugar water gets too full of bugs, pour it down the drain and make up a new batch.

Continue to check outdoors for signs of animal intrusion (See January Problem-Solve, page 31). Reapply repellents after severe weather. Try switching repellents as critters can become desensitized to one repellent over time and will start munching the plants. Try scare tactics like whirligigs, noisemakers, and even coyote urine (available commercially). Many urban animals have become used to the noise of the city and aren't affected by scare tactics that make sounds.

BULBS

Carefully check summer bulbs in storage for signs of rot, mildew, or soft spots (including cannas, calla lilies, dahlias, and gladiolus). If you find any, discard the bulbs.

LAWNS

Continue checking for areas where snow and ice linger (see January Problem Solve, page 33). If snow has melted, note any damage.

ROSES

Keep an eye out for deer. If it has been a rough winter, they like nothing better than some nice rose canes to nibble—and they can eat them all the way down to the ground if there's no snow. The best way to keep them out of the garden is with an 8- to 10-foot-high electric fence. Deer netting of the same height may be equally effective and more pleasing to the eye.

TREES & SHRUBS

Do not shake ice or frozen snow off plants. Your good intentions can do more damage than nature. Make note of any damage that could have been prevented with winter protection and add it to your to-do list for fall.

Check for winter damage and note it for immediate or future pruning.

Continue checking for overwintering insects as described in January Problem-Solve (page 33).

If you had a problem last year with galls (harmless but unsightly bumps on leaves), aphids, mites, or scale, spray with dormant oil. Apply it only on days when temperature will be above 40 degrees Fahrenheit or above for at least 12 hours after the application. Do it yourself if you have the equipment or hire a professional. Routine spraying of *all* trees is costly and unnecessary.

■ *Galls, the nasty-looking bumps on leaves, can be controlled by spraying with dormant oil in late winter.*

March

It can be challenging to draw a landscape plan, but even more challenging to remember what is where, so if you aren't already doing it, document your garden with pictures and videos. This is an ideal time to start, as the garden is mostly asleep. You can see the "bones" (the hardscape—anything that isn't plant material, including buildings, structures, paths, and walkways) and the shape of the beds clearly. Get some overall shots now and continue taking pictures at least once a month, if not more often. Try to get pictures from the same vantage points so you can really see the garden's progress from month to month. This has been made much easier with smartphone technology—no heavy camera and tripod to lug around. Jot down plant names; the more information you can add, the better. Of course, if you create a video, you can narrate as you go.

Finalize your landscape and garden plans and start your planting list. Take advantage of nice days to stake out new planting beds and measure existing gardens. Calculate the square footage of new and existing beds (multiply the length by the width). Jot this down on your plans; it's a helpful bit of information to use later on in determining the number of plants that can go into the space and for determining how much fertilizer you need.

Be sure you have room in your compost pile for all the trimmings of your garden cleanup. If not, it's time to start another pile.

March can be a pivotal month, beginning the transition from winter to spring. But there's no telling what the weather will do. It could be a month of blizzards, ice storms, and freezing weather. But whatever March brings, it's time to start getting your garden (and yourself) in shape. Get out your pruners, loppers, hedge shears, lawn rake, wheelbarrow, and other tools you'll need to start cleaning up the garden and get them ready for emerging plants and new arrivals. The winter vacation from gardening is *over*. On your mark, get set, go!

PLAN

ALL

Cultivate relationships with your local nurseries, garden centers, and home-improvement centers. As you finish your planting list, check the availability of plants you want. They may special order new or unusual plants for you. Shop early to find sources.

Continue to monitor and record seed-starting results in your journal; document with photos.

Think about where you want to locate new planting beds. Mark them off. You can start preparing them as soon as the soil can be worked.

■ *The results of your soil test provide you with information on what soil amendments you need to add.*

If you didn't do it last fall, perform soil tests on new areas after the ground thaws. Established areas only need testing every three to five years unless problems develop. Soil tests give information about soil (pH and nutrients in the soil) and suggest how much fertilizer (and what type) and organic matter to add. This helps you choose and apply the right fertilizer and avoid damaging plants through under- or overfertilizing. Contact your local Cooperative Extension Service for information on testing. Some local nurseries and garden centers perform tests. DIY kits often just test pH and not nutrient levels.

ANNUALS & BIENNIALS

Look at the seed racks in stores as you shop. You can find seeds for annuals and biennials as well as edibles in grocery and hardware stores, nurseries, garden centers, and home-improvement stores. Some gift stores even carry them. See if there is anything you have overlooked and want to grow.

BULBS

Consider planting alliums in garden beds. They come in a wide assortment of sizes, shapes, and colors. As members of the onion family, some have a somewhat pungent scent, which makes them a good pest deterrent. Pick out some interesting varieties and order them right away. The bulbs will be delivered in time for late-summer planting.

■ *Alliums range in size and color from 12-inch-tall, yellow summer-blooming* Allium moly *to spring-blooming, 4- to 5-foot-tall purple giant allium,* A. giganteum *(pictured).*

EDIBLES

Save leftover seeds from any plantings (indoors and out). Store them in a clean, dry envelope. Note when you opened the seed packet.

LAWNS

Now is a good time to get your lawnmower ready for the season ahead. Take it to a repair shop, or get out the owner's manual and do it yourself (see next page).

PERENNIALS & ORNAMENTAL GRASSES

Take one last look at the winter garden and note any changes that should be made. Make those adjustments, such as plants that need to be replaced or moved.

Keep your plans simple if you are either a beginner gardener or a more experienced gardener with

HERE'S HOW

TO READY YOUR LAWNMOWER FOR SPRING

If you haven't done this before, have an experienced friend guide you through the first time.

■ *Changing the air filter is an important part of getting your lawnmower ready for the mowing season.*

1. For safety reasons, whenever you're working on a lawnmower, always disconnect the spark plug wire.
2. Clean or replace the spark plug and air filter.
3. Drain the oil from the crankcase of a four-cycle-engine mower (this isn't necessary with two-cycle engines). Refill with oil; follow the owner's manual for the type and amount needed.
4. If the blades are damaged in any way (bent or cracked), replace them. Otherwise, sharpen the blades. Do it yourself or have a professional sharpen them.
5. Check tires for wear; replace if necessary.
6. Check for loose nuts, bolts, and screws. Tighten those that are loose.

limited time. See "Here's How To Design for Lower Maintenance" (page 39) for good tips.

Finalize your plant list. Include the number of each plant that you need. A plant list is like a grocery list: they both keep you from buying the wrong items or more than you need. You may still succumb to the temptation of new plants, but the list will help keep overbuying to a minimum.

ROSES

Lay in some straw in case of a late freeze; straw is available at feed stores year-round. A light covering can make the difference between a plant that thrives and one that succumbs to a late winterkill.

Start a master list of the roses you have. Include the basics: name (botanic if it's a species); type (such as hybrid tea, shrub, or floribunda); when planted; and color (use the catalog or tag description; change it later if it's not accurate). Add new varieties as you plant them. Cross plants off if they die. Keep it simple: date of bloom; repeated bloom (if applicable); overall look and health (vigorous, spindly, well-branched, many flowers); fragrance (none, mild, strong and a descriptive word such as rose, spicy, or apple); and any pests and/or diseases and treatment. Allow space for comments: for example, "lots of flowers," "must have more," or "dig up and toss."

TREES & SHRUBS

Take a long, hard look at the large trees and shrubs in your landscape. Have any grown out of bounds, grown so tall they shade other plants (or the whole back yard), or require too much pruning to keep them at the size you want? If so, consider removing or transplanting it. Transplanting large specimens should be done by a professional and can be costly. Landscapers who specialize in moving large plants may buy yours to put in someone else's garden.

■ *Climbing hydrangeas are heavy vines growing to 20 feet or more and can be trained to grow up a large tree.*

MARCH

SUCCESSFUL GARDENING: GROWING ROSES

Before you buy any rose, read and follow these guidelines. Otherwise, you may end up with an expensive annual that *may* bloom its first season, but is unlikely to come back in future years.

- **Location, location, location**—first and foremost! Choose a space that gets at least six hours of *direct sun*. Roses need room to breathe, so pick a spot that allows for good air circulation. Don't crowd roses—together or with other plants. Keep them away from large plants that shade them and compete for soil nutrients. Provide well-drained, fertile soil. Add compost, well-rotted manure, or leaf mold to make the soil richer. Mix in builder's sand and compost to enhance drainage.

- **The right plant for the right place.** Make sure the plant is rated hardy for your zone.

■ *Grow roses in the right spot, in good light, feed and mulch them, and they will reward you with beautiful blooms.*

When possible, purchase a rose grown on its own rootstock (sometimes called "own-root" roses), which are generally hardier than grafted roses. The "knob" near the base of the main stem (bud union) is where the flowering rose was grafted to hardy rootstock. Choose the sturdiest, healthiest plant you can find that is in sync with the current outdoor conditions. For example, don't buy a container-grown rose that has leafed out if the soil is frozen; you can't plant it. Choose a plant with at least three healthy canes that are broader than a pencil.

- **Roses need TLC**. Give rose plants tender loving care. This includes mulching, feeding, watering, weeding (often unnecessary if the plant is mulched well), pruning, preparing the plant for winter dormancy, and controlling pests and diseases.

VINES & GROUNDCOVERS

Consider letting a few vines run horizontally as groundcovers. Use non-aggressive plants that won't suffocate their neighbors or strangle the stems and trunks. Climbing hydrangea, euonymus, and other vines can climb tree trunks for added interest. Do not use twining vines, such as bittersweet, which can girdle and kill a tree.

PLANT

ALL

Wait until soil thaws and dries before getting out your shovel. Test the soil by gently squeezing a handful, then tap it with your finger. If it breaks into smaller pieces, it's ready to work. Working wet soil causes damage that can take years to repair.

Use a transplant solution at planting, which helps get plants off to a good start, encouraging strong root growth. Follow mixing directions on the label.

ANNUALS & BIENNIALS

Continue starting seeds indoors. See February Plant (page 41) for detailed seed-starting instructions. From early to mid-March, plant coleus, dusty miller, flowering tobacco, pinks, snapdragon, and verbena. From mid- to late March, sow alyssum, moss rose (portulaca), and salvia seeds.

Plant geraniums that were stored in a cool, dark location for winter. Use lightly moistened, sterile potting mix and a clean container with a drainage hole. Cut plants back to 4 to 6 inches tall. Water the soil thoroughly, allowing the excess to run out the bottom of the pot.

SUCCESSFUL GARDENING: HARDENING OFF

■ *When using a cold frame for hardening off, be sure to open it in the daytime and close it at night.*

Indoor-grown transplants, plants that overwintered inside, and tender plants need to be hardened off (acclimated) before moving them into the garden. Without slowly adapting the plants to life outside, they would likely die of shock.

Two weeks before planting time, stop fertilizing and allow the soil to dry slightly before watering again. Move the plants to a shaded, protected location outside. Slowly introduce plants to full sun conditions. Move into the sun for one or two hours the first day. Increase the amount of sun time the plants receive each day. Move indoors or cover with a polyspun row cover or a light blanket if frost threatens. Move back outdoors or remove the cover the next morning. The plants will be ready to go into the garden in two weeks.

BULBS

Start canna rhizomes as you would caladiums. Check the rhizomes for any signs of rot (soft spots, discoloration) or evidence of mold or mildew. Cut the rhizome so there are one or two buds per piece. Plant the piece of rhizome and cover it with 2 inches of planting medium. Follow the rest of the instructions as for caladiums on page 54.

EDIBLES

If you live in the warmer parts of our region (Oklahoma, Kansas, southern Iowa, and southern Nebraska), start the hardiest plants—those that can withstand a frost—indoors the first three weeks of this month. This includes most of the mustard family (brassicas): broccoli, cauliflower, cabbage, kale, mustard, and Brussels sprouts. In the cooler areas, start them the last two weeks of March and the first week of April. Plant them in pots, peat pots, yogurt containers, seed flats, or milk cartons cut to half their height. These are suggestions for seed-starting containers; you will undoubtedly come up with other good planters. Poke a couple of drainage holes in the bottom of non-porous containers.

Follow the instructions for seed starting in February Plant (page 41). Sow two or three seeds in an individual container. Label the containers. Sometimes one seed doesn't germinate, but the other one does. Once they are up and starting to put out true leaves, remove the weaker or smaller one. If you can't bear disposing of any living thing, repot the smaller seedling; keep or give to a fellow gardener. Grow indoors until planting time, or move to a cold frame when it has reached a good size.

PERENNIALS & ORNAMENTAL GRASSES

Ordering some of the newer and harder-to-find perennial varieties as plants could blow your

■ *Thin plants when they have two sets of leaves, cutting the smaller ones off at soil level.*

MARCH

HERE'S HOW

TO PLANT CALADIUMS

Start caladiums indoors six to eight weeks before the last frost date.

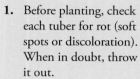

■ *Plant caladium bulbs with the rounded side up.*

■ *Caladiums are eye catching even as the leaves begin to emerge.*

1. Before planting, check each tuber for rot (soft spots or discoloration). When in doubt, throw it out.
2. Fill 6-inch pots (or use a flat for mass plantings) to within 3 inches of the rim with damp milled sphagnum moss or vermiculite. If you plan to grow the caladiums in a container outdoors, start them in that pot.
3. Place the tuber on the soil round side up; allow 1 inch between tubers. Cover the tubers with 1 inch of potting medium. Water well. Set on a sunny windowsill or under fluorescent lights.
4. Keep the pots between 80 to 85 degrees Fahrenheit (use a heating mat) until the tubers sprout, and keep the soil lightly moist until planting time.

Caladiums are magnificent in a hanging basket. Fill a moss-lined basket with damp, milled sphagnum moss. Plant one tuber on the top, and poke several tubers into the soil on the sides and bottom of the basket. As the leaves grow, the outside of the basket will be aglow with the showy, variegated leaves.

garden budget for the year. The only affordable way to get them is to grow them from seed. Check seed packets for starting times. Continue planting seeds and transplanting seedlings.

Bare-root plants generally arrive right about planting time. Plant them directly in the garden if the soil is workable. If the plants arrive early or winter stays late, store dormant bare-root plants in a cool, dark location. A root cellar or refrigerator works fine. Keep the roots lightly moist. If the plant started to grow during shipping or storage, pot it up and grow indoors in a sunny window or under artificial lights. Plant outside after the danger of frost has passed.

ROSES

A bare-root rose can be put in the ground before the last frost date as long as the ground is workable, not too wet, and the plant is dormant. As soon as you get it, unwrap and soak in water with a handful of soil mixed in for at least eight hours before

planting. If you cannot plant within 24 hours, wrap in wet newspaper and store at 40 degrees Fahrenheit in the dark for up to a week. If it is likely to be longer, plant it temporarily in a large container filled with lightly moistened potting soil and keep it cool. If the rose has already leafed out, pot it up. Keep it in a cool, bright place until danger of frost has passed, and then plant it outside. Otherwise, the tender leaves and buds could freeze.

TREES & SHRUBS

Late winter and early spring are the best times to transplant trees and shrubs—when the ground has thawed, the soil is moist, and before the plant leafs out. Plan ahead; at least two working days before digging, call 811 (a free service that arranges for a utility company to come and mark underground utilities so you don't cut into an electric, phone, water, cable, or gas line). Get some strong friends to help you transplant; wet soil is heavy and moving plants is awkward. It's worth the expense to hire an experienced

HERE'S HOW

TO PLANT A BARE-ROOT ROSE

Dig a hole several inches deeper and wider than the root system. Fill the hole with transplant solution and give it an hour to soak in. If there is still solution in the hole after an hour, dig deeper and wider. Mix in builder's sand and organic matter to increase drainage.

1. Mix the soil from the hole with an equal amount of compost and 1 cup each of rock phosphate, bone meal, and blood meal. Put enough amended soil in the hole to form a cone to support the roots.
2. Prune out any small canes (thinner than a pencil), leaving three or four healthy canes. Cut back any damaged or disproportionately long roots.
3. Place the rose so that the roots fan out over the cone.
4. Adjust the rose so the bud union (bump on stem above roots where hybrid was grafted onto rootstock) is about 2 inches below soil level. Add amended soil until the hole is two-thirds full. Add 2 to 3 quarts of transplant solution and let it soak in.
5. Fill in the rest of the hole; gently firm the soil with your hands.
6. Water in with transplant solution.
7. Cover two-thirds of the exposed plant with moist soil to protect it from wind and weather. The extra moisture allows the plant to develop properly. Keep an eye on the rose. When the new growth is 1 to 2 inches long, gently remove the extra soil, smoothing it out to soil level. Mulch well.

professional with the right equipment to move large plants. If the plant is not special or a favorite—merely overgrown or in the wrong place—consider replacing it. You'll save money and have a young, healthy plant—the right plant for the right place.

VINES & GROUNDCOVERS

Before creating a new planting area, get the soil tested so you can add the recommended amendments when you dig the area. (See Plan at the beginning of this chapter for more details.)

See "Here's How To Prepare a New Bed for Groundcovers" on page 57.

CARE

ALL

A cold frame is versatile for getting a jumpstart on the gardening season in spring, starting seeds outdoors, hardening off transplants, and extending the gardening season in fall. See "Here's How To Build a Cold Frame" on page 58.

TO TRANSPLANT A SHRUB

1. Loosely tie up branches with twine to prevent you from damaging them.
2. Dig the shrub slightly wider and deeper than the rootball size. (For a 2-foot-tall shrub, 12 inches in diameter × 9 inches deep; 3-foot-tall, 14 × 11 inches; 4-foot to 6-foot, 16 × 12 inches).
3. Use a sharp spade to undercut the rootball; use hand pruners or loppers to cut tough roots.
4. Slide a tarp or piece of burlap under the rootball. Use your strong friends to help lift it out of the hole and move it to its new home.
5. Dig a hole as deep as the rootball and two to three times as wide. Carefully place the shrub in the hole and slide out or cut away the tarp.
6. Backfill the hole and water-in with at least 1 gallon of transplant solution. Add a 2-inch layer of organic mulch, taking care to keep it at least 2 inches away from the base of the plant.

■ *Dig a hole slightly deeper and slightly wider than the rootball of the plant.*

Check plants in the cold frame daily. Vent it on sunny days to prevent heat damage. Close the lid in late afternoon to keep plants warm on cold nights. Automatic venting systems are available from garden centers and online. Unless you are home 24/7 to monitor the temperature in the cold frame, an automatic vent is worth the investment, especially as the temperature can fluctuate so drastically within a few hours.

Row covers of spun polypropylene fabric can also extend the season. They help trap heat around the plants while allowing air, water, and light to pass through. Loosely drape fabric over the plants. Anchor on the sides, leaving enough slack in the fabric to allow for plant growth or create a tunnel with fabric-draped wire hoops.

ANNUALS & BIENNIALS

Harden off pansies started indoors. A cold frame will protect them from frost and will allow them to adjust to the cooler, harsher outdoor conditions. Reduce watering and stop fertilizing until they are planted in their permanent location.

Pinch out the growing tips of leggy annuals to encourage branching. Pinched plants will develop stouter stems and more branches.

Continue to take 4- to 6-inch cuttings from annuals you want to propagate. See February Care for detailed instructions.

BULBS

Although minor bulbs (such as snowdrops, glory-of-the-snow, and Siberian squill) are not usually thought of as cut flowers, a group of eight to twelve flowers is charming in a small container like an antique inkwell or salt shaker.

Cut off any brown or yellow leaves from forced bulbs.

EDIBLES

Once the brassicas and other cool-season vegetable seeds germinate, move the flats and pots into a cool, bright place. If kept at regular house temperatures, they need a longer period to harden off before going in the garden.

Enjoy your delicious indoor salad greens. Try drizzling them with balsamic vinegar and orange juice as a fat-free, easy-to-prepare dressing.

LAWNS

Once the snow and ice melt, and the water dissipates into the soil, you can begin lawn care.

Working on frozen or waterlogged soil damages grass and can kill it. Clean up any leaves and debris.

PERENNIALS & ORNAMENTAL GRASSES

Check unmulched gardens for signs of frost heaving. Replant any perennials that were pushed out of the soil. Wait until temperatures are consistently above freezing before removing mulch. However, if plants are starting to grow, remove the mulch. Keep some mulch and a floating row cover handy to protect the tender tips of emerging hostas, primroses, and other early plants that may be damaged by a sudden drop in temperature.

Cut back ornamental grasses as described in February Care (page 42).

If the foliage on Japanese sedge grass looks weather-beaten after winter, cut it back to the crown. If it still looks good, remove any brown or dead leaves by combing through with your fingers.

Cut back any ratty foliage on Japanese forest grass.

ROSES

Light frosts can kill tender growth, so don't remove winter protection too early. Look under the mulch to see if there is evidence of new growth. When danger of frost has passed, gently remove the mulch. Avoid injuring tender (and small) new growth. If a freeze threatens, cover the plant with straw, blankets, or a floating row cover.

If you used a Styrofoam cone as protection, vent the rose during the day. Slowly harden off the rose, removing the cone for a few hours each day and returning it at night. Gradually, over a period of two weeks, the cone can remain off.

Start spring pruning. Begin by cutting off any dead or broken canes, cutting down to live wood. You can tell if it's alive by scratching the cane lightly with your thumbnail. If the area is green, it's alive; if it's brown, it is dead. Make cuts at a 45-degree angle above outward-facing bud eyes (small nubs on the stems from which leaves will emerge). For more detailed information on pruning roses, go to Appendix (page 196).

TREES & SHRUBS

Damage from animals, snow, and ice becomes more obvious as snow melts. Rabbits and voles often leave teeth marks on the lighter area on the trunk where they have gnawed. Gnawing around most of the trunk girdles it, keeping nutrients and water from flowing up from the roots to the rest of the tree. Wait and see if the plant leafs out.

HERE'S HOW

TO PREPARE A NEW BED FOR GROUNDCOVERS

You can prepare the soil for a new area when the soil thaws and is dry enough to work. Do not till or dig deeply under established trees and shrubs.

1. Start by removing or killing (with a total vegetation killer) any existing weeds and grass. Leave the dead grass intact on hillsides where erosion is a concern.
2. Work the recommended fertilizer (from your soil test results) and 2 to 4 inches of organic matter into the top 6 to 12 inches of soil.
3. Rake the bed smooth and wait for the soil to settle before planting. See May Plant (page 86) for details on planting.

■ *Rake the area smooth, water it gently, and let the soil settle for several days before planting.*

HERE'S HOW

TO BUILD A COLD FRAME

Use plywood to make the walls and an old window sash or a wood frame covered with plastic for the top. Most cold frames are 6 feet long and 3 feet wide or made to fit the size of the top.

1. Depending on how high you want the cold frame to be (consider the size of the plants you'll be putting in it), make the back wall 18 to 30 inches tall and as wide as the cover.

■ *A cold frame can be put together easily using an old window as the cover.*

Make the front wall slightly lower—12 to 24 inches tall with the same width as the cover.
2. Cut side walls to the same length as the cover with a slanted top that matches the height of the front and back walls.
3. Use 2 × 2s for the corners. Make the posts longer than the sides if you want to use them to anchor the frame into the ground. Use galvanized nails to attach the walls to the 2 × 2s.
4. Place the cover on the frame or attach it with hinges.
5. Face the front of the cold frame toward the south for maximum light and heat. Placing the cold frame next to the house screens it from the wind and adds some warmth from the foundation.

Prune or remove damaged branches. If a tree or shrub is severely damaged, it is best to remove it.

Finish pruning dormant trees and summer- and fall-blooming shrubs before they leaf out. Do not prune spring-blooming shrubs like forsythia and lilacs (except to remove damaged branches); you will cut off the flower buds. Read the Appendix (page 192) for detailed pruning information and directions.

■ *Prune small branches back to within ½ inch of their attachment to larger branches.*

VINES & GROUNDCOVERS

Start cleaning out beds. Remove debris and leaves. Cut off winter-damaged leaves and stems. Check shallow-rooted groundcovers, such as woolly thyme, sea thrift, and dianthus, for frost heaving. If they have risen out of the soil, gently press them back down, and water lightly.

Edge planting beds with a sharp spade or edging tool. This helps keep the groundcovers in and the surrounding grass out of the beds.

Start pruning vines and groundcovers. Remove dead and damaged stems and branches. See specific directions for when and what to prune in the Appendix (page 192).

WATER

ALL

Check seedlings every day. Water whenever the soil surface begins to dry. Apply enough water to thoroughly moisten the soil. Avoid overwatering, which can lead to root rot and damping-off disease. As plants grow and develop larger root systems, they will need less frequent watering.

SUCCESSFUL GARDENING: TO CUT OR NOT TO CUT PERENNIALS

■ *Cut woody perennials back to within several inches of the ground.*

It can be confusing to know which perennials need to be cut back before they start growing in spring. If you cut too much, especially from evergreen perennials, such as ferns, hellebores, and lungwort, you risk losing all the foliage. Take care not to damage leaves of early-emerging plants. Follow this cutting guide:

- **All stems to within several inches of the soil:** Russian sage (cut stems at 45-degree angle above an outward-facing bud)
- **Dead leaves only:** Evergreens like barrenwort, coral bells, lamb's ear, lungwort
- **Dead tips of stems:** Candytuft, lavender, thyme
- **Dead foliage and stems:** All other perennials

Check the cold frame daily. Monitor soil moisture with your finger or a soil probe and water as needed. Plants in a cold frame need less-frequent watering when hardening off.

As the soil thaws, if it is dry and there is no rain in the forecast, water so that plants get 1 inch of water a week.

ANNUALS & BIENNIALS

Water potted annuals whenever the top few inches of soil start to dry. Apply enough water so that some runs out the drainage holes. Pour off any water in the saucer; the water could lead to root rot.

BULBS

Crocus, snowdrops, Siberian squill, and glory-of-the-snow need to be lightly moist during their growing season. If snow melt doesn't provide this, water the plants.

When hyacinths, daffodils, and other spring bulbs forced in pots finish blooming, keep the plants watered until the soil is workable and you can plant them outside.

EDIBLES

Follow January's watering regimen (see page 30).

LAWNS

Water grass along sidewalks, drives, and steps—any areas where deicing salts had been applied—to flush the salts off the lawn and out of the soil. Otherwise the salts can kill the lawn.

Water any lawn that was sodded, seeded, or overseeded last fall to keep young roots growing.

PERENNIALS & ORNAMENTAL GRASSES

Keep the packing material around stored bare-root plants lightly moist until you can plant them.

ROSES

Keep newly planted bare-root roses evenly moist until they are established.

TREES & SHRUBS

Once the ground has thawed, wait until the top 4 to 6 inches of soil are dry before watering. Apply 1 inch of water a week.

Thoroughly water any plants that were exposed to deicing salts to help wash the salts away from the roots.

Whenever the soil in aboveground planters is thawed and dry, water them thoroughly.

VINES & GROUNDCOVERS

Continue the watering regimen for vines overwintered indoors described in February Water.

■ *Pelletized, slow-release fertilizer—added to new plants or when transplanting—eliminates the need for monthly feeding.*

FERTILIZE

ALL

When using any fertilizer, always follow all package instructions for proper application, frequency, concentration, and mixing/dilution.

ANNUALS & BIENNIALS

Start fertilizing recently transplanted annuals when new growth appears. Use a dilute solution of any flowering houseplant fertilizer.

Fertilize or foliar feed seedlings every other week with a dilute solution of any complete water-soluble fertilizer.

BULBS

As bulbs emerge, sprinkle bulb food around the planting area. Water it in well. Be sure to wash any fertilizer from the leaves or flowers.

ROSES

Save used coffee grounds. (If you don't drink coffee, many coffee shops will give grounds if you ask for them.) Dry them completely and put in a zipper storage bag in the freezer. Add them to alkaline soil to provide nourishment, give it more friability, and lower the pH. Save banana peels, which are high in potassium. When the ground has thawed, dig peels in around roses—about 4 inches deep and 8 inches away from the base of the plant. Each rose can use about five banana peels; add them clockwise around the plant so you remember where the last one went.

VINES & GROUNDCOVERS

Fertilize after the ground thaws and before growth begins. Use the type and amount of fertilizer recommended by the soil test report.

PROBLEM-SOLVE

ALL

Watch for damping off in seedlings. See February Problem-Solve for more information and treatment.

Check the label before mixing and applying any pesticide, insecticide, herbicide, repellent, or any other chemical.

ANNUALS & BIENNIALS

Watch for whiteflies, fungus gnats, aphids, scale, and mites. See January Problem-Solve (page 32) for complete information on these pests and how to control them.

BULBS

Check any forced bulbs you are saving to plant outdoors for signs of rot or mildew. If you find any, throw away the bulb—soil and all.

EDIBLES

Incorporate some of these herbs among your edibles to attract beneficial insects, which can control insect pests, and pollinators: caraway, catnip, daisy, dill, fennel, hyssop, lemon balm, lovage, mint, parsley, rosemary, thyme, and yarrow.

LAWNS

Rake grass briskly with a leaf rake to reduce the risk of snow mold. Raking fluffs the grass and allows it to dry.

If there is evidence of voles (slightly raised, 2-inch-wide runways across the lawn), gently step on the areas to compress the runway and re-establish contact of grass roots with the soil.

ROSES

Some gardeners apply dormant oil in early spring to ward off blackspot and powdery mildew. Use plain horticultural oil with no insecticide or pesticide additives, that oils used on trees often contain. Spray only when the temperatures are above 40 degrees Fahrenheit; otherwise, you can damage the plants.

Rose rosette disease (RRD) has become the scourge of home gardeners and professional rose growers. It is an incurable, systemic viral disease that infects an entire plant—roots and all—and kills it. The most obvious symptoms are closely bunched multiple bright red shoots with clusters of soft, pliable thorns, small leaves, and deformed or no blooms. RRD is transmitted by microscopic mites that can spread on the wind and through contaminated clothing and equipment. The mites (*Phyllocoptes fructiphilus*) are endemic on multiflora roses (*Rosa multiflora*), which grow wild and rampant. Once a rose has RRD, destroy it. Bag the infected plant and dig up the entire root system, extending the bag over the root mass. Clean up any leaves on the ground and bag them. Put the bags in the trash. Do not plant another rose in that place for two years, as any small piece of root left behind will infect the new plant. Clean any tools used, as well as your garden gloves, with a disinfectant such as Lysol; wash your clothes in hot water. As yet, there are no disease-resistant roses, except two species, *R. setigera* and *R. carolina*. For prevention, remove and destroy any multiflora roses growing in the vicinity (or kill them with a systemic herbicide). Some experts recommend also removing any roses growing near the infected rose. Some gardeners are abandoning rose gardens in favor of incorporating roses with other plants, which may reduce the spread of the disease. Others are thinning their gardens so there is plenty of room between roses.

TREES & SHRUBS

Spray trees with dormant oil if you had a problem last year with galls (harmless but unsightly bumps on leaves), aphids, mites, or scale. Routine spraying of *all* trees is costly and unnecessary. Apply *only* when the temperature will be above 40 degrees Fahrenheit or above for at least 12 hours after the application. Do it yourself if you have the equipment or hire a professional.

Monitor and destroy egg masses of Eastern tent caterpillar, gypsy moth, and tussock moth (see January Problem-Solve, page 33, for details).

Cankerworms (inchworms) are 1-inch-long brown or green insects that feed on elm, apple, hackberry, linden, oak, boxelder, maple, and ash, as well as shrubs growing beneath heavily infested trees. If birds and the weather don't control these pests, apply sticky bands around trunks of trees defoliated last year and any currently infested. Place bands from mid-March through mid-June and again from mid-October to mid-December. Use store-bought sticky bands or make your own with a length of fabric treated with a commercial sticky material, such as Tanglefoot, and tie it around the tree trunk.

VINES & GROUNDCOVERS

Monitor animal damage. Apply repellents if animals are present and food supply is limited.

April

Celebrate Arbor Day. Nationally—and in Nebraska (where it started in 1872 and is a state holiday), Iowa, Kansas, and South Dakota—it's celebrated on the last Friday in April. North Dakota's is the first Friday in May, while Oklahoma has Arbor Week (the last full week of April). Individual states set their own date. The date may even differ in some cities; check with the Arbor Day Foundation (www.arborday.org). Find out when your community celebrates Arbor Day and participate. At least plant a tree—or two or three—on your property, for a friend, or join in a community planting.

They say, "April showers bring May flowers." But in our region it can just as easily be snow or drought. And if it's rain, it can be of epic proportions. Yet if you drive around during a rain, you may notice some sprinklers spewing water on lawns and gardens. If you have an automatic watering system, make sure it includes a rain sensor. If you see a sprinkler running in the rain, consider leaving a note suggesting that the homeowner get a rain sensor. Water is too precious (and costly) a natural resource to waste.

The changeable weather is hard on gardens and anxious gardeners. Make sure the air *and* soil are warm before planting. Only seeds of frost-tolerant plants can withstand the cold soils of April—if it is thawed. Invest in a soil thermometer (they cost very little) to keep from second guessing whether or not the time is right to plant.

Visit local garden centers and nurseries to get fresh ideas and see new plants. Find a vacant space in your garden or add a few planters to accommodate these late additions to your plan. If you have the luxury of space, consider adding a "newbie" garden that can serve as a temporary home (and trial garden) for new plants until you decide where their permanent location should be. This is much better for the plants than having them sitting by the house or driveway waiting to be planted, getting stressed and becoming rootbound in their original containers.

PLAN

ALL

Keep your garden journal up to date. Record the name, variety, and source for the plants you add to your landscape. Note pruning and trimming done on new and established plants.

Record weather conditions, seed-starting dates, successes, failures, discoveries, pests, significant weather events, and other helpful garden information. Compare the current season with past years' garden records. Make needed adjustments in planting times and other tasks based on current weather and past experience.

Start a bloom chart to keep track of the name and bloom times of various plants in your landscape. This will help you fill any flowering voids when planning next year's additions. After a few years, you'll have a picture of what will bloom where and when.

Take a walk through your landscape. Note what survived and what may need replacing. Adjust your landscape plans to accommodate these changes.

ANNUALS & BIENNIALS

Talk to friends about what they are growing. It's likely they will have plants you want (and vice versa). You can organize a swap when the plants get big enough. Throw a seed-starting party so each person grows certain plants for everyone, especially annuals you may not want in large numbers.

BULBS

Don't be disappointed if the bloom of the glory-of-the-snow you planted last fall is not as spectacular as you had hoped. Leave the bulbs in place. They self-seed freely; within a couple of years, you'll have a starry carpet to dazzle friends and neighbors.

EDIBLES

Even though we think about plants as food to enjoy through the sense of taste, don't ignore the senses of smell and sight—even in the garden before it comes to the table. Imagine the citrusy scent of lemon balm in summer and how rainbow chard looks like stained glass when the early morning or late afternoon sun shines through its colored stems and veins.

Every garden needs some fragrant foliage; site plants where you may lightly brush them as you pass. Many culinary herbs fit the bill; each has a distinctive aroma: anise hyssop, beebalm, borage, chamomile, chervil, chives, coriander, dill, fennel, lavender, lemon grass, lemon verbena, marjoram, oregano, parsley, sage, sweet woodruff, and tarragon. Some herbs, such as mint, have many varieties, each with a unique scent. Other multi-aromatics include basil, rosemary, and thyme.

■ *One-gallon plastic jugs act as individual hothouses allowing you to plant tender crops up to one month earlier.*

If you are in a hurry to plant tender vegetables and herbs, you can fashion individual hothouses from plastic 1-gallon milk jugs. Cut the bottom off the jugs. Four to six weeks before normal planting time, set the jugs where you plan to grow individual plants. Push them into the ground a bit so they don't fly off in a heavy wind. Screw the cap on and let it warm the soil for a couple of weeks. Remove the jug quickly to get the plant in the ground and then replace the jug. During the day, if it is warm, remove the cap to let the jug vent. Recap before nightfall.

LAWNS

Depending on the weather, mowing can begin anytime this month. Make sure your lawnmower is ready to go. See March Plan (page 51) for details on preparing your mower for the season.

SUCCESSFUL GARDENING: HEIGHT MATTERS

■ *Before you plant, track how the sun moves over the garden. Put the tallest plants in the "back" so they don't shade smaller ones.*

Be aware of the mature heights of the herbs and vegetables you put in the garden. Don't place tall plants in the front or edge of the garden, shading the small plants behind. As in any garden, taller plants like lovage, tomatoes, corn, and fennel go in the back (or center in the case of a round bed) with decreasing height as you go toward the front. Thyme, parsley, lettuces, additional salad greens, strawberries (even though they are fruit), radishes, carrots, and other low-growing herbs and vegetables are excellent along the edge of an informal bed, softening any hard edges.

ROSES

One option to poor drainage is to install drains if there is a place to send the water. However, that can be time-consuming and costly.

A raised bed is the best solution. If it's not as easy as it used to be for you to bend down, dig, and work at soil level, consider making a 2-foot-tall (or higher) raised bed with a broad edge so you can sit and garden. The bed can be as long as you like; make it narrow enough so you can reach into the middle from both sides. A raised bed has an advantage besides good drainage—the soil warms up earlier in spring so you can start enjoying your flowers before your neighbors do.

TREES & SHRUBS

As you walk around your neighborhood or visit others, take note of trees and shrubs that are blooming. Note their shape and size, as well as their leaves. When you get home, you can do some research online and find out more about the plant. Since the blooms may only last a few weeks, it's important for a tree or shrub to have other attributes that make it worthy of further consideration, including multi-seasonal interest, fall or winter color, form, and edible fruit or berries. Start making a new wish list.

Check local nurseries and garden centers for the more unusual and hard-to-find shrubs. (See March Plan, page 51.)

HERE'S HOW

TO TEST SOIL DRAINAGE

Roses need soil with good drainage. Before planting, do a perc (percolation) test:

■ *When doing a perc test, if there's water in the hole after one hour, you need to dig deeper and retest.*

1. Dig hole that is 10 inches deep and wide, fill it with water and wait.
2. If there is water in the hole after an hour, dig 6 inches deeper. Amend the soil taken from the hole with builder's sand and organic matter (compost, well-rotted manure, or leaf mold).
3. Add 6 inches of amended soil back into the hole. Refill the hole with water.
4. If the hole still retains water, this is not a good place for roses. However, it would be ideal for a bog garden.

SUCCESSFUL GARDENING: FRAGRANT ROSES

To some, a rose is not a rose if it has no scent. While hybrid tea roses can dominate any list of fragrant roses, they are not reliably hardy in Zone 5 and colder. Look to the tougher shrub, miniature, and floribunda roses to add their sweet scent in the cooler climes.

- 'Fourth of July™' (Cl)
- 'Abraham Darby' (Sh)
- 'Alchymist' (Sh)
- 'Angel Face' (F)
- 'Apricot Nectar' (F)
- 'Blossomtime' (Cl)
- 'Candy Stripe' (Ht)
- 'Chrysler Imperial' (Ht)
- 'Don Juan' (Cl)
- 'Double Delight' (Ht)
- 'Elle®' (Ht)
- 'Europeana' (F)
- 'Gertrude Jekyll' (Sh)
- 'Harison's Yellow' (Sh)
- 'Honey Perfume' (F)
- 'Iceberg' (F)
- 'Memorial Day™' (Ht)
- 'Mister Lincoln' (Ht)
- 'Perfume Delight' (Ht)
- *Rosa eglanteria* (Sp)
- *Rosa rugosa* (Sp)
- 'Royal Sunset™' (Cl)
- 'Scentimental' (F)
- 'Sundowner' (G)
- 'Sunsprite' (F)
- 'Sun Sprinkles' (M)
- 'Tiffany' (Ht)
- 'White Lightnin' (G)

■ *If it's fragrance you want, 'Gertrude Jekyll' (and many of the other David Austin roses) is a top choice.*

Key:

Cl – Climber	G – Grandiflora	M – Miniature	Sp – Species
F – Floribunda	Ht – Hybrid tea	Sh – Shrub	

If you're planning any planting or transplanting, call 811 at least two business days ahead of time so they can mark any underground utilities on your property.

PLANT

ALL

Use a transplant solution whenever you're planting. This diluted solution helps get plants off to a good start, encouraging strong root growth. Follow mixing directions on the label.

See "Here's How To Prepare a New Bed for Planting" on page 67 and "Here's How To Prepare Existing Beds for Planting" on page 68.

ANNUALS & BIENNIALS

Start zinnia, marigold, calendula, celosia, and blanket flower seeds indoors in mid-April (in early April in Kansas and Oklahoma). Transplant seedlings from flats to individual containers as soon as the first set of true leaves appear. Label everything.

Sow seeds directly in the garden for cleome, cosmos, four-o'clocks, globe amaranth, gloriosa daisy, morning glory, moss rose, and snapdragon. Follow planting and spacing directions on the seed packets.

Plant hardened-off frost-tolerant annuals, such as pansies, dusty miller, and snapdragons, outdoors in late April. Let the weather and soil temperature be your guide for your garden. Keep mulch or row covers handy to protect transplants from unexpected drops in temperature.

It's nice to add a splash of seasonal color under trees with annuals. To minimize root disturbance, sink old nursery pots in the soil with the upper lip even with the soil surface. Set a slightly smaller container filled with colorful annuals or edibles inside the buried pot. It's easy to change them out each season without disturbing the tree roots.

BULBS

Plant the hyacinth bulbs you forced indoors in the garden, and they will bloom the following spring. The flowers won't be as showy, but the fragrance will be as lovely as when they first bloomed. Plant other forced bulbs, including crocus, daffodils, and tulips. They should come back strong next year.

See "Here's How To Start Tuberous Begonias" on page 68.

Grow hardy cyclamen beneath shrubs, around trees, in rock gardens, or mixed borders. It thrives in well-drained, moist, slightly alkaline soil in light shade. Plant tubers concave side up (round side down), ½ inch deep, and 6 to 8 inches apart. Protect from harsh, heavy rains, but do not let tubers dry out. Once established, don't disturb them and they will slowly multiply.

Give dahlias a head start by planting them in pots indoors four to six weeks before last frost. Separate the tubers from the stalk. Leave 1 inch of stalk attached to each tuber; be sure the tuber has an eye or bud, which is essential for bloom. Pot dahlias in individual pots in a damp mix of equal parts peat moss and vermiculite with the tuber about 1 inch below soil level.

HERE'S HOW

TO PREPARE A NEW BED FOR PLANTING

Start the planting process for a new garden or bed by properly preparing the soil.

■ *Define the edge of the bed by using a straight shovel to cut inside the hose outline.*

■ *Another way to smother grass is to lay sheets of newspaper (six deep) on the area, water well, and wait.*

1. Remove existing grass with a sod cutter. Use the grass to patch problem areas in the lawn. Or treat the grass with a total vegetation killer. The grass and weeds must be actively growing for these chemicals to be effective. Wait four to fourteen days (check the label) before completing soil preparation. If you're not in a hurry to start planting, cover the area with black plastic and weigh or pin down the edges. The weeds and grass will die over a period of four to eight weeks—without the use of chemicals.

■ *Install edging to make mowing around the bed easier.*

■ *Add organic matter to feed the soil.*

2. Work the soil when it is lightly moist but not wet. Grab a handful of soil and gently squeeze. Open your fist and tap on the clump. If it breaks into smaller pieces, the soil is ready to be worked. If it stays in a clump, it is too wet; wait a few days and do the "fist test" again.

3. Add 2 to 4 inches of organic matter to the top 8 to 12 inches of soil. Use compost, peat moss, leaf mold, or well-aged manure to improve the drainage of clay soil and to increase water retention of sandy soil. Follow soil test recommendations for amendments. Recent research indicates that amended soils need little if any fertilizer. If you feed the soil (adding lots organic matter and using an organic mulch that will eventually break down), the soil will feed the plants.

4. Rake the garden smooth and allow the soil to settle. Lightly sprinkle the prepared site with water to speed up settling.

APRIL

HERE'S HOW

TO PREPARE EXISTING BEDS FOR PLANTING

Annuals can deplete the soil of nutrients. If you didn't get the soil tested last fall, do it now so you can add the recommended amendments. (See March Plan, All, page 50 for more details.)

1. Check the soil moisture; grab a handful of soil and gently squeeze it into a ball. Open your hand and lightly tap the soil ball. If it breaks up, the soil is ready to work. If it stays in a wet ball, wait a few days and try again.
2. Once the soil is dry enough, work 2 inches of aged manure, compost, or peat moss into the top 6 to 12 inches of garden soil. The organic matter will improve the drainage of heavy clay soils and increase the water-holding capacity of sandy soils.
3. Incorporate any fertilizer or other soil amendments as recommended by the soil test.
4. Rake the garden smooth, sloping the soil away from any building or the center of island beds. Lightly sprinkle with water or wait a week to allow the soil to settle.

EDIBLES

If you live in the cooler parts of our region—northern Iowa, northern Nebraska, and the Dakotas—continue starting brassicas (broccoli, cauliflower, cabbage, and Brussels sprouts) and other cool-loving vegetables indoors the first week of this month. (See February Plant, page 41, for information on seed starting.) Grow them indoors until planting time, or start them and then put them in a cold frame when they have reached a good size.

Use the planting chart on page 23 (January Plan) or follow the instructions on the seed packets for starting seeds of certain warm-weather plants indoors, including tomatoes, eggplants, peppers, basil, cilantro, and most other annual herbs. Wait until the soil is about 60 degrees Fahrenheit before direct-sowing the larger-seeded vegetables or any root vegetables directly into the garden—they don't transplant well.

HERE'S HOW

TO START TUBEROUS BEGONIAS

■ *Tuberous begonias, which bloom in summer and give a tropical look, are not hardy and are best started indoors.*

The ideal time to start tuberous begonias is at least six weeks before the last frost. If you're weary of winter foliage and eager for a tropical look, you can start them earlier and enjoy their magnificent leaves indoors before moving them outside.

Short on space? Use a flat to plant begonias *en masse*, otherwise use individual 4- to 6-inch pots. If the begonia is going to be in a container outdoors, start it in that container to avoid transplanting stress and the probability of breaking off a stem or two.

1. Fill the pot or flat to within 2 inches of the rim with a soilless potting mix.
2. Plant the tuber round side down. Cover with 1 inch of soil. Tamp down gently and water well with transplant solution.
3. Put the pot in a warm, semi-shady area at about 70 degrees Fahrenheit. Bottom heat (try using a heating cable) helps the tubers root.
4. Keep the soil moist but not soggy.
5. When all danger of frost has passed, transplant outdoors being careful not to disturb the roots.

■ *It is easier to direct sow small seeds if you pour them into your hand and sprinkle them onto the soil.*

Be creative: don't plant in soldierly rows. As soon as the soil is workable and not too wet, plant peas of all kinds: sugar snap, snow peas, and traditional English peas.

■ *Brassicas (cabbage, kale, broccoli, and Brussels sprouts) thrive in cool weather and can be planted before the last frost date.*

Harden off the brassicas you started inside and plant them. Direct seed kohlrabi and other brassicas in the garden. Sow seeds of lettuces and

other salad greens, including arugula, corn salad, mâche, mizuna, and mustard outdoors. Plant them singly or mix together for a personal mesclun mix. In addition, sow Asian greens, arugula, kale, rainbow Swiss chard, spinach, and Japanese red mustard.

Consider edging a path or bed with a salad mix. Put it where the neighbors can see it—but not their dogs. Show your friends how to harvest— outer leaves first—as you'll have more than enough to share. Don't worry about the varying heights of the plants; you will be harvesting them all when they are young.

LAWNS

The grass is turning green so you can readily see any problem areas and fix them. You can purchase lawn repair kits that have seed and mulch. Or, make your own by combining a handful of quality lawn seed mixture (choose the mix that is best suited for the specific area you're repairing) with a bucketful of topsoil. Remove the dead grass, loosen the soil (amend it if needed), and spread the seed/ soil mix (about ½ inch thick) on the patch. Water gently so the seeds are not disturbed. Mulch to conserve moisture.

Start laying sod once the ground thaws and is dry enough to work. Test by grabbing a handful of soil and squeezing it into a ball. Open your hand and lightly tap it. If the ball breaks up, the soil is ready to work; if it doesn't, wait a few days and try again.

See "Here's How To Lay Sod" on page 72.

PERENNIALS & ORNAMENTAL GRASSES

Begin planting once the soil is prepared (see this month's Plant for complete instructions) and plants are available.

Purchase plants as bare-root, field-grown in pots, or greenhouse-grown plants. Do not buy perennials in bloom, especially at this time of year, as they will have been forced. Most perennials bloom for a short time and only once a year. If you buy it in bloom, there will only be foliage for the rest of the season—no flowers at the normal bloom time.

HERE'S HOW

TO PLANT A TREE OR SHRUB

Before planting, gently pull soil away from the trunk of the tree until you see the root flare (where roots flare out from the trunk). Measure the height of the rootball from the bottom to the root flare; that is the depth of the rootball. For a shrub, the rootball is the entire mass in the container or wrapped in burlap. Trees need to be planted with the root flare at or just above ground level; shrubs should be planted at the same soil level they were in the container or in the burlap. Otherwise, planting is the same for both.

Studies have shown that trees and shrubs have much better root systems when planted in "native" soil than if the soil in the planting hole is amended. In amended soil, the roots don't reach out past the planting hole. In native soil, roots spread into the surrounding area.

Start by digging a hole as deep as the root system and at least two to three times as wide. Roughen the sides of the hole with a fork or shovel.

■ *When digging the planting hole, break up any clods of soil.*

CONTAINER-GROWN

1. While it's still in its container, soak the plant in a bucket of transplant solution for several minutes.
2. Remove the plant from the container. If it is packed in tightly, which indicates it may be rootbound, cut the container from around the root mass with scissors and, if necessary, unwind any roots. If it's very rootbound, with roots spreading all over the sides, use a knife to make four ½-inch-deep vertical slits equidistant around the rootball. This loosens the roots, allowing them to grow into the surrounding soil.
3. Place the plant in the hole, adjusting the amount of soil underneath so the root flare is at or slightly above soil level (for a shrub, so it is at the same level it was in the container). Water with a gallon of transplant solution.
4. Fill in with remaining soil. Gently tamp the soil down with your hands.

■ *Before removing the plant from its container, set it in the hole to check that it will be at the right depth.*

■ *Once the plant is in the ground, make a water basin to direct water to the roots.*

5. Make a 3-inch-high ring of soil—creating a water basin—around the planting hole, and water with a gallon or two of transplant solution, depending on the size of the tree or shrub.
6. Add a 2- to 3-inch layer of wood chips or twice-shredded bark as mulch, keeping it several inches away from the base of the plant.
7. Cut off any broken or damaged branches.

BARE-ROOT

1. Soak the roots overnight in cool water.
2. Make a cone of soil so the roots can spread down around the cone with the root flare at or slightly above ground level (for a shrub, the top of roots will be at or just below ground level). Place the plant on the cone and make any adjustments necessary.
3. Follow steps 4 to 7 from Container-Grown (at left).

BALLED-AND-BURLAPPED

1. Loosen the tie around the top of the burlap. Place the plant in the hole, and by angling and lifting it, remove all of the burlap—and the metal or plastic mesh basket, if there is one. The root flare should be at or slightly above soil level (for a shrub, plant it at the same level as it was growing).
2. Once the plant is positioned at the proper height, water with several gallons of transplant solution.
3. Follow steps 4 to 7 from Container-Grown (at left).

■ *Once the plant is in the hole, carefully remove all the burlap and any material under the rootball.*

ROSES

Continue planting bare-root roses, following the instructions in March Plant (page 55). The roses in cardboard boxes are usually bare root; you can tell by how light they are. Remove the rose from the box before planting. If it has leafed out, plant it temporarily in a large container and keep in a cool, bright place until it is warm enough to plant outside without frost damaging its tender growth.

TREES & SHRUBS

Finish transplanting shrubs before they leaf out. See March (page 56) for complete instructions.

Start planting trees and shrubs as soon as plants are available. Keep them in a cool, shaded location until you can plant them. Cover the roots of balled-and-burlapped plants with woodchips. Water often enough to keep the roots moist.

VINES & GROUNDCOVERS

Plant bare-root plants as soon as they arrive. If you can't plant right away, pack the roots in moist peat moss, and keep the plants in a cool, frost-free location until planted. Plant so that the crown (the point where stem joins the roots) is even with the soil.

Start annual vines from seeds indoors. Starting them indoors results in earlier flowering for a longer bloom period. See February Plant (page 41) for directions on growing from seed.

CARE

ANNUALS & BIENNIALS

Adjust grow lights over seedlings. The lights should be about 6 inches above the tops of the young plants. Lower the lights if seedlings are long and leggy. Raise the lights as seedlings grow.

Cut back on indoor watering and stop fertilizing the first transplants.

Prune back leggy annuals as needed. Use the cuttings to start additional plants for this

HERE'S HOW

TO LAY SOD

Before you purchase sod, calculate the square footage of the area to be sodded. A roll of sod (measuring 1½ feet wide by 6 feet long) covers 9 square feet. Choose sod that has been grown on soil similar to yours, is healthy and green, is a blend of several grasses, and most important—is freshly cut. Arrange to pick it up or have it delivered the day you plan to plant it. Store the sod in the shade; keep it rolled and moist until you're ready to plant. Bring only one or two rolls out to the planting area at a time. *Note:* Don't stand on sod; instead, use a kneeling board to work.

1. Establish a bed 1 inch below grade so the new lawn will be even with surrounding areas. Follow instructions in this month's "Here's How To Prepare a New Bed for Planting" (page 67).
2. Lay the first length of sod along a straight edge, such as a sidewalk or driveway. Unroll the grass strip gently, placing it snugly against the walk. Start the second roll so its end neatly abuts the first.
3. Lay subsequent rolls so the end seams are never flush with those in adjacent rows. Coax the edges as close together as possible, but don't stretch them.
4. Use a sturdy knife to cut sod to fit irregular spaces.
5. Tamp the sod or gently use an empty lawn roller to establish good root contact with the soil, pushing it 90 degrees from the direction the sod runs. Fill any gaps with loose soil.
6. Water the area so the sod and top 3 to 4 inches of soil are moist. Keep the area moist until the sod is rooted.
7. Once the sod is firmly rooted, it can be mowed. Continue watering, but not as often.

■ *Make sure the underlying soil is lightly moist before laying sod.*

summer's garden. See August Plant (page 132) for instructions.

Check seedlings and transplants growing in cold frames. Open the lid on sunny days to prevent heat buildup. Lower the lid in late afternoon to protect cold-sensitive plants from cold nights. Consider buying an automatic vent.

BULBS

Take any forced bulbs from storage. Use some for indoor enjoyment. Move a few of the potted bulbs from cold storage directly outdoors to planters and window boxes. This is a great way to brighten up drab areas and create a surprise in the spring landscape.

Remove winter mulch as the bulbs begin to grow and the weather consistently hovers near or above freezing. Keep some mulch handy in case of sudden and extreme drops in temperature.

Replant or firm frost-heaved bulbs back into place. Frost heaving occurs in unmulched gardens or those with inconsistent snow cover. Fluctuating temperatures in exposed soil cause the soil to shift, pushing bulbs and other plants out of the ground.

Deadhead daffodils or cut down the flower stems when the bloom fades. Do not cut down or braid the foliage. Photosynthesis in the leaves rejuvenates the bulbs, allowing them to store food for the next year.

After flowering, remove the seedheads of tulips; allow the stem and foliage to die back naturally.

EDIBLES

If a light frost threatens—especially within a week of transplanting or as young seedlings are emerging from the ground—or a heavy frost threatens at any time, cover the plants. Use bent hangers as hoops to prevent the cover from squashing tender seedlings. To conserve heat, use floating row covers, sheets, blankets, large garbage bags—anything that will protect the plants. In the morning, if frost is visible on the covering, remove the cover when the mercury rises above freezing. You don't want the frost to melt and drip through onto the plants or refreeze.

After a few more harvests from your indoor salad garden, move it outdoors into dappled shade. As long as the plants aren't pulled out or cut so short there are no leaves, the gardens will keep producing for a month or more, depending on the weather.

■ *Brush staking is an economical and environmentally friendly way to support peas using branches cut from trees and shrubs.*

Give peas and beans some support for their tendrils to wind their way upward. One of the easiest ways is to brush stake them using small, cut branches (brush from pruning and winter deadfall). Simply stick them in the ground and let the peas climb. Another easy way is to drive screws or nails 4 inches apart into stakes up to the maximum height of the plant. Then place the stakes along the rows and run string or fishing line from one screw or nail to the other. Or get a bit more high-tech and put 5-foot stakes in every 24 to 36 inches along the row of peas. Attach the support—chicken wire, turkey wire, or bird netting—to each of the stakes in progression.

LAWNS

Rake out any dead grass. Grass roots may resprout, so wait until the grass greens up before filling in these areas.

Start mowing as soon as the grass greens up and starts to grow. Keep the grass at least 2½ inches tall, but preferably 3 to 3½ inches tall. Mow often enough so that you remove no more than one-third of the total height—this may be several times a week in spring (especially if you fertilize now).

PERENNIALS & ORNAMENTAL GRASSES

Finish cleanup early in the month. See March Care (page 57) for tips on what to cut.

Continue removing winter mulch. Let the weather and plant growth be your guide. Remove mulch as temperatures consistently hover above freezing and as soon as plants begin growing. Keep some mulch or a floating row cover handy to protect semi-hardy plants from sudden and extreme drops in temperature.

Watch for late-emerging perennials, such as butterfly weed. Be sure to label them or consider adding spring-flowering bulbs next fall to mark the location to avoid accidentally planting over or damaging them in spring.

ROSES

For a bare-root rose planted earlier in the season, gently remove the extra soil above ground level when the plant begins to break dormancy (showing the first signs of leaves and bud). Add a 2- to 4-inch layer of organic mulch around the plant; keep the mulch at least an inch away from the stems. However, if there is a threat of a freeze after the soil has been removed and the plant is still relatively tender, cover it with a floating row cover or a light blanket for the night. Remove the covering the next day, mid-morning is ideal, so you don't let the plant overheat during the day.

Finish pruning hybrid teas, floribundas, grandifloras, and miniatures. (See March Care, page 57, for details.) If you didn't get around to pruning before they leafed out, prune them as soon as you can; you don't want to cut off flower buds. Always prune at a 45-degree angle just above an outfacing bud or leaf; each bud can produce up to three branches. Prune ever-blooming shrub roses if they get too large by cutting the previous year's growth back by about one-third. You can cut older canes to within 6 inches from the ground, if you want.

TREES & SHRUBS

Remove screening and any winter protection and store it until fall. Leave hardware cloth protection if it's not rubbing against the bark or threatening to girdle the trunk.

Move plants growing in aboveground planters out of winter storage. If they started to leaf out, keep them safe until the temperature is consistently above freezing.

Renew mulch by adding a 2- to 3-inch layer of twice-shredded bark or woodchips. Only buy mulch that is labeled as certified by the Mulch and Soil Council. That tells you that what is labeled *on* the bag is actually what's *in* the bag. Mulch helps conserve moisture, reduce weeds, and add organic matter.

Keep mulch several inches away from the base of trees and shrubs so insects and pests don't have easy entry. Avoid colored mulches, which have artificial dyes added.

Finish dormant pruning before buds begin to open and plants start to leaf out. Wait until the plants are completely leafed out and leaves are full sized to prune any more (see Appendix).

VINES & GROUNDCOVERS

Remove damaged or dead leaves on groundcovers.

Prune plants according to timing directions in the Appendix (page 196).

WATER

ANNUALS & BIENNIALS

Keep potted annuals, seedlings, and transplants growing and thriving with proper watering. Check seedlings and young transplants daily. Water potted annuals thoroughly every time the top inch of soil starts to dry.

Check plants growing outdoors in the cold frame and garden. Water only when the soil is slightly dry. Overwatering can lead to root rot.

BULBS

Keep crocus, snowdrops, Siberian squill, and glory-of-the-snow lightly moist during their growing season. Water hyacinths now and throughout their growing season. Water crown imperial deeply in spring.

EDIBLES

Make sure that new transplants are lightly moist; if they are too wet, they are prone to fungal problems.

For indoor plants, continue the watering regimen described in January Water (page 30).

LAWNS

Continue water regimen from March Water (page 59).

Keep the soil surface moist in newly sodded or seeded areas.

PERENNIALS & ORNAMENTAL GRASSES

Thoroughly water-in transplants and divisions with transplant solution.

Water when the top few inches of soil begin to dry, thoroughly enough to wet the top 4 to 6 inches of soil. Reduce watering frequency as the plants become established.

ROSES

Water if the season is dry, providing about 1 inch of water a week. You don't want to start the season with roses stressed from insufficient water.

SUCCESSFUL GARDENING: UNDERSTANDING THE MYSTERIOUS THREE NUMBERS ON FERTILIZER BAGS

Many gardeners don't know what the three numbers on fertilizer packages mean. These numbers, such as 5-10-5, represent the percentage of the elements nitrogen, phosphorus, and potassium in the fertilizer. This is called the N-P-K ratio (the letters are the chemical symbols for the elements).

Each element affects plants in a specific way. Nitrogen encourages leaf growth. Phosphorus promotes strong roots, speeds up maturity, and is essential for seed and fruit development. Potassium, also called potash, is necessary for cell division in roots and buds.

If you don't want to use commercial fertilizers, there are several organic choices. Nitrogen is readily available in blood meal, cottonseed meal, fish meal, and fish emulsion. Bone meal and rock phosphate contain phosphorus. The best sources for potassium are granite dust and ash from hardwoods.

■ *The three numbers on a bag of fertilizer represent the percentage of nitrogen, phosphorus, and potassium in the food.*

TREES & SHRUBS

Start watering trees and shrubs after the ground thaws and when soil is dry. Established plants only need watering during dry periods. Provide 1 to 2 inches of water when the top 6 to 8 inches of soil start to dry. Check plants in clay soil weekly, those in sandy soil twice a week.

Give any plants that were exposed to deicing salts a thorough watering to help wash the salts through the soil and away from the roots.

Water newly planted trees often enough to keep the top 12 inches of soil moist but not wet.

Continue to water trees and shrubs in aboveground planters. Water until the excess drains out of the bottom of the pot. Check containers at least twice a week and water as needed.

VINES & GROUNDCOVERS

Continue to water as described in February Water.

Keep the soil moist around new plants.

FERTILIZE

ALL

Always follow package instructions for proper application, frequency, concentration, and mixing/dilution for *all* fertilizers.

ANNUALS & BIENNIALS

Incorporate fertilizer into the soil prior to planting. Follow soil test recommendations.

Continue fertilizing indoor plants and transplants every two weeks. Use a diluted solution of any complete water-soluble fertilizer or foliar feed with a solution of fish emulsion or kelp.

BULBS

Feed crocus weekly with compost tea.

LAWNS

Do not fertilize; wait until late May in Zones 6, 7, and 8 and June for Zones 3, 4, and 5. Fertilizing now encourages lush, succulent leaves at the expense of root growth. This means more watering and mowing—more time and money spent unnecessarily.

SUCCESSFUL GARDENING: SPRING BOOST FOR ROSES

Like people, established roses benefit from a springtime pick-me-up to get them off to a good start. (Do not give this to newly planted roses.)

2 to 3 cups compost or other well-rotted organic matter (leaf mold or manure)
½ cup bone meal
½ cup bloodmeal
⅓ cup rock phosphate
1 cup all-purpose organic fertilizer (optional)
Epsom salts (for watering-in)

Sprinkle each ingredient around the base of each plant in a circle about 12 inches in diameter in the order listed. Water-in with a solution of 1 to 3 tablespoons Epsom salts dissolved in 1 gallon of water. The magnesium in Epsom salts strengthens the canes (it is also beneficial to tomato plants). Top it off with 2 to 4 inches of organic mulch (twice-shredded bark, cocoa hulls, ground leaves, coffee grounds, or others). When you're done, run a warm bath, add a ½ cup of Epsom salts, immerse yourself, and soak away any aches from a good day's work.

PERENNIALS & ORNAMENTAL GRASSES

Perennials grown in properly amended soil need little fertilizer. Always follow soil test recommendations.

Spread several inches of compost or aged manure over the surface of existing gardens. Lightly rake this into the soil surface. Use organic matter as mulch and most perennials will thrive. Replenish the mulch as it breaks down.

ROSES

Hybrid teas, floribundas, and grandifloras need at least three feedings a year—the first feeding as early in spring as the rose starts to leaf out. Species, shrub roses, ramblers, and climbers need only one feeding—before they leaf out. Strong plants are less likely to become infested with insects or disease—survival of the fittest.

TREES & SHRUBS

Do *not* fertilize newly planted trees and shrubs for at least a year; fertilizer can harm new roots.

Fertilize established plants in spring before they leaf out—only if they need it. Trees often get fed inadvertently from lawn fertilizers and grass clippings left on the lawn. Shrubs get fed from decomposing mulch and fertilizer applied to nearby plants in the same bed.

Poor growth and off-color leaves may indicate the need to fertilize. Check the results of the soil test and fertilize following the recommendations given. If soil tests are not available, use a slow-release fertilizer containing just nitrogen (like 20-0-0) or three times more nitrogen than phosphorus and potassium (like 30-10-10). Check the fertilizer analysis on the bag.

To fertilize trees growing in the lawn, remove small cores of soil 6 inches deep and 2 to 3 feet apart throughout the area surrounding the tree (starting 2 to 3 feet from the trunk and continuing several feet beyond the drip line. Divide the recommended fertilizer amount evenly between the holes. Water until the top 12 inches of soil are moist.

For plants growing in beds, sprinkle fertilizer around the root zone, rake it through the mulch, and water well to send the fertilizer down to the roots.

VINES & GROUNDCOVERS

Incorporate fertilizer into the soil prior to planting. Fertilize existing plants before growth begins.

Select a fertilizer with little or no phosphorus, since our soils tend to be high to excessive in this nutrient. Calculate the amount of fertilizer you need to add to your planting area.

PROBLEM-SOLVE

ALL

Continue to monitor for damping off in seedlings. See February Problem-Solve (page 46) for more information and treatment.

SUCCESSFUL GARDENING: LET OTHER CREATURES CONTROL PESTS

When you think of critters in the garden, you imagine them creating problems, not as the solution. Yet these creatures wield control over the true pests. So, when you see a bat, snake, bird, or spider, thank it for its efforts on your behalf.

The little brown bat eats moths, caddis flies, midges, beetles, and mosquitoes.

In their intricate webs, spiders catch a wide variety of insects and tie them up with their silk to eat later.

Snakes are more valuable than we care to admit. Garter snakes, green snakes, grass snakes, and brown snakes eat slugs, snails, and insects. Corn snakes and milk snakes dine on mice and rats.

It pays to keep a bird feeder and a birdbath to attract feathery friends. Flycatchers, swallows, warblers, nuthatches, and others consume huge numbers of insects.

■ *Unless they are in the way, leave spiderwebs alone. Spiders do a great job of catching insects that are pests.*

Follow the label instructions before mixing and applying any pesticide, insecticide, herbicide, repellent, or any other chemical.

ANNUALS & BIENNIALS
Continue monitoring for fungus gnats, mites, aphids, scale, and whiteflies. See January Problem-Solve (page 32) for detailed information about of these pests.

Outdoors, pull or lightly hoe annual weeds as soon as they appear. Pull and destroy ground ivy, quackgrass, and bindweed to prevent rerooting. Consider treating badly infested gardens with a total vegetation killer prior to planting. Begin preparing the soil for annuals 4 to 14 days after treatment.

BULBS
If deer are a problem, you know that there is a limited menu of plants that deer will snub. What they refrained from eating last year they may relish this season—especially if winter was harsh. One of

the lesser-known stalwarts in the ongoing battle is crown imperial (*Fritillaria imperialis*). The skunky

■ *Crown imperial is a unique-looking, hardy, summer-blooming, deer-resistant bulb. Plant it to repel deer from nearby plants.*

aroma of the leaves and bulbs (never use it as a cut flower), makes this underutilized bulb a great deer deterrent. As it emerges from the ground and grows upward, single stems resemble lilies, but the smell is a dead giveaway. The stem rises 3 to 4 feet tall and produces a cluster of orange (or red or yellow) 1- to 2-inch bell-like florets that ring the stem. A topknot of green leaves bursts above the flowers. You will smile when you see this unique beauty—if not for its looks, for the knowledge that it will keep the deer away from the garden when planted at the perimeter.

EDIBLES
See "Successful Gardening: Let Other Creatures Control Pests" on page 77.

LAWNS
To reduce the risk of snow mold, rake the grass briskly with a lawn rake in areas where ice and snow had collected. Fluffing the grass allows it to dry.

Prevent crabgrass by mowing the lawn high (3 to 3½ inches) and watering during dry spells. If this

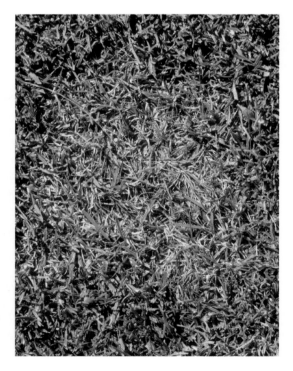

■ *Snow mold is seen in early spring. Avoid having piles of snow on the lawn that are slow to melt.*

hasn't worked, consider applying a pre-emergent on problem areas when bridalwreath spirea blooms. Pre-emergents prevent lawn grass seeds from sprouting as well as crabgrass, so don't use them if you plan to seed or overseed. Corn gluten pre-emergents provide organic crabgrass control.

SUCCESSFUL GARDENING: CONTROLLING JAPANESE BEETLES WITH MILKY SPORE

■ *Japanese beetles are persistent garden pests that eat leaves and flowers in the adult stage and lawn roots as larvae (grubs).*

If Japanese beetles threaten your roses, the best way to control them is milky spore disease (*Bacillus popilliae*). Japanese beetles overwinter in the form of grubs. Although grubs are most commonly found in lawns, they are also in garden soil. As soon as the soil is workable, inoculate the soil and lawn: Put 1 teaspoon of milky spore disease powder on the lawn or soil every 4 feet, creating a checkerboard pattern. Water it in lightly. Milky spore infects grubs, killing them, which releases new spores. Although it may take three years or more to establish, the bacteria can thrive in the soil for 25 years. However, any pesticide will kill the milky spore bacteria—all the more reason for keeping your lawn and garden organic.

PERENNIALS & ORNAMENTAL GRASSES

Complete garden cleanup. Sanitation is the best defense against pest problems.

Inspect new growth for signs of pests, including aphids or any caterpillars. Remove insects and disease-infested leaves as soon as they are found. Make this a regular part of your gardening routine.

Use netting and repellents to protect emerging plants from animal damage. Start early to encourage animals to go elsewhere to feed. Reapply repellents after severe weather or as recommended on label directions.

ROSES

For problem caterpillars, get help from another bacteria, Bt (*Bacillus thuringiensis*), available commercially. It comes in powder and liquid form. Spray it on the caterpillars as well as the tops and bottoms of leaves. When ingested by a feeding caterpillar, the bacteria paralyzes the digestive tract, and the caterpillar dies of starvation.

Be vigilant for signs of rose rosette disease. Remove infected plants (see March Problem-Solve for detailed information).

■ *Remove branches extending beyond the tent, cover tent with a large plastic bag, and then cut the branch(es) at the base of the tent.*

TREES & SHRUBS

Continue to monitor for cankerworm and apply sticky bands if needed. See March Problem-Solve (page 61) for detailed information.

To reduce the spread of spruce gall on small trees, prune out the small swollen sections (they look like miniature cones or pineapples on a stem) while they are green and the insects are still nesting inside.

Check trees for signs of Eastern tent caterpillars. The eggs hatch and the caterpillars start building their webbed tents in the crotches of branches. Prune out or knock down the tents with a long stick and destroy them. Never try to burn out the tents.

Birch leaf miners feed between the upper and lower leaf surfaces, causing the leaves to brown. This stresses the tree, making white-barked birches more susceptible to borers. Apply a soil systemic labeled for use on birches to control leaf miner to prevent infestations. Do *not* treat trees previously treated with a soil systemic.

Stop applying dormant oil when new growth appears, as it can harm the expanding buds.

Avoid mower blight (tree decline caused by machine damage) by keeping weed whackers and lawnmowers away from tree trunks. Surrounding trees with mulch or groundcovers or planting them in beds avoids the problem altogether.

The emerald ash borer (EAB) is an exotic insect, which in the larval stage feeds beneath the bark. This disrupts the flow of water and nutrients within the tree and eventually kills it. A soil drench (applied yearly by a professional) can be used as a preventative. However, once EAB has been identified, the tree has to be destroyed. Some gardeners are removing their ash trees in hopes of curbing the spread of this scourge. Although it has not yet been seen in all states, it is spreading quickly. Consult your local Cooperative Extension Service to find out if it is in your area.

VINES & GROUNDCOVERS

Pull weeds as soon as they appear.

May

Everywhere you turn, there are plants for sale, beckoning with their beautiful blooms. But beware. Growers are producing perennials that are in flower when you buy them (annuals have been sold that way for years). It's good marketing—what you see is what you get. However, most perennials have a limited flowering season (although a few rebloom if you cut them back, the majority won't). That means when you buy them in mid-spring, they will look pretty in the garden for a short time (most bloom from two to six weeks) and revert to foliage plants. When summer comes—the plant's normal bloom time—there are no flowers. You'll have to wait until next year.

If you buy plants at large garden centers or home-improvement stores, find out when they receive their plant shipments. Plan to go there that day or the next when the plants are at their best and least stressed. Some stores take good care of their plants (they have real gardeners who understand plants' needs), so they thrive despite harsh conditions; others neglect plants once they have been unloaded from the truck.

Keep your landscape plan and garden journal handy. Refer to the plan whenever you visit a nursery or garden center. All those beautiful plants, attractive tags, and promises of beauty can be tempting. It's easy to succumb to temptation and end up with too many or the wrong type of plants for the available space.

Even in the coldest parts of our region, the garden comes to life this month. It's a riot of color from bulbs to early annuals, perennials, shrubs, and groundcovers. The burgeoning garden demands more time. Spring cleanup is done, but routine tasks like mowing, weeding, and watering come to the fore. May can also be a whirlwind of planting. But don't just stick everything in the ground. Plants that are properly sited will thrive, benefitting from being given the optimum conditions in which to grow. Get growing and enjoy all the beauty that is your garden this month and in the months to come.

PLAN

ALL

Check the garden for losses and voids that need filling. Look at them as an opportunity to try something new.

ANNUALS & BIENNIALS

Hopefully you made a plan before you started planting and plant shopping. Or maybe you had a plan but the labels and pictures of other plants were too tempting to resist. Join the club! Take inventory and reevaluate planting space and garden locations.

BULBS

It's time to start shopping for hardy spring-blooming bulbs. Check out catalogs and shop online. Take notes of new bulbs you want to grow for next spring. Refer to your journal and look at pictures to see what performed well this year and what didn't. Think back to March and April; where would you like to see a splash of color in otherwise barren earth? Consider adding a large bed of hardy bulbs for a dynamic spring display. Add small groups of bulbs throughout your perennial gardens. As the bulbs fade, the perennials hide the declining bulb foliage and provide additional bloom. Use bulbs to dress up shrub beds and groundcovers while adding color and an element of surprise. Naturalize early-blooming bulbs in deciduous wooded areas—they will be in full sun until after they finish blooming. Plant some early crocus in the lawn and let them naturalize and

spread. (Don't mow the lawn until the bulb leaves start to die back.) There are lots of possibilities.

EDIBLES

Winter squash and pumpkins are ideal sunny hillside groundcovers; the vigorous vines keep the soil from eroding without bullying other plants. The dark green leaves are attractive, and the variety of shapes and colors of squash and pumpkins provide interest throughout autumn. Unlike summer squash that need daily picking, you can ignore these (except for watering) until the leaves start to die back in fall.

LAWNS

The pace is picking up with mowing and planting. Think about the time, energy, and money spent maintaining a lawn, and whether it is worth it. Consider downsizing the lawn into a native plant garden or prairie—little to no maintenance and watering (after the first year).

■ *Going to a garden center can be like letting a kid loose in a candy shop. Shop with a wish list to avoid overbuying.*

PERENNIALS & ORNAMENTAL GRASSES

Use your landscape design as a working document. We all make changes to our plans. Sometimes the plants we wanted are not available—and then there are those unplanned additions that we just could not resist at the garden center.

ROSES

Consider incorporating some lavender or blue fescue plants among your roses. The blue-gray

■ *Pumpkins make an eye-catching, easy-to-grow groundcover and provide erosion control on a sunny hillside.*

foliage highlights the roses. These plants will not steal nutrition from the rose plants.

TREES & SHRUBS

A large expanse of neatly mulched trees and shrubs can be boring. Add some spring surprise with a mass planting of crocus, grape hyacinth, and squill. You'll get a carpet of color. Intersperse some daffodils, tulips, and hyacinths for height and additional color. Consider using perennials to create seasonal interest. A mixture of spring-, summer-, and fall-blooming flowers can complement the seasonal interest that trees and shrubs provide.

If you're planning any planting or transplanting, call 811 at least two business days ahead of time. This free service will arrange to have the underground utilities on your property marked. This can avoid any potential expensive and dangerous accidents that can occur from severing phone, electric, water, cable, or gas lines.

VINES & GROUNDCOVERS

Try shallow-rooted perennial groundcovers, such as deadnettle, bishop's hat, hosta, and vinca, to mask mulch and create a good growing environment. This month and next are ideal times for planting them.

PLANT

ALL

Use a transplant solution, which helps get plants off to a good start, encouraging strong root growth. Follow directions for mixing.

ANNUALS & BIENNIALS

Continue planting frost-tolerant annuals. Plant cold-tolerant annuals, such as calendulas, dianthus, sweet alyssum, and sweet peas, in the garden after all danger of frost has passed. (To find your last spring frost date, visit http://davesgarden.com/guides/freeze-frost-dates/#b and enter your zip code. This site also lists the first frost date in fall.) Wait until the air *and* the soil are warm (above 60 degrees Fahrenheit) to plant warm-weather annuals.

Removing flowers when planting encourages root development, branching, and better looking, healthier plants in the long run. If you're doing a mass planting

TO TRANSPLANT ANNUALS & BIENNIALS INTO THE GARDEN

■ *Setting a rootbound plant like this in a bucket of transplant solution before planting makes loosening the roots easier.*

Harden off indoor-grown transplants prior to planting them in the garden (see March Plant, page 53 for directions on hardening off).

Space plants according to the directions on the plant tag or seed packet. The spacing may look too wide, yet before you know it, the transplants will fill right in. Overplanting reduces air circulation, increasing the risk of pests and diseases. Use extra plants for container gardens, herb gardens, shrub beds, or to fill bare spots in perennial gardens. Or share them with friends or neighbors. Plant one at a time so you don't risk the plant drying out as it lays on the soil with roots exposed.

1. Dig a hole the same depth and width as the root mass of the plant.
2. Carefully remove the plant from its container. Squeeze the container and slide the plant out. Do *not* pull it out by the stem. Gently and ever-so-slightly loosen the roots if the plant is rootbound.
3. Place the plant in the hole at the same depth as it was growing in the container. Add soil around the plant and gently tamp to remove air pockets. Water-in with transplant solution.

and can't bear to remove those beautiful flowers, you can compromise. Remove the flowers on every other plant or every other row before planting. Remove the remaining flowers the following week. Then it will not seem so long before the new flowers appear.

BULBS

Plant lily bulbs once the danger of frost has passed. Choose a sunny spot with well-drained, porous, sandy soil enriched with compost. Lilies prefer full sun with the ground shaded to keep the soil moist. Plant 6 to 8 inches deep and 6 inches apart in groups of three or five, taking care not to break off any stalks or growth that may be on the bulb.

Begin planting gladiolus in Zones 7 and 8.

Plant tuberoses when the weather is relatively warm—60 degrees Fahrenheit or more at night. Space bulbs 8 inches apart and 1 to 2 inches deep. Water-in with transplant solution. Feed after the foliage appears. Tuberoses are very fragrant; avoid planting them near other sweet-scented flowers, as two different perfumed aromas can clash.

EDIBLES

After all danger of frost has passed and the soil temperatures are consistently over 60 degrees Fahrenheit, harden off and transplant tomatoes and other warm-weather plants outside. Be sure to use transplant solution to water them in. See March Plant, page 53 for directions on hardening off.

In Zones 5 to 8, sow tomato, eggplant, peppers, basil, and other annual herb seeds directly in the garden, labeling as you go. In all zones, direct-sow the other warm-weather plants that grow too quickly to start inside, including beans, corn, cucumber, squash, and Malabar spinach. Make successive sowings of corn and beans every two weeks to extend the harvest. Follow directions on the seed packet for depth and spacing.

HERE'S HOW

TO PLANT GLADIOLUS

Thrips can be serious pests for gladiolus. Avoid them by soaking the corms in a solution of 4 teaspoons Lysol® mixed in 1 gallon water for two to three hours just before planting.

1. Dig a 6- to 8-inch-deep trench or large round or oval hole, depending on how you want to group (nine or more corms) the glads.
2. Add 1 inch of organic material (compost, well-rotted manure, leaf mold) and 1 cup of bone meal per 10 feet and mix in.
3. Top with 1 inch of builder's sand to ensure good drainage.
4. Firmly place the corms in the trench, pointed end up, spacing them 6 inches apart.
5. Fill in with soil. Press the soil down firmly with your palms—do not compact soil.
6. Water well with transplant solution.
7. Top with 2 inches of mulch to keep the roots cool and conserve moisture.
8. To extend the period of bloom, plant some corms every two weeks until 90 days before your first fall frost date. In windy areas, consider staking gladiolus, especially tall ones. Place the stake at the same time you put the corm in the ground; staking later risks damaging the corms.

■ *Gladiolus is a great cut flower. Keep it fresh by removing spent flowers (they bloom from the bottom of the stem up), re-cutting the stem, and changing the water every few days.*

HERE'S HOW

TO PLANT POTATOES

If you are using cut potatoes with eyes, lightly dust them with sulfur before planting to discourage any soilborne diseases, rot, or mold.

1. Dig a 12-inch-deep trench; put the soil along both sides of the trench.
2. Mix in 2 inches of compost at the bottom of the trench.
3. Plant seed potatoes or potato eyes spacing them about 2 feet apart. Cover with 2 inches of soil and water in with transplant solution.
4. As the potato shoots begin to emerge in the trench, cover them with 2 inches of soil.
5. Repeat step 4 every couple of weeks until all the soil is on the plants.

■ *Plant seed potatoes or potato pieces with an eye in a 12-inch-deep trench and cover with 2 inches of soil.*

Sow carrots and radishes together. Radishes grow faster than the carrots, so they help loosen the surrounding soil while marking the row of the slower-germinating carrots.

LAWNS

This is a good time to seed or overseed lawns (although mid-August through mid-September is best). Chooses a grass mix appropriate for your sun/shade condition. For full sun, use a grass mix that is 60 percent bluegrass, 30 percent fine fescue, and 10 percent turf-type perennial ryegrass. For a shady area, use grass mix that is 60 percent fine fescue, 30 percent bluegrass, and 10 percent turf-type perennial ryegrass. Look for a mix that has several varieties of each grass type.

See "Here's How To Start a Lawn" on page 86. This is still a good time to install sod. See April Plant (page 72) for details.

PERENNIALS & ORNAMENTAL GRASSES

Complete soil preparation. Invest time now to ensure many years of success with your perennial garden. See April Plant (page 67) for instructions on preparing the soil.

Harden off plants started indoors or in a greenhouse before planting (See March Plant, page 53 for directions on hardening off).

When using little bluestem (*Schizachyrium scoparium*) in a large area (for a prairie or native plant area, erosion control or groundcover), save money by growing it from seed. After broadcasting the seed, push the seeds down into the soil using a water-filled soil roller. Keep soil lightly moist until this low-maintenance grass sprouts and is established.

HERE'S HOW

TO PLANT A BARE-ROOT PLANT

Plant dormant bare-root plants as you get them. If you can't plant right away, pack the roots in moist peat moss and keep the plants in a cool, frost-free location until planted.

1. Soak the roots for two hours—no more—in room-temperature water.
2. Trim off any broken roots.
3. Dig a hole large enough to accommodate the roots. Form a cone of soil to support the roots.
4. Place the plant on the cone and spread out the roots. Cover the roots with soil and fill the hole, keeping the crown of the plant (where stem joins the roots) just below the soil surface.
5. Gently firm the soil with the palm of your hand. Water-in with transplant solution.

HERE'S HOW

TO START A LAWN

Proper soil preparation is the key to creating a healthy lawn that can withstand the rigors of our weather.

1. Follow instructions in "Here's How To Prepare a New Bed for Planting," (page 67). Rake the area, but leave it rough; do not smooth it.
2. Water the area and wait several days for any newly surfaced weed seeds to germinate and grow. Remove the weeds.
3. After a week of weeding, sow the grass seed, following the package instruction. Water lightly to moisten the seeds and the soil.
4. Lightly cover the area with straw or polyspun landscape fabric to help maintain moisture in the seedbed and prevent birds from feasting on all the seed.
5. For optimum germination, keep the grass seed consistently moist. The new grass will grow through the straw or push up the light fabric as it grows.
6. Keep watering, less frequently but more heavily, as roots continue to grow. When the grass is 3 inches tall, remove the fabric or gently rake up the straw, and lightly mow.

■ *When using a drop spreader to seed a new lawn, follow the directions on the seed package for proper application rates.*

■ *After seeding a new lawn area, water gently, lightly cover it with straw, and keep it lightly moist with frequent waterings.*

ROSES

The soil should be warm and dry enough to start planting container-grown roses. When purchasing roses, look for ones that are breaking dormancy (with leaves). Avoid those that are in bloom; too often they are stressed from being forced into flowering early.

See "Here's How To Plant Container-Grown Roses" on page 88.

TREES & SHRUBS

Balled-and-burlapped and container-grown plants can be planted throughout the growing season. See April Plant (page 71) for detailed instructions.

Amend planting beds in areas that have been problematic. Add organic matter to the top 6 to 12 inches of the bed—not in the planting hole.

VINES & GROUNDCOVERS

Grow vines, such as clematis, wintercreeper, and Goldflame honeysuckle, in containers to add vertical interest on patios and decks.

Set aboveground containers among groundcovers under trees to add height, structure, and color without damaging the tree roots.

Use annual vines in place of spiky plants (like dracaena) for vertical interest in container gardens. Check out your favorite nursery, garden center, or home-improvement store for small trellises and obelisks that can fit inside containers.

CARE

ALL

Thin direct-seeded seedlings to their ideal garden spacing as directed on the seed packet.

Do not use weed barriers under bark, wood chips, and other organic mulches. The barriers are only a temporary fix against weed growth and can create long-term maintenance headaches. As the mulch on top of the weed barrier decomposes, it creates a perfect place for weeds and grass to grow, often

HERE'S HOW

TO PLANT A CONTAINER-GROWN PLANT

Plant container-grown plants in the garden anytime from spring to early fall.

1. Before planting, set the plants on the bed to determine the best placement. Odd-numbered groupings look most natural. Allow enough space between plants for them to grow and mature for several years; check the plant tag for spacing.
2. Place the container in a bucket of transplant solution for a few minutes.
3. Dig a hole large enough to accommodate the rootball when it's taken out of the container.
4. Gently remove the plant from the pot. If necessary, cut the pot to free the root mass. Loosen any tangled roots; if it is very potbound, make four vertical slashes about ½-inch deep equidistant around the rootball.
5. Set the plant in the hole so the top of the rootball is level with the surrounding soil.
6. Fill the hole with soil. Gently firm the soil and water in well with transplant solution.
7. Add a 2-inch layer of mulch (chopped leaves, compost, cocoa hulls, or other fine-textured organic matter) around the plant. Keep the mulch at least an inch from the stem to keep insects from attacking the plant.

sending roots down through the barrier. A weed barrier also prevents the decomposed mulch from improving the soil beneath it. Make sure everything is well mulched.

ANNUALS & BIENNIALS

Thin or transplant annuals directly seeded into the garden. Leave the healthiest seedlings properly spaced in their permanent garden location. Move extra transplants to other areas with bare space.

Place stakes next to tall annuals and biennials, such as foxgloves, larkspur, and hollyhocks, which need staking. Early support placement prevents later

HERE'S HOW

TO PLANT CONTAINER-GROWN ROSES

Container-grown roses are easy to plant.

1. Dig a hole a few inches wider and deeper than the container. Amend the soil from the hole with several handfuls of organic matter (compost, leaf mold, humus, or well-rotted manure), and 1 cup each of rock phosphate, bone meal, and blood meal.
2. Add about 6 inches of amended soil to the hole.
3. Remove the rose from its container (even cardboard boxes that say to plant the entire thing). Keep the surrounding soil intact unless the plant appears rootbound (then gently tease the roots apart).
4. Pour a quart of transplant solution in the hole and let it absorb into the surrounding soil.
5. Position the rose at the same soil level it was in the container unless it is a grafted rose. You can distinguish a graft by the knoblike protrusion on the stem—the bud union where the rootstock and main plant were joined. For the growers' convenience, the bud union is above soil level on *all* container-grown plants—ideal for mild winter climates, but not here (except for Zone 8). Make sure that bud union is 2 to 3 inches *below* soil level once planted.
6. Fill the hole halfway with soil and gently firm to eliminate any air pockets. Water with a quart of transplant solution. Add soil to fill the hole; water-in with 2 quarts of transplant solution.
7. Gently firm the soil with your palms (do not step on the soil, or it becomes too compacted). Top off with additional soil, if necessary. Form a watering basin.
8. Mulch the planting area with 2 to 3 inches of organic matter. Keep the mulch 1 inch away from the stem. Before you know it, you'll be smelling the roses!

root and plant damage caused by staking established plants that are already flopping over.

BULBS

Some hyacinths are magnificent the first year, but subsequently have fewer florets. If this happens, move them to a less prominent area. It's wonderful to come along them at a woodland's edge. Their fragrance will lead you right to them.

Remove the dead flowerheads from crown imperials before they go to seed. Cut off individual spent florets to keep the topknot intact or cut the stem just below the flowers.

After tulips bloom, cut off the spent flower, but allow the stem and foliage to die back naturally.

EDIBLES

If you're short on space, but long on plants, grow up. Many vines can be trained skyward as long as the resulting fruit or vegetable is fairly lightweight. Try cucumbers, pole beans, pumpkins, runner beans, squash, and zucchini. With squash, melons, and pumpkins, choose the small-fruited varieties, often described as "mini" or "baby." Or use a pantyhose "sling" to support the fruit.

After all danger of frost has passed, start hardening off warm-weather herbs and vegetables started inside. See March Plant for detailed instructions.

Begin harvesting asparagus as soon as the spears are the length you prefer. With a sharp knife, cut the spear just above ground level. With enough plants, you can have asparagus every other day for at least a month.

LAWNS

See "Successful Gardening: Thatch No More" on page 90.

PERENNIALS & ORNAMENTAL GRASSES

See "Here's How To Divide Perennials" on page 91.

Cut back any overgrown and leggy transplants. Prune the stems back by one-third to one-half at planting. This encourages new growth and results in a fuller, sturdier plant.

SUCCESSFUL GARDENING: CHIVES

■ *Chives are so pretty; plant them where they can be seen. Keep picking the edible flowers, and they will rebloom.*

Chives are must-haves in any garden, both for their grasslike, oniony leaves and their lilac-pink pompom flowers. Keep cutting the flowers of these perennial plants, and they'll bloom intermittently for months. When you're cooking with the flowers, break them into florets (the individual flowers that make up the flower head), or the flavor can be too intense. One flower can be the equivalent of an entire bulb of garlic. Rub the flower around the inside of a wooden bowl to release its essence when making a salad of mixed greens. Add some fresh-squeezed orange juice and balsamic vinegar for a quick and easy, flavorful, fat-free salad dressing. Include chive florets in marinades for meat, fish, and chicken. Brush on marinade during cooking (craft a "brush" from chive stems and flowers), and sprinkle a few florets on the finished dish.

Watch for late-emerging perennials, such as butterfly weed. Be sure to label them or consider adding spring-flowering bulbs next fall to mark the location to avoid accidentally planting over or damaging it in early spring.

As blue fescue plants age, the mound dies out in the center. Dig the plant up, cut it into sections (eliminating the dead center) and replant.

Put stakes, peony cages, and trellises in place. Tuck young plants in place or carefully tie them to the support as needed. Loop twine or other soft bindings around the stem and then around the support in a figure-eight. It's easier to train young plants through the cages than manipulate mature ones into submission.

Wait for the soil to warm before adding mulch. Apply a thin layer of compost, leaf mold, well-rotted manure, twice-shredded bark, or chopped leaves to the soil surface. Do not bury the crowns of the plant; this can lead to rot.

Mulch blue fescue with pebbles or sand (not organic matter) to increase drainage.

Remove side buds from peonies for larger flowers.

Shear phlox, pinks, and candytuft to encourage a new flush of foliage.

Pinch back mums and asters. Keep them 4 to 6 inches tall throughout May and June. Pinch back Shasta daisy, beebalm, garden phlox, and obedient plants to control height and stagger bloom times.

Thin garden phlox, beebalm, and other powdery mildew-susceptible plants when the stems are 8 inches tall. Remove one-quarter to one-third of the stems (leaving at least four to five). Thinning increases light and air to the plant, decreasing the risk of powdery mildew.

Deadhead early-blooming perennials.

Trim any unsightly frost-damaged leaves.

Foliage is the main attraction on Japanese grass sedge. If you want, cut the flower spikes (use in a flower arrangement) to show off the leaves.

ROSES

Cut some flowers to bring inside and enjoy. Cutting a long stem (at a 45-degree angle just above the lowest out-facing five- or seven-leaflet leaf) is good for the plant (encouraging new growth and another bloom).

TREES & SHRUBS

Trees and shrubs benefit from mulch, which helps maintain soil moisture, cut down on weeds, and

SUCCESSFUL GARDENING: THATCH NO MORE

Thatch is a brown layer of partially decomposed grass. It is normal on lawns and only becomes a problem when it builds up, forming a thick, spongy layer that is like a barrier, keeping water and nutrients from reaching the grasses' roots. To prevent thatch buildup:

- Don't overwater or overfertilize the lawn.
- Avoid using insecticides, which can reduce earthworm populations—nature's aerating machines.
- Leave short grass clippings on the lawn to decompose (and feed it in the process).
- Remove and compost long grass clippings (if they are herbicide-free).
- Test for thatch by taking out several 3-×-3-inch plugs of grass from different areas. More than ½ inch of thatch is a problem. Core aeration removes plugs of soil,

■ *When thatch is a problem, aerate by hand or rent a core aerator to pull plugs out of the grass.*

allowing the thatch to break down. The soil openings also help repair compaction. Dethatching involves renting equipment or hiring a professional to physically remove this layer.

feed the soil when it breaks down. Use a 3-inch-thick layer of twice-shredded bark or wood chips that extends to the drip line.

Wait until the plants are leafed out and leaves are full sized to do any major pruning. Pruning oaks other than in dormancy increases the risk of oak wilt.

Prune spring-flowering shrubs when they're done blooming and up to early June. Later pruning may prevent the plants from setting buds for next year

Perform renewal pruning on suckering shrubs such as forsythia, bridal wreath spirea, and lilacs. Remove one-third of the older stems to ground level. See Appendix, page 194, for instructions.

Cut off spent blooms from lilacs, azaleas, and rhododendrons to enhance next spring's flowering.

VINES & GROUNDCOVERS

Move tender vines you overwintered inside, including mandevilla and passionflower, outside once the danger of frost has passed, gradually acclimating them to the outdoors.

Dig and divide groundcovers whenever they are overcrowded, fail to bloom, the center dies, or you

want to start new plants. Use a shovel or garden fork to dig a large plant. Use a sharp knife or two shovels to divide the clump into smaller pieces. Add organic matter to the original planting site and return one division to this space. Use the others to start new plants or share with friends.

Propagate groundcovers and vines by division, cuttings, and layering. Cuttings and layering are best done with relatively tender new growth in mid- to late spring (see page 92 for instructions). This is a great way to share special plants and family heirlooms with relatives and friends.

WATER

ALL

Check new plantings often. Water thoroughly to wet the roots and surrounding soil. Keep the soil lightly moist, but not wet.

ANNUALS & BIENNIALS

Cut back on watering as you prepare the plants to move outdoors. See April Plant, page 53 for details on hardening off transplants.

Check new transplants every few days. Water when the top inch of soil starts to dry. Cut back on frequency as the transplants establish.

BULBS

Keep crocus, snowdrops, Siberian squill, and glory-of-the-snow lightly moist during their growing season.

Stop watering crocus as soon as their leaves yellow.

Water caladiums frequently. Water crown imperials and hyacinths deeply. Keep tuberoses lightly moist.

EDIBLES

Water new transplants; most need at least an inch of water a week. Established plants need less.

LAWNS

Newly planted lawns need extra attention. Keep the soil surface moist until the sod is well rooted or the grass seed has sprouted. Established lawns require 1 inch of water each week.

PERENNIALS & ORNAMENTAL GRASSES

Check new plantings several times a week and water only as the top few inches of soil start to dry. Established plants need less frequent watering.

ROSES

Avoid creating the conditions that encourage blackspot. Water at ground level early in the day to

HERE'S HOW

TO DIVIDE PERENNIALS

Spring is the best time to divide overgrown summer- and fall-blooming perennials or those you want to propagate. The ideal time is just as new growth appears and the plants are less than 3 to 4 inches tall. Cut back taller plants to reduce the stress of transplanting. Wait until after flowering or late August to divide spring-flowering perennials.

1. a) Use a shovel or garden fork and dig up the clump to be divided. b) Lift the clump and set it on the ground.
2. Using a sharp knife or two shovels or garden forks, divide the clump. Cut the plant into several smaller pieces.
3. Amend the soil in the planting holes with organic matter by mixing in several cups of compost, peat moss, or leaf mold into the soil.
4. Replant one of the divisions in the original hole and use the other pieces to fill in voids, start new gardens, or share with friends.
5. Plant the division at the same depth as it was growing originally. Gently tamp the soil, and water-in with transplant solution to remove any air pockets and stimulate root growth.
6. Provide shade for any plants showing signs of transplant stress.

give leaves time to dry before the cool of the evening. Problems increase if roses are watered too often.

HERE'S HOW

TO PROPAGATE PLANTS

Experiment a little with cuttings of vines and groundcovers. Herbaceous plants (with soft stems) are easier to propagate this way than those with woody stems. Some root best from new growth in spring, while others root better from cuttings taken in winter.

FROM CUTTINGS

1. Take 3- to 6-inch-long cuttings from new growth. Dip the cut end in a rooting hormone and place it 1 inch deep in a container filled with moist vermiculite.
2. Place it in a warm, bright (no direct sun) location. Keep the vermiculite moist. Wait several weeks for the plant to root.
3. Plant the rooted cutting in a container filled with well-drained potting mix.
4. Plant it in its permanent location outdoors once the plant roots have filled the small pot and weather allows.

LAYERING

This is the most successful method of rooting woody vines.

1. Bend a long, flexible stem to the ground. Remove the leaves from the portion of the stem located between 6 and 12 inches from the tip.
2. Make a cut halfway through that portion of the stem. Treat with rooting hormone.
3. Dig a shallow trench and bury this portion of the stem in moist soil. Leave the growing tip, with leaves attached, above the ground.
4. Keep the soil slightly moist throughout the season while the buried stem forms roots. It will continue to get water and nutrients from the parent plant through the attached stem.
5. Next spring, cut the long, flexible cane where it enters the soil. Dig and transplant the newly rooted vine.

■ *Before doing any planting or transplanting, make up enough transplant solution to water plants in.*

TREES & SHRUBS

Keep the rootball and top 10 to 12 inches of soil of newly planted trees and shrubs slightly moist, but not wet. Water when the soil begins to dry—every seven to ten days in clay soil and twice a week in sandy soil.

Established trees and shrubs need less water due to their larger root systems. Give them a thorough watering every two weeks during dry periods. Check birches, willows, and other moisture-loving trees weekly during dry weather. Water when the top 6 inches of soil begin to dry.

Check aboveground planters regularly; when the top few inches of soil start to dry, water until excess water drains out.

VINES & GROUNDCOVERS

Water established plantings during dry weather. Soak the top 6 to 8 inches whenever the top 4 to 6 inches are dry. Apply needed water once every seven to ten days in clay soils and split it into two waterings a week in sandy and rocky soils.

Water potted plants thoroughly as needed.

FERTILIZE

ALL

When using any fertilizer, always follow all package instructions for proper application, frequency, and dilution/concentration.

ANNUALS & BIENNIALS

Stop fertilizing indoor- and greenhouse-grown transplants two weeks prior to planting outdoors.

Mix organic matter into the soil prior to planting. Follow soil test recommendations.

Incorporate a slow-release granular fertilizer into the potting mix for container gardens. A small amount of fertilizer is released each time you water throughout the next several months. This constant feeding is good for both you and the plants, as it saves you some work.

BULBS

Stop feeding amaryllis when you move it outside into a partially shady spot after all danger of frost has passed.

Follow these recommendations using organic products:

- Foliar feed caladiums once with a solution of kelp or fish emulsion.
- Fertilize lilies monthly until they finish blooming.
- Feed tuberoses after the foliage appears.
- Foliar feed autumn crocus leaves when they emerge. They will only be there for a month or so. Mark the spot so you don't accidentally plant anything in the same space.

EDIBLES

By the middle of May, if the temperatures have been mild enough and the warm-season vegetables have been transplanted into the garden, begin foliar feeding edibles every two weeks with a solution of fish emulsion or liquid kelp.

LAWNS

Apply a slow-release, low-nitrogen fertilizer if you live in Zones 6, 7, or 8.

PERENNIALS & ORNAMENTAL GRASSES

Perennials need very little fertilizer. Topdress established plantings with several inches of compost as the mulch breaks down and becomes incorporated into the soil. Feeding the soil, feeds the plants.

ROSES

Give hybrid teas, floribundas, and grandifloras their second feeding the moment they start to bloom. Foliar feed with a solution of fish emulsion or seaweed. Don't spray if the temperature is over 80 degrees Fahrenheit or if rain threatens. Wait three months before foliar feeding newly planted roses.

TREES & SHRUBS

Wait at least a year before fertilizing new plantings.

Run a soil test or consult a tree care professional if your trees do not look healthy.

Fertilize aboveground planters with a complete plant fertilizer, such as 10-10-10 or 12-12-12.

Finish feeding shrubs. Only fertilize plants that are showing signs of deficiencies, those which the soil test report indicates a need to fertilize, or young plants that you are trying to encourage to grow. Use a slow-release formulation to reduce risk and improve results.

VINES & GROUNDCOVERS

Fertilize existing plantings if needed; follow soil test recommendations.

PROBLEM-SOLVE

ALL

Be on the lookout for signs of voles (a.k.a. meadow mice), especially 2-inch-wide runways just below the surface of lawns. They thrive where there is lots of debris and dense vegetation. Eliminate much of their habitats and food by keeping the lawn mowed, garden beds weeded, and avoiding dense plantings like creeping juniper. Keep mulch several inches away from the base of plants. Try trapping voles with snap traps baited with peanut butter and oats. Tuck the traps in a pipe or under cover to prevent birds and desirable wildlife from accidental injury. Keep in mind there may be more than 400 voles per acre. That's a lot of peanut butter and snap traps!

Get a good insect ID book that shows good and bad bugs so you know what you have in the garden.

Walk around the garden and look closely at the plants—stems, leaves (top and bottom), flowers, fruit—with an eye to any critter that may be lurking, or signs that something has been nibbling. Identify the pest. If you can't find the culprit in the daytime, go out hunting at night with a flashlight; some, such as slugs and snails, are nocturnal. Decide whether the damage is enough to warrant control. Handpick what you can.

"If it's not broke, don't fix it." Routine spraying is unnecessary unless pests or disease are seen.

Neem oil has many uses, including controlling some insect pests, blackspot, and powdery mildew. However, some plants can be killed by Neem oil, especially if it is applied heavily. Before spraying the entire plant, test a couple of leaves. Wait 24 hours and check if the leaf has any damage. If there is no damage, then the plant will not be harmed by the Neem oil. Apply Neem oil only in indirect light or in the evening to allow the preparation to seep into the plant while avoiding burning the foliage.

ANNUALS & BIENNIALS

Protect new plantings from cutworm damage. These insects chew through the stems of young transplants. They are most common in planting beds recently converted from lawn. Use cutworm collars made of metal or plastic. Remove the bottoms of shallow pet food and tuna cans and use them as collars around the new transplants. Sink them at least an inch deep or close to the rim down into the soil.

Watch for aphids, mites, spittlebugs, and slugs.

Earwigs are a mixed curse and blessing. They can decimate seedlings, evidenced by missing all or parts of the leaves and stem. To be sure earwigs are the culprits, go out at night to see them feeding. But they are also important predators of aphids. If damage is extensive, control them by trapping. Sink low-sided cans (cat food or tuna) with ½ inch of oil in them (tuna oil, or vegetable oil with a drop of bacon grease) in the ground so the top of the can is at soil level. Dump the oil and replace when it's full of earwigs.

Pull or dig out weeds as soon as they appear. Be careful not to damage the fragile roots of transplants while weeding.

Watch for gnawed plants and chewed-off new growth—sure signs of deer, rabbits, and woodchucks. These animals also appreciate a few fresh greens— your new transplants—in their diets. Repellents applied before they start feeding may give you control. Fencing small garden areas may help keep out deer, as they do not seem to like to feed in small, fenced-in areas. A 2-foot-high fence anchored in the ground will help keep rabbits out. Fencing may not be the most attractive remedy, but it beats having no flowers at all.

Protect hanging baskets from birds and chipmunks. Cover baskets with bird netting. Secure the netting

■ *Use cutworm collars, such as paper towel rolls cut to size, on spring transplants in the vegetable garden, especially brassicas— broccoli, cauliflower, cabbage, collards, Brussels sprouts, and kale.*

HERE'S HOW

TO DIVIDE TULIPS AND DAFFODILS

■ *Easy bulb planting: push trowel into soil, pull towards you, drop in bulb, remove trowel, and pat down soil.*

1. Dig up the clump of bulbs.
2. Gently tease the bulbs and roots apart.
3. Replant the bulbs at a depth that is three times their height. Space them two to three times their width (center to center) apart.
4. For fast planting, use a bulb trowel that is marked in inches. Put the trowel in the soil to the desired depth. Pull the trowel toward you and drop the bulb in the hole. Remove the trowel and firm the soil.
5. Water well with transplant solution.

above and below the container. Do this at the first signs of a problem. Quick action discourages birds and animals so they will find a better place to go. Remove netting once wildlife is no longer a threat.

BULBS

If hungry animals and early frost aren't to blame for tulips or daffodils not blooming despite healthy leaves, it's time to divide them.

EDIBLES

Cutworms can make short shrift of new transplants. Use cutworm collars as detailed in this month's Problem-Solve.

LAWNS

Check your lawn's health by noting changes in color, density, and overall vigor. For help diagnosing problems, contact your local Cooperative Extension Service (free) or a lawn care professional.

Sod webworm larvae can cause thin patches or brown trails. To test for them, mix 1 tablespoon of dishwashing detergent in 1 gallon of water. Sprinkle the soapy water over 1 square yard of lawn. Conduct the test in several areas, in both damaged spots and areas adjacent to the damaged grass. Check the treated areas several times over the next 10 minutes for sod webworms to appear. Treat if one or more sod webworm larvae are present. Contact your local Cooperative Extension Service for recommended treatments.

See "Successful Gardening: Weeds: Good and Bad" on page 96.

PERENNIALS & ORNAMENTAL GRASSES

Monitor the garden for pests. Remove infected leaves when discovered. Watch for four-lined plant bugs, slugs, and aphids. Check the upper and lower leaf surfaces and stems for aphids and mites. These pests suck out plant juices, causing leaves to yellow and brown. Attack insect pests early, while they are young, to avoid an infestation. Spray plants with a strong blast of water to dislodge these insects.

Insecticidal soap works well for whiteflies, aphids, caterpillars of many kinds, and Japanese beetles. You can purchase a ready-to-spray solution or concentrate (more expensive, but lasts a long time), or you can make your own. See January Problem-Solve (page 33) for complete directions on making your own. Neem oil is also an effective control.

Pull weeds as soon as they appear. Dandelions, thistle, and quackgrass are among the first to appear. Removing weeds before they set seed saves pulling hundreds more next year.

Continue to minimize animal damage by fencing and using repellents on susceptible plants.

SUCCESSFUL GARDENING: WEEDS: GOOD AND BAD

■ *Creeping Charlie is a beautiful, but persistent, lawn weed that can take several years to eradicate successfully.*

A weed by definition is a plant growing where you don't want it; a rose could be a weed in an onion patch. Do you have to have a pristine, weed-free lawn? Are dandelions so bad? If you don't spray chemicals on your lawn, you can eat both the greens and young flowers. Chickweed leaves are a nice addition to a salad as are purslane leaves. White clover fixes nitrogen, which feeds the lawn. Learn to identify the weeds and then decide which (and how much of that weed) are acceptable.

The best defense against weeds is a lush, healthy lawn. Mowing high shades the soil so weed seeds are less likely to germinate. Pull or dig out weeds when you first see them; be sure to get all the roots. Or use a broadleaf weedkiller to spot-treat the problem.

Creeping Charlie, also known as ground ivy, has round scalloped leaves that smell minty when crushed. It can be pernicious. Spot treat it with broadleaf weedkiller when the purple flowers appear in May. It may take a couple of years to eradicate.

ROSES

Walk around the garden and take a good look at the roses. After their spring pruning and feeding, they should be looking great—healthy and

HERE'S HOW

TO MAKE BAKING SODA SOLUTION TO TREAT BLACKSPOT

1 tablespoon baking soda
3 drops Ivory dish liquid *or*
   1 teaspoon light horticultural oil
1 gallon water

Mix well. Spray at first sign of blackspot. Be sure to get the tops and bottoms of the leaves as well as the stems. Do not spray if the temperature is over 80 degrees Fahrenheit.

vigorous, getting ready to bloom. If any aren't up to snuff, look closely to see what's wrong. Did the graft die and the rootstock has taken over? Is the plant weak and spindly? Are there signs of major pests or disease this early in the season? Be especially vigilant for rose rosette disease (see March Problem-Solve, page 61, for detailed information). Decide whether it is worth the time and effort to coddle the plant. If it was a plant from grandmother's garden, do whatever needs to be done to save it. Otherwise, this is a perfect time to pull it up and replace it. If the problem was pests or disease, choose a different planting site for the replacement. Plant onions, chives, or garlic in the space; they will thrive.

■ *Blackspot can be a major problem in roses with our humid summers. Avoid it by choosing resistant varieties.*

Treat blackspot at the first sign—small black spots on the leaves—if the fungal disease has been a problem in the past. Spray with baking soda solution as soon as the plant leafs out. Baking soda changes the pH slightly so conditions are not optimal for fungal growth. Spray the entire plant, including leaves and canes, every seven to ten days. It will not eliminate blackspot that already exists but can keep other leaves from becoming infected. Remove affected leaves and clean up around the plant. Another treatment for blackspot is to spray with a solution of Neem oil.

Holes in the leaves or skeletonized leaves are the first signs of caterpillars. Often you will find them feeding on the underside of the leaves. Spray with insecticidal soap (see recipe for making it yourself on page 33, January Problem-Solve) or a solution of Neem oil.

TREES & SHRUBS

Continue monitoring for the insects described in April Problem-Solve (page 79), including cankerworm, Eastern tent caterpillar, birch leaf miner, and emerald ash borer.

Look for gypsy moth caterpillars on trees. They are distinctive, growing to 2 inches long with black bristles and two rows of colored spots on their backs (blue near the head, red lower on the back). They feed at night; use sticky bands to catch them as they come down the tree trunk in the daytime.

Check pines for colonies of wormlike European pine sawflies. Wear a leather glove to squash them, or prune out the infested branches and destroy them. Also look for pine needle scale. Spray insecticidal soap or Neem oil when bridal wreath spirea is in bloom; repeat in seven to ten days.

Control aphids and mites with a strong blast of water from the hose. Lady beetle (ladybug) larvae feed on aphids. Neem oil is a good control for aphid and mite infestation if water does not work.

Look for phomopsis blight on junipers and Russian olives, especially if spring is cool and wet. Signs are

■ *Always prune out any cankers (they resemble oozing sores on branches) at least 9 inches away from them.*

branches with sunken, discolored cankers and brown/dead needles/leaves. Prune out infected branches 9 inches below the canker and destroy or discard them. Disinfect tools between cuts with rubbing alcohol or a solution of 1 part bleach to 9 parts water.

Fireblight can infect crabapples, apples, pears, firethorn, and quince, turning leaves black and curling branch tips. Splashing water, pollinating bees, and infected tools can spread the disease. Avoid pruning during wet periods. Cut out infected branches 12 inches below the canker.

Oyster shell scale can affect poplars, dogwoods, cotoneasters, lilacs, and other deciduous trees and shrubs. The aptly named hard-shelled insects resemble miniature oyster shells. Spray stems and leaves with ultrafine oil or an insecticide labeled for use on shrubs with scale. Spray when the bridal wreath spirea is in bloom and again when the hills-of-snow hydrangea flowers turn green.

VINES & GROUNDCOVERS

Monitor wintercreeper vines for euonymus caterpillar webbed nests. Remove and destroy them. Or spray nests and surrounding foliage with Bt (*Bacillus thuringiensis*). This bacterial insecticide will kill caterpillars, but it will not harm people, pets, or wildlife.

June

June marks the heightening of tornado season when severe weather can occur, bringing strong winds, heavy rain, and lightning. Be prepared for winds by supporting plants. Be sure the supports (anything from stakes and cages to trellises and arbors) are securely anchored deeply in the ground or fastened to a building or structure. For example, to stake tomatoes 6 feet high, use an 8-foot stake and pound it at least 18 inches into the ground.

Get a good rain gauge for an accurate measurement of weekly rainfall. Remember to empty it at the end of each week. (You can also use it to monitor snowfall.)

If the weather has been warm and damp, your mulch may be turning into compost faster than you realize. Save money and help the environment and shred junk mail (nothing glossy, black-and-white only), the excess printed matter your computer generates each day, and black-and-white newsprint to use as mulch. Attack a small area (up to 4 feet × 4 feet) at a time. Pull back existing mulch and spread a 6-inch layer of shredded paper around and between plantings. Water it well. Cover lightly with decorative mulch so ribbons of paper do not show through.

Keep yourself inspired. Visit nearby botanic and public gardens (where you know that plants will be labeled correctly) to see new and different plants. Participate in local garden tours. This is a great way to support community beautification efforts and charities while getting a peek into fellow gardeners' backyards. Ask questions. People are flattered to have their gardens admired. Offer to swap something from your garden in exchange for a cutting or division. Note planting combinations that you want to use in future gardens and take lots of pictures.

As the old song goes, "June is busting out all over!" Roses are in their first gorgeous flush of bloom, early daylilies (especially a few night-blooming varieties) are flowering, and the vegetable garden is getting into harvest mode—Asian greens, radishes, carrots, lettuces, and broccoli. If you're really lucky, you may even be savoring tomatoes (small cherry types) before the end of the month.

PLAN

ALL

Record visitors to your garden: note the birds, butterflies, frogs or toads, and beneficial insects stopping by to nest or feed. You may want to add water, bird feeders, birdhouses, frog shelters, and butterfly houses to encourage your welcomed guests to stay.

Summer is a great time to plan next year's garden. Evaluate the success and beauty of your spring garden. Be sure to take photos and videos of your ever-changing landscape.

Start a wish list for new plants for future gardens. Add to this throughout the season. Record the name, bloom time, size, hardiness, and other features of the plant. This will help when planning new additions.

ANNUALS & BIENNIALS

Take a walk around the yard. Look for bare or drab areas that would benefit from a boost of annual color. Use annuals (as well as early-blooming perennials) to hide spring bulbs as their leaves turn yellow and brown. Consider adding a pot of annuals on your patio, deck, or entranceway. You will be amazed at the difference a few plants can make.

BULBS

If you haven't already ordered fall- and spring-blooming bulbs, do it now. As convenient as the Internet is, nothing beats slowly going through the catalogs, using sticky notes to mark plants that pique your interest. Go through a process of elimination, whittling the list down until it is affordable and can fit in the garden. You're likely to discover some bulbs that are new to you, like autumn crocus, the true fall-blooming crocus, star of Bethlehem, and the wonderful range of alliums. Bulbs are shipped at the proper planting time, so you don't have to worry about summer storage.

Add lilies to your bulb order. Lilies make superb container plants, especially the dwarf varieties. The selection is much more varied when you shop through mail-order and online sources, but local nurseries, garden centers, and home-improvement stores offer a dozen or more different lilies. Consider Orienpet lilies, which easily weather late Midwestern frosts without bud kill, and have the sweet fragrance and shape of Oriental lilies.

EDIBLES

In a moist, boggy area, you can grow the best celery you will ever eat. Watercress flourishes in a small stream. There are a surprising number of edible aquatics, including wild rice, lotus (unripe seed and tubers), water mint, taro (tubers), water cilantro, water chestnuts, and more.

It is not too early to start thinking about fall vegetables. First, take a hard look at the garden, realizing that the existing plants will fill in a lot of the bare space. If there is room or if there are plants that will be completely harvested by early July, start making your list. The best fall crops are the same as the early spring crops—greens of all sorts and brassicas. For a splash of color, include some pansies (fall varieties can last through the winter). Find out if your local nursery, garden center, or home-improvement store carries starts of any of the plants you want. Go online or get out the catalogs and order seeds now, unless you have seeds leftover from spring planting.

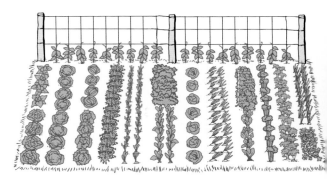

■ *A fall vegetable garden can contain a myriad of greens from lettuces to Asian vegetables—and even peas.*

PERENNIALS & ORNAMENTAL GRASSES

Harvest flowers for arrangements and drying. Experiment with different flower combinations. If they look good together in a vase, they will probably look good as planting partners in the garden.

SUCCESSFUL GARDENING: PROFESSIONAL TREE CARE

Summer storms can wreak havoc, leaving shredded leaves, broken branches, and uprooted trees and shrubs in their wake. Keeping plants healthy and properly pruned can minimize some storm damage.

Consider having a tree care professional (certified arborist) come now to assess your property and develop a long-term plan to maintain or improve your trees' storm resistance. Then put that person's number in your phone's contact list in case disaster strikes.

Keeping trees healthy and well pruned by a professional can avoid tragedies like this shallow-rooted oak uprooted after heavy rains.

To find a certified arborist, ask friends, neighbors, and relatives for recommendations. Go to the International Society of Arboriculture website (www.isa-arbor.com/findanarborist/findanarborist.aspx) to find an arborist in your area or check to see if someone is certified. Quality tree care companies participate in professional organizations such as the International Society of Arboriculture and National Arborist Association. They also provide staff with training and educational opportunities.

ROSES

As you visit other gardens, take the time to smell the roses. Discover new scents to include in your garden. Check catalogs and online nurseries for availability of fragrant roses.

If you have a separate rose garden, consider incorporating roses into other areas—perennial beds, borders, cottage garden, and even your vegetable and herb gardens.

TREES & SHRUBS

"Change is good" and "change happens" could be garden mottos. Adjust your plans and make notes as they occur. You may find these changes actually improve the original plan.

VINES & GROUNDCOVERS

Consider replacing annual plantings under trees with perennial groundcovers. This means less root disturbance for the tree and less work.

PLANT

ALL

Early June is peak planting time. The air and soil have finally warmed. Transplants quickly adjust to these warmer outdoor conditions.

Reduce transplant shock by planting in early morning, late afternoon, or on a cloudy day. Always water in with transplant solution. This solution helps get plants off to a good start, encouraging strong root growth. Follow mixing directions on the label. Proper planting and post-planting care will help transplants adjust to their new location. See May Plant for tips on transplanting, planting, and care.

ANNUALS & BIENNIALS

Finish planting frost-sensitive annuals early in the month for the best and longest possible flower display. Check out local nurseries, garden centers, and home-improvement stores for larger transplants. Use these for a quicker show or for later plantings.

BULBS

Transplant caladiums outdoors when all danger of frost has passed and the soil is at least 60 degrees Fahrenheit. Plant the tubers 1 inch deep and 8 to 10 inches apart in full to partial shade.

Transplant cannas outdoors at the same time as caladiums. Cannas can take very moist soil; grow them at the edge of your pond and in the garden. Site colorful-leafed cannas such as 'Tropicanna®' so the early-morning or late-afternoon sun can shine through the leaves, making them look like stained glass. Space 18 inches apart.

Begin planting gladiolus in Zones 3 to 6 and continue planting them in Zones 7 and 8. See page 84 for detailed planting instructions.

■ *Peacock orchids are underused, summer-blooming bulbs. They're a great addition to an evening garden with their brilliant white flowers and nighttime fragrance.*

Start planting peacock orchids (botanical name *Gladiolus callianthus* or *Acidanthera bicolor murielae*). Similar to gladiolus, they bloom from the lower part of the stem up. White, with deep burgundy at the throat, they are a fragrant addition to an evening garden; in moonlight they appear to be fluttering moths. Plant the corms in clusters of five or seven (or any larger odd number) 4 to 6 inches deep and 3 to 5 inches apart. Stagger the planting to extend the season; plant several clusters every two weeks for six to eight weeks. Water well.

EDIBLES

Plant some herbs, salad greens, and one or more tomatoes in large containers near your kitchen door. Easy accessibility means you are likely to pick them for immediate use, no matter what the weather—very hot, rainy, or even a delightfully comfortable day. Yield on these plants is very high; as you keep picking, you encourage new leaf and fruit formation.

Make successive plantings of summer greens; change to heat-tolerant New Zealand spinach and lettuces labeled for summer. They will get ample light and stay cooler in dappled sun or a place that has morning sun with shade from noon on.

LAWNS

Continue to lay sod, if necessary. It will need extra water if the weather turns hot and dry.

PERENNIALS & ORNAMENTAL GRASSES

Keep planting. The soil is warm, and there are still lots of perennials available at local garden centers, home-improvement stores, and nurseries. Label new plantings, write their locations on your garden plan, and record critical information in your garden journal. See the plant tag for any specific planting and care information. Consider saving the tags for future reference.

ROSES

If there are any "holes" in the garden, now is the time to fill them with roses. Give the rose a head start by soaking the container overnight in transplant solution. Take care to gently loosen or tease any roots that may be encircling the rootball. See May Plant (page 88) for detailed planting instructions.

TREES & SHRUBS

Balled-and-burlapped and container-grown plants can be planted throughout the growing season. See April Plant (page 70) for detailed instructions.

SUCCESSFUL GARDENING: BEFORE PLANTING TREES AND SHRUBS

There is probably still a good selection of balled-and-burlapped and container-grown trees and shrubs at local nurseries, garden centers, and home-improvement stores. Use these tips for increasing your planting success:

- Call 811 at least two business days ahead of time so they can mark any underground utilities on your property.
- Bring a large enough vehicle to pick up the plant. Borrow a van, SUV, or pickup from a friend (bring the friend along to help).
- Look closely at the plants. Choose healthy specimens with leaves free of brown spots. Avoid plants with dry edges or other signs of pest damage and neglect.
- Get the plant home safely. Bring a tarp, drop cloth, or blanket to wrap the canopy of a tree (branches of a shrub). This will protect new leaves and prevent breaking branches while bringing your tree home. If transporting the plant in a truck, drape a tarp over the entire plant to prevent it drying on the windy trip home, which can add to its stress.
- Store the plant in a shady spot until you are ready to plant.
- Check the plants daily. Water frequently enough to keep roots and soil moist.
- Cover the rootball with woodchips if you're not planting within a few days.

■ *Container-grown trees and shrubs, which are readily available locally from spring to fall, can be planted anytime.*

VINES & GROUNDCOVERS

Anchor the trellis in place before planting a vine. Gently tie vines to the trellis with soft cloth or non-wire ties to get them started climbing on their new support.

Finish hardening off and transplanting annual vines into the garden. See March Plant (page 53) for detailed information about hardening off.

Keep planting. Container-grown vines and groundcovers can be planted throughout the growing season.

CARE

ALL

After a heavy rain or storm, assess any damage in the garden. Restake plants, if necessary, using a stronger support set deeper into the ground.

ANNUALS & BIENNIALS

Mulch transplants. Use compost, well-rotted manure, fine wood chips, pine needles, shredded

■ *Deadheading annuals keeps them blooming all summer long. Use hand pruners on cosmos to cut off several spent flowers at once.*

leaves, or other organic material as mulch. Keep mulch 1 to 2 inches away from stems. A 1- to 2-inch layer of mulch helps conserve moisture, moderates soil temperature, and reduces weeds.

Finish staking tall annuals that need a little added support. Stake early in the season to reduce the risk of damaging taller, more established plants.

Deadhead flowers as they fade. Pinch or cut the flowering stem back to the first set of leaves or flower buds. Use a knife or garden shears to make a clean cut on tough stems. This improves a plant's appearance and encourages continual bloom.

Ageratum, cleome, gomphrena, New Guinea impatiens, narrow-leaf zinnias, impatiens, wax begonias, and pentas are self-cleaning. They drop their dead blooms and do not need deadheading.

Pinch out flower stalks on coleus as soon as they appear to keep the plants full and compact.

Pinch back leggy petunias to encourage branching all along the stem. Cut stems back above a set of leaves.

Cut off spent begonia and ageratum flowers during wet weather to reduce disease problems.

BULBS

If not done last month, move potted amaryllis outside after all danger of frost is passed. Place them in semi-shade or under a shrub.

Pinch dahlias back, especially dwarf or compact varieties, so they will retain their low, compact size. If you want later-blooming, larger dahlia flowers (like the dinner plate ones you see at flower shows), pinch off most of the buds (disbud), leaving only one or two flower buds on each stem.

Remove the dead flowerheads of crown imperial before they go to seed.

Do *not* deadhead Siberian iris. Leave seedpods to provide added interest in the summer, fall, and winter garden.

EDIBLES

Stake or cage tomatoes, if you didn't do it when they were planted. Tomatoes are one of the few vines that cannot climb unaided. You can let it run along the ground, but put some straw or other material under the vine to improve air circulation and to keep it from touching damp soil, which can lead to fungal diseases.

■ *To avoid damaging the roots, set tomato cages or stakes when you put in the plants. Straw is an inexpensive mulch.*

Train tomatoes to a single stem by pinching out any side shoots, which emerge between the main stem and a branch. The result is fewer—but larger—tomatoes on the plant, better air circulation, and fewer fungal diseases.

Cloth strips or old pantyhose are ideal for tying tomatoes and other plants to supports. These loose-fitting, slightly stretchy materials are unlikely to cut into the vine as it grows and expands. Make a loose figure-eight around the stem and support. Tie every 8 to 12 inches.

Stop harvesting asparagus and let some stalks grow their delicate, ferny foliage. Plants are dioecious (there are male and female plants); the females will bear red berries during summer.

Depending on how temperate the winter and spring were, you may start getting something tasty besides lettuce and other leafy vegetables out of your garden.

Pick snow peas before the pods start to enlarge. Sugar snap peas are best once the pods are about half to three-quarters filled out, although they are fine for cooking when completely ripe. Harvest English (garden peas), when the pods are completely filled out.

As herb plants grow, cut off what you need. Pick chive blossoms, crumble them and use them like onions. Keeping the flowers picked off results in more flowers over a longer period of time.

Check broccoli and the other brassicas (except for Brussels sprouts, which won't be harvested until fall). If the weather is forecasted to turn hot for more than a few days, harvest broccoli and cauliflower even if they have not reached mature size. Otherwise, they will start to flower (bolt). Give cabbages another few days, and if the mercury is still soaring, cut them too. Pull carrots and radishes when they are fairly young, as they can get pithy as the temperature rises. If the weather is cool, cut the broccoli and cauliflower, but leave at least an inch of stem on the plant; it will develop small, tasty sideshoots.

Begin to harvest garlic when the leaves start to yellow. Choose a dry, sunny day, with a three-day forecast of more of the same. Gently pull or dig the bulbs out of the ground, lay them on top of the ground for one to two days. Braid or store the garlic in a cool, dry area. Save some bulbs for planting in fall.

■ *Mowing high helps conserve soil moisture and shade out weeds. Leave clippings on the lawn to feed the soil over time.*

LAWNS

Mow often enough so that you remove only one-third of the total grass height at each cutting. Removing less leaf surface minimizes the stress on the plant. Keep the grass 2½ to 3½ inches tall. The taller grass shades the soil, keeping grass roots cool and preventing weed seeds from sprouting.

PERENNIALS & ORNAMENTAL GRASSES

Put stakes and cages in place. Tuck plants in place or carefully tie them to the support as needed. Twine or other soft bindings work best. Loop the twine around the stem and then around the support in a figure-eight.

Thin garden phlox and other overgrown perennials subject to mildew and leaf spot diseases. Remove one-third of the stems.

Pinch back perennials to control height or delay bloom. Keep mums and asters at 6 inches through this month and then stop pinching them.

Remove dead or declining foliage on spring-blooming perennials. Add this material to the compost pile unless it died from pests or disease.

Mulch perennials with at least 2 inches of compost, leaf mold, well-rotted manure, twice-shredded bark, or shredded leaves to conserve moisture and reduce weeds. Keep the mulch 1 to 2 inches from the base of the plant; be careful not to bury the crown.

Continue deadheading to prolong bloom, prevent unwanted seedlings, and improve a plant's overall appearance.

Consider removing lamb's ear flowers as soon as they form. This encourages better foliage; removing flowers leads to open, more attractive growth.

Create a living support for purple coneflower, heliopsis, garden phlox, balloon flower, and veronica by cutting back an outer ring of stems on the plant. The shorter, pinched-back stems will bloom later.

Cut back any unsightly foliage after plants bloom.

ROSES

Whether deadheading or cutting a bloom to enjoy indoors, the technique is the same as basic pruning: make the 45-degree cut just above the lowest, outward-facing, five- to seven-leaflet leaf.

TREES & SHRUBS

Prune trees for repair this month. Cut out branches that cross or are damaged or diseased. See Appendix (page 192) for detailed instructions.

Last call for pruning spring-flowering shrubs. Later pruning could prevent next year's flower buds from developing.

Shape hedges after new growth appears so that the bottom is wider than the top. This allows the sun to reach the entire plant.

If a tree or shrub is surrounded by lawn, consider removing the grass and creating planting beds around the plant. It will be better off without the competition for nutrients and water and the possibility of damage from mowers and weed whackers. Or remove the lawn and surround the plant with mulch.

Renew mulch if necessary to maintain a 3-inch layer.

VINES & GROUNDCOVERS

Mulch 2- to 3-inches deep around groundcovers and vines with shredded leaves, cocoa hulls, leaf mold, woodchips, or twice-shredded bark. Keep mulch at least 2 inches away from the base of the plants to avoid burying the crowns.

Lightly mow or shear bugleweed when it finishes blooming to improve its all-over appearance and to keep it from setting seed.

Prune creeping phlox back halfway (if it's not already done) to encourage healthy new growth.

WATER

ALL

Most plants need a minimum of 1 inch of water a week. Remember to include any rainfall.

■ *A single rain barrel can usually provide ample water for plants in containers, depending on weather conditions.*

ANNUALS & BIENNIALS

Check new plantings several times per week. Water when the top inch of soil starts to dry.

Water established plants thoroughly when the top few inches of soil start to dry. Adjust the watering schedule to fit the plant's needs and growing conditions.

Water in early morning to reduce disease caused by wet foliage at night, leaf burn due to wet leaves in midday, and moisture loss due to evaporation.

Using a watering wand or drip irrigation system waters the soil without wetting the foliage. This puts the water where it is needed and helps reduce the risk of fungal disease.

Drooping leaves can indicate drought stress; however, it is also one way that some plants conserve moisture. Wait until evening to see if the plants recover. Always check the soil moisture before reaching for the hose.

BULBS

Keep caladiums, cannas, calla lilies, tuberoses, and peacock orchids lightly moist. Don't let soil dry out.

Water crown imperials and hyacinths deeply.

EDIBLES

If your rain gauge measures less than 1 inch of rain per week, supplement watering.

LAWNS

New lawns need to be kept lightly moist. Established lawns generally need 1 inch of water a week if rain doesn't supply it. A lawn tells you when it needs water: it loses its vibrant color and becomes dull and blue-gray, the grass blades begin to roll, or you'll leave a footprint when you step on it. Less frequent, but thorough, watering encourages deeper roots.

■ *Using a watering wand conserves water. Aiming directly at the roots at soil level keeps leaves dry, thwarting fungus.*

PERENNIALS & ORNAMENTAL GRASSES

Perennials, like annuals, may wilt in the heat of day to conserve moisture. By evening, the plants perk back up without watering

Check new plantings several times a week. Water thoroughly whenever the top 2 to 3 inches of soil start to dry. Do not overwater.

Check established plantings weekly.

Most ornamental grasses need no supplemental water and thrive just on what nature provides. Japanese grass sedge and tufted hair grass need regular watering, however. Keep the soil uniformly lightly moist. Don't let it dry out.

ROSES

Water weekly or as needed.

If you are going on vacation and don't have an automatic sprinkling system, your roses can still get watered. This is not the most aesthetically pleasing solution, but it will keep the plants going. First, water the garden well. Take a plastic, 2-liter soda bottle and make small pinholes on the bottom and around the lower 2 inches of the bottle. About a foot away from the crown, dig a 3-inch-deep hole wide enough to hold the bottle. Fill the bottle with water and recap it. Place it in the hole and pack the excess soil around it. That should quench any thirst for at least a week—up to two weeks in cooler temperatures.

TREES & SHRUBS

Weather, the age of the plant, soil type, and mulch all affect how much water trees and shrubs need. In general, when the top 6 inches of soil begin to dry, thoroughly soak the top 10 to 12 inches of soil. Check young plants once or twice a week. Established plants need water infrequently. During extended dry periods, water them every two weeks thoroughly enough to moisten the top 10 to 12 inches of soil. Paper birch, willows, and other moisture-loving plants require weekly watering when the weather is dry. Check plants in clay soil every seven to ten days and those in sandy soil every four to five days.

VINES & GROUNDCOVERS

Check container plantings daily. When the top 2 inches of soil starts to dry, water until the excess runs out the bottom.

Water new plantings often enough to keep the soil around the roots slightly moist. Gradually decrease watering frequency and check plants growing in clay soil weekly, and those in sandy soil twice a week. When the top 2 to 3 inches of soil start to dry, soak the top 6 to 8 inches of soil.

Established plants need less frequent watering. Check them during extended dry periods. When the top 3 or 4 inches are dry, water enough to wet the top 6 to 8 inches of soil.

FERTILIZE

ALL

When using any fertilizer, always follow all package instructions for proper application, frequency, concentration, and mixing/dilution.

ANNUALS & BIENNIALS

Incorporate a slow-release, complete fertilizer in the potting mix for your containers. Every time you water, you will be fertilizing. Or, foliar feed with a solution of fish emulsion or kelp every two weeks.

BULBS

Foliar feed caladiums, calla lilies, and cannas monthly with a solution of kelp or fish emulsion.

Fertilize lilies monthly until the plants stop blooming.

EDIBLES

Give Mediterranean herbs one foliar feeding early in the month and everything else twice a month.

LAWNS

Apply a slow-release, low-nitrogen fertilizer if you live in Zones 3, 4, or 5.

PERENNIALS & ORNAMENTAL GRASSES

Perennials and ornamental grasses usually get enough nutrients from the soil and need very little supplemental fertilization.

Topdress established beds once every two to four years with 2 to 4 inches of compost. If plants need a quick boost, foliar feed with kelp or fish emulsion or use a liquid fertilizer.

ROSES

Start foliar feeding roses planted in March.

Feed hybrid teas, floribundas, and grandifloras the moment they start to bloom. Foliar feed with fish emulsion or seaweed. Don't spray if the temperature is over 80 degrees Fahrenheit or if rain threatens. Feed early in the day so that leaves can dry. You don't want to be setting them up for fungal problems.

■ *Fish emulsion and liquid kelp (diluted according to package directions) are excellent organic fertilizers to use for foliar feeding.*

If using traditional fertilizer, give plants their second feeding when the flowers are in bud, just before they open. For granular fertilizer, remove the mulch from around the plant, sprinkle the fertilizer evenly around the plant, water well, and then replace the mulch. Or you can spread fertilizer over mulch and water and rake it through the mulch and into the soil. Add more mulch if it has broken down and it is less than 3 inches deep. If using liquid fertilizer, follow package instructions for dilution. No need to remove the mulch, just water around the plant with the diluted food.

TREES & SHRUBS

If the plant has signs of nutrient deficiency like yellow or off-color leaves, do a soil test. It will tell you what type and how much of each nutrient you need to add. Adding unnecessary nutrients can harm plants and the environment, as well as waste your time and money.

For aboveground planters, use a complete fertilizer, such as 10-10-10 or 12-12-12, to replace the nutrients washed away by frequent watering.

VINES & GROUNDCOVERS

Fertilize established plantings if recommended by a soil test. Too much fertilizer can result in excess leaf growth, poor flowering, disease problems, and root damage.

Fertilize vines growing in containers with a dilute solution of any flowering plant fertilizer.

PROBLEM-SOLVE

ANNUALS & BIENNIALS

Monitor the garden for insects. Instead of pesticides, turn to beneficial insects for control of pests. The fewer pesticides used, the more beneficials you'll find. Look for ladybugs, lacewings, praying mantises, and other insects that eat aphids and other troublesome pests. Also watch for bees, butterflies, and hummingbirds that come to visit your garden. Protect and encourage these visitors by minimizing your use of pesticides. See July Problem-Solve, page 123, for ideas on controlling unwelcome insect pests.

■ *It pays to have a good insect ID book. This delicate-looking lacewing is a good defense against aphids.*

Pull weeds as they appear. It is much easier to keep up with a few weeds than it is to reclaim an entire garden. Pull and destroy quackgrass, creeping Charlie, crabgrass, and other perennial weeds; do not compost them.

Continue the regimen for animal pests in May Problem-Solve (page 94).

Remove spotted, blotchy, or discolored leaves, which can be caused by fungal disease, as soon as you see them. Discard or destroy leaves; do not compost. Sanitation is the best way to control and reduce the spread of disease.

BULBS

If your daffodils and tulips had lots of leaves but fewer flowers than in previous years, they are too crowded. See May Problem-Solve (page 95) for details on dividing them.

EDIBLES

Did you know that some garden caterpillar pests metamorphose into beautiful, prized butterflies and moths that flit through the garden gathering nectar? The striped parsleyworm or celeryworm, which voraciously eats parsley, celery, dill, and carrots, eventually turns into the lovely black swallowtail butterfly. Unaware of this transformation, you could unwittingly kill off the potential butterflies by spraying the plants with Bt (*Bacillus thuringiensis*), insecticidal soap, or Neem oil. Plant extra parsley in another space for the hungry larvae; if they get out of control in your veggies, handpick and move them to the new feeding ground.

LAWNS

See page 90 for detailed information on thatch.

A cool, wet spring can set a lawn up for disease, especially fungus. Dry weather can reverse it or stop it from spreading. Avoid stressing a lawn (which can make it more prone to disease) by watering during droughts and mowing high (3 to 3½ inches). Overseed any damaged areas in late August or early September.

Warmer weather seems to bring out the weeds in force. Unfortunately, the quick fix of weedkillers (herbicides) is not an option in summer as they can damage a lawn when applied in hot, dry weather. Go back to the tried-and-true method of digging up weeds. Be sure to get all of the roots. Don't want to dig? Remove any flowers so the weeds can't produce seeds. Maybe you can convince a child or grandchild to "unplug" and dig weeds for a price.

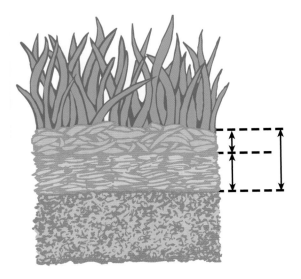

■ *A thatch layer should be no more than ½ inch thick. Rake lawn vigorously to loosen top layer.*

■ *Sickly or over-fertilized plants can be magnets for pests like aphids, which suck the juice out of the plant.*

Dogs may be the culprits when you see brown spots of dead grass. Their nitrogen-rich urine burns the lawn just like applying too much fertilizer does. Treat both problems by thoroughly watering the area. This dilutes the urine and washes it through the soil. The surrounding grass will eventually fill in any brown spots.

PERENNIALS & ORNAMENTAL GRASSES

Remove spotted, blotchy, or discolored leaves, which can be caused by fungal disease, as soon as you see them. Discard or destroy leaves; do not compost. Sanitation is the best way to control and reduce the spread of disease.

Monitor for aphids, leafhoppers, mites, and spittlebugs, which suck out plant juices. Leaves turn yellow, brown, and die. Treat infested plants with insecticidal soap (for directions on making your own insecticidal soap, see page 33, January Problem-Solve) or Neem oil. Repeat weekly as needed.

Use a flashlight to look for nighttime marauders. Slugs, snails, and earwigs feed at night, eating holes in leaves and flowers. Hostas are a delicacy. Treat slugs and snails by applying snail bait granules around affected plants. Making a ½- to 1-inch-wide ring of diatomaceous earth or wood ashes also works by scratching the tender underbellies of slugs and snails. Some gardeners derive satisfaction from hunting snails at night, picking them off the ground or plants, and stomping on them (there's that crunch). See May Problem-Solve for information on earwigs and their control.

Check the garden for signs of wildlife. Deer and rabbits love hostas, phlox, and other perennials. Apply repellents or use scare tactics such as noisemakers and whirligigs. Fence gardens to discourage feeding.

Pull weeds as soon as you see them.

ROSES

If blackspot persists, remove and destroy afflicted leaves. Check the stems for spotting. If they are affected, cut them off and destroy them. Clean up around the plant, picking up any dead leaves on the ground. Spray the entire plant, including leaves and canes, every seven to ten days with baking soda solution (see May Problem-Solve [page 96] for directions on making the solution) or Neem oil.

If you garden without chemicals, remember that everything does not have to look picture perfect. If you see a few caterpillars, beetles, cabbage moths, or other pests, decide what is your tolerance level. Not every bug is a pest. Armed with your insect book, identify the bug and find out what it will evolve into—some caterpillars turn into monarchs, other beautiful butterflies, or moths. Then decide if removal or treatment is necessary

Many caterpillars are easily handpicked and can be disposed of in a zippered plastic bag. Japanese beetles are also easily handpicked, especially early in the morning as they are late risers. If you're squeamish, gently shake the assaulted flower into a zippered bag. Early in the day, the beetles will just drop off. Some gardeners love to squash them. Read about other Japanese beetle controls in April Problem-Solve (page 78).

TREES & SHRUBS

Continue to monitor for cankerworm and apply sticky bands if needed. Refer to March Problem-Solve (page 61).

Distorted, spotted, and discolored leaves may indicate you have an insect or disease problem. See April Problem-Solve (page 79) for tips on controlling Eastern tent caterpillars and emerald ash borers. See May, Problem-Solve (page 97) for information on controlling aphids and mites.

Japanese beetles skeletonize leaves on trees and shrubs too. Handpick or use Neem oil or insecticidal soap on them. For directions on making the soap yourself, see January Problem-Solve (page 33). For heavy, repeated infestations on large trees, call a

tree care professional. Treat the beetles in the grub stage by applying milky spore (See April Problem-Solve [page 78] for detailed information).

Continue monitoring for gypsy moth caterpillars. They are larger now, getting to their mature 2 inches. In addition to sticky bands, wrap a 12- to 18-inch-wide strip of burlap around the tree trunk at chest height. Tie a string around the burlap 6 inches from the top. Let the top 6 inches of burlap flop over the string. Check under the burlap every day between 2 to 6 p.m. Use gloves to remove caterpillars; drop them in soapy water to kill or into a zippered plastic storage bag to dispose.

Monitor for fireblight and phomopsis blight as detailed in May Problem-Solve (page 97).

VINES & GROUNDCOVERS

Record problems encountered throughout the season. List the plant affected, the pest problem, and the control methods used. Evaluate and record the results. This will help you avoid and control future problems.

Check for euonymus scale on wintercreeper—tiny, hard-shelled insects on stems and leaves. Spray with insecticidal soap or ultrafine oil when Japanese tree lilacs are flowering. Repeat twice at 10- to 12-day intervals.

Remove and discard (do not compost) spotted leaves and stems on lily-of-the-valley and pachysandra. Control fungal leaf spot and blight diseases with sanitation including raking fallen leaves off the plantings.

Check clematis for wilt, evidenced by wilting leaves that turn black (as do areas of the stem). Cut infected stems down to the ground. Disinfect tools between cuts with rubbing alcohol or a solution of 1 part bleach to 9 parts water.

July

As the song goes, "Summertime, and the living is easy. . . ." It is for people with air-conditioned homes, cars, and workplaces. But plants have no such luxury; they have to tough out the heat and dryness (only to have torrential rains come down during severe weather). Look back one hundred years or more, and much of this region was still prairie and grasslands. The plants, by necessity, were drought tolerant. Grasses turned tan or brown in summer, going dormant. Take some hints from our forebears as you continue to evaluate and plan changes to your garden and include more of those native plants and grasses.

Nature is fickle, especially when it comes to providing water at this time of year. It may be dry as a bone for weeks on end and suddenly there's a massive thunderstorm. That's when you appreciate mulch, for preventing the soil from drying out. Without a thick layer of mulch around your plants, the soil is likely too dry for rain to penetrate. Water runs off and is lost down storm drains. If you haven't mulched, do it now, but give the ground a thorough soaking beforehand.

This is a sensuous time for the sights, scents, and flavors in the garden. Daylilies, which captivate those three senses, are at their peak—in colors from white through yellow, orange to red, and mauve to green (single, bicolor, and tricolor)—growing from 8 to 60 inches tall. Some are fragrant, even blooming at night. Many are tasty too. Even the lowly ditch lily is prized in Chinese cookery (in hot and sour soup and stir-fries) as golden needles. Get out in the garden and indulge your senses.

Many herbs are hitting their stride now. Even so, it is impossible to use them all fresh. Consider drying them (cut leaves and lay them on a screen in a warm, dry area—I dry them by my dehumidifier). Or pulse the leaves in a food processor with a small amount of water. Pour into ice cube trays and freeze. Put frozen cubes in freezer bags and store for up to six months.

PLAN

ALL

Continue evaluating the garden. Note in your journal the successes, failures, and what is just acceptable. Document your garden with photos and videos to help you remember specifics. Consider changes you want to make. Look for ways to reduce maintenance and improve plant health. Start a to-do list of tasks, including lawn repair, pruning, and so forth.

Start a list of new or replacement plants to add to in the garden now, in fall, or next spring.

Go on garden tours in your area. Beautification committees, Master Gardeners, and other not-for-profit groups sponsor these. Support their efforts and gain some insight from landscape designers, expert gardeners, and plant lovers like yourself at the same time.

When you travel, besides visiting botanic gardens and public parks, which are often showplaces, walk around neighborhoods and see what real folks are doing in their gardens. If someone is in the garden, ask questions and compliment the garden. People appreciate having their work acknowledged.

On a really hot day, plan a trip to a really cool place—your local air-conditioned library. Flip through the latest gardening magazines and books for new ideas: style, design, plant combinations, new plants, and using all or part of the garden as an extension of the house—a summer living room.

ANNUALS & BIENNIALS

Plan for late summer and fall color. Look online and at local nurseries, garden centers, and home-improvement stores for new annual plants or seeds. Fall-planted pansies can bloom right up until the snow flies.

BULBS

Most minor bulbs (the small, early bloomers) need full sun. When planning the site for planting these bulbs in fall, think full sun for when they are up and blooming, not full sun at planting time. While it may be shady under a deciduous tree or shrub in late summer or fall, it will be sunny when the early bulbs flower because the tree or shrub will not yet have leafed out.

Whatever your source for grape hyacinths, get them early (by mid-August) and plant within the next two weeks. They need time to develop a strong root system and send up their leaves before the weather turns cold. Grape hyacinths are unique among spring-blooming bulbs in that they send up leaves in late summer.

EDIBLES

It's not too early to start thinking about a winter garden. You can eat fresh greens through much of winter if they are grown in a cold frame. You can buy fancy ones or make a cold frame yourself. There are different kinds from very basic manual ones to preconstructed frames with automatic vents. Have it electrified, heated, or not. It depends on how much time and money you want to spend. See March Care (page 58) for information on building a cold frame.

LAWNS

As you evaluate your lawn, note areas that are thin, have died, or are overseeding in mid-August to mid-September.

Think about the time, energy, and money spent on the lawn and whether it is worth it. Consider downsizing the lawn into a native plant garden or prairie, which has little to no maintenance and watering (after the first year). Or eliminate some areas that are difficult to mow, replacing the lawn with groundcovers.

Plan for someone to take care of the lawn if you're on vacation for more than a week. Grass needs to be watered and mowed unless you have let the lawn go dormant. Learn more about dormancy in this month's Water section.

PERENNIALS & ORNAMENTAL GRASSES

Consider adding more ornamental grasses throughout your landscape. The ultimate low-maintenance plants, you can find them in a size that is perfect for any location—from 8-inch-high blue fescue to big bluestem that can reach 6 to 10 feet tall. When you go to a nursery, don't be

When shopping for ornamental grasses, be aware that colors change throughout the season. The brownish plant is a perfectly healthy sedge.

talking to an arborist about thinning, limbing up, or even removing the tree(s). See June Plan for information on hiring a professional.

VINES & GROUNDCOVERS

As you visit botanical gardens, arboreta, parks, and neighborhoods, note how they use vines and groundcovers. Take a few pictures, sketch some ideas, and start making a list of additions and changes you want to make.

Consider groundcovers as an alternative to grass. They add interesting texture, colorful foliage, and even flowers to the landscape. They do not require frequent mowing, but they do require weed control. Groundcovers may be a little more time consuming than lawns until they are established. After that, you can relax and enjoy all the time not taken up by mowing the lawn.

PLANT

deceived by some tan grasses like the one in the photo. On first look, you may think it's dead, but that's just the normal color of sedge in late summer.

ROSES

Roses, especially miniatures, make great container plants. Grow them alone or combine them with other plants, such as Wave® petunia, blue lobelia, peach alyssum, or even lettuces. Choose a complementary plant that contrasts to the shape and form of the rose; a trailing plant does that well.

TREES & SHRUBS

As you evaluate your landscape, ask yourself if you have the right trees and shrubs in the right locations to do the jobs you intended. Are those on the east and west side of your house big enough to help shade it and keep in cooler in summer? What about trees for shade in outdoor leisure and play areas?

If you have lived in your home for a number of years, you may realize that your once-sunny backyard or vegetable garden is now mostly shaded. Trees, even slow-growing ones, get taller and broader without our awareness. Consider

ANNUALS & BIENNIALS

There is still time to plant. Stop by your favorite nursery, garden center, or home-improvement store. Many offer late-season transplants as replacements or late additions. You might even find a bargain or two. Avoid plants that look stressed, are very rootbound, or have any discolored leaves (signs of pests, diseases, poor watering, or lack of fertilization).

BULBS

Continue planting gladiolus every two weeks until 90 days before the first frost date.

EDIBLES

Although you can direct-seed fall plants, germination may not be very good as the soil is quite warm, and you're trying to get cool-season plants started. In Zones 3 and 4, start them indoors or outside the first few weeks of July. In the rest of the region, wait until the end of the month or the beginning of August. Outdoors, start them in flats or containers in full shade; once the seeds have germinated, move them to dappled shade. Refer to the Planting Chart in January Plan (page 23).

SUCCESSFUL GARDENING: PLANTING & TRANSPLANTING IN SUMMER

■ *If you give plants some extra TLC, you can successfully plant and transplant throughout the summer.*

Although summer is not the ideal time to add new plants to the garden or move established plants, you can be successful if you take the time to do it right.

- Prepare the planting area. Dig it up, break up any clods, and mix in soil amendments (if needed). Water the area well with transplant solution so it is lightly moist at least a foot down. This diluted solution helps get plants off to a good start, encouraging strong root growth. Follow mixing directions on the label.
- Give the plant you're planning to move a good drink of transplant solution.
- Wait until the next day—late afternoon when the sun is getting low in the sky or anytime if it's overcast. Plant the new plant or dig up and move an established one. Settle it in, and water once more with transplant solution. Add a 2- to 3-inch layer of mulch.

LAWNS

You can still lay sod. Use fresh sod and install it as soon as possible. Stored sod can overheat and damage or kill the grass plants. Once installed, the new lawn will need extra care. Make sure the soil surface stays moist until the sod roots into the soil below. Once rooted, it will still need thorough, though less frequent, watering.

PERENNIALS & ORNAMENTAL GRASSES

Keep planting as long as you have space, time, and plants. Give July transplants extra attention during hot dry spells. Mulch new plantings to conserve moisture and keep soil temperature cool. Label, map, and record all new plantings. This will make spring cleanup and weeding much easier.

Dig and divide spring-blooming perennials. See May Care for directions on dividing perennials.

ROSES

Keep planting container-grown roses. See May Plant (page 88) for detailed instructions.

■ *Before planting groundcovers in a new bed, lay them out to get the spacing between plants the same.*

TREES & SHRUBS

Continue to plant container-grown and balled-and-burlapped trees and shrubs. Before buying, check the plants for signs of stress. Avoid any with brown leaves and/or bare branches and stems.

VINES & GROUNDCOVERS

Continue to plant container-grown and balled-and-burlapped vines and groundcovers.

Dig and divide overgrown and declining plants. See May Care for detailed information on dividing plants.

CARE

ALL

Deadhead flowers for continual bloom and beauty. Pinch back leggy plants to encourage branching and more flowers.

■ *Deadheading makes the garden look neater and encourages plants—even some perennials—to rebloom.*

Stagger pinching within each flowerbed to avoid colorless areas and keep you in flowers all season.

Remove and discard any declining, diseased, or insect-infested leaves and stems.

Add any healthy garden trimmings (including deadheaded and spent flowers, pinched stems, and

SUCCESSFUL GARDENING: REDUCE SUMMER STRESS TO PLANTS

July and August are usually the hottest times of the growing season. Extreme heat can cause plants to stop blooming, decline, and even die. Reduce stress to plants with a little preventative care.

- The heat of summer not only dries out the soil, it also slows rooting. Be sure that all plants are well mulched after a thorough watering. This will help keep the soil and roots cool and moist and cut down on weeds. Use shredded leaves, compost, well-rotted manure, pine needles, twice-shredded bark, wood chips (trees and shrubs only), or other organic mulch.
- Water plants slowly and deeply, but less often. This encourages deep roots that are more drought tolerant.
- Stop fertilizing during extremely hot, dry weather. Feeding can damage already stressed plants.
- Use heat- and drought-tolerant plants for the hot spots in your landscape.

small prunings) to the compost pile. Destroy (burn, if allowed) or discard any that may have pests or diseases. Don't add weeds to the compost.

ANNUALS & BIENNIALS

Stake tall plants that tend to flop. Use twine or cushioned twist ties to loosely secure the stems to the stake.

Cut flowers for indoor enjoyment in early morning. Use a sharp knife or hand pruners to cut the stem above a set of healthy leaves. Indoors, recut the stems just prior to placing the flowers in a vase filled with room-temperature water (cold water is too shocking). Cut a few extras to share with friends and neighbors.

Cut flowers for drying at midday. Pick flowers before they fully open. Remove the leaves and gather a few stems into a bundle and secure it with a rubber band. Then use a spring-type clothespin to hang the bundle from a line or rack in a dry, dark location. The best flowers include bells of Ireland, bachelor's button, clarkia, cockscomb, larkspur, love-in-a-mist, and strawflower.

Cut back lobelia and heat-stressed alyssum halfway. Continue to water; as the weather starts to cool, they will spring back and rebloom.

BULBS

Spray caladium leaves frequently during hot, dry weather. Cut off any faded leaves.

Lily pollen easily drops off the flowers and can stain anything it touches. When cutting lily flowers for an arrangement, you may want to remove the anthers. For a more natural look, just cut off the ends with the pollen.

When lilies finish flowering, remove only the blooms, not the stems or leaves. Enjoy the green foliage for another month or more. Allow it to die back naturally.

Gladiolus is a superb cut flower stem, blooming from the bottom of the stalk up. The stem can last at least a week when you treat it right. Pull out faded blossoms. Change the water and cut ½ inch off the stem every couple of days.

Deadhead cannas to prolong bloom.

Continue to pinch and disbud dahlias until the middle of the month as described in June Care (page 104).

EDIBLES

By this time of year, chives tend to get a bit tough. Cut them down to within 1 inch of the ground to spur new growth of tender, young leaves.

If you are growing tomatoes on stakes or in a cage, pinch out the side shoots that grow out at an angle between a branch and the stem as soon as you see them. This practice will limit your harvest a bit. You may have fewer fruit, but the tomatoes will be larger than on unpinched plants.

Pinch or cut off flower spikes from basil as they appear. The small flowers are edible, but if the

■ *In our climate, pinching out the sideshoots on tomatoes helps increase air circulation, which can cut down on fungal problems.*

plant goes into full flower the leaves change flavor—and not for the better. That said, let at least one plant go to flower so you can enjoy eating the blooms. Sprinkle them on salads, vegetables, pizza, or chowders. With enough flowers, you can even make white pesto.

■ *Remove basil's flower spikes to extend the harvest. Also, cut the stem back an inch to encourage fresh new leaves.*

Cut handfuls of herbs—with stems as long as possible. Gather them (a single variety at a time) with a rubber band and hang them upside down in a dry area. Once they are dry, you can keep them in bunches or remove the leaves and store them in a glass bottle to use all winter.

Pick vegetables as they ripen. Don't forget about root crops, including beets, carrots, and radishes. Refer to the Planting Chart in January Plan (page 23) for approximate times to harvest.

LAWNS

Keep mowing the lawn high—3 to 3½ inches. This leads to a deeper root system that is more drought tolerant. Taller grass is generally healthier, more drought tolerant, and can shade out any germinating weed seeds. Cut off no more than one-third of a leaf blade at a time.

PERENNIALS & ORNAMENTAL GRASSES

Finish staking. Carefully maneuver plants around trellises and into stakes.

Continue deadheading and pinching back straggly plants, such as lavender.

Prune back Silver Mound artemisia before it blooms. Cut it back to fresh new growth to avoid open centers.

Cut back old stems of delphiniums to the fresh growth at the base of the plant. This encourages new growth and a second flush of flowers.

Yellow foliage on bleeding heart is normal—the plant is going dormant until spring. Cut it down to the ground and add the cut material to the compost pile.

Cut flowers for drying at midday. Pick flowers at their peak. Remove the leaves and gather a few stems into a bundle and secure it with a rubber band. Then use a spring-type clothespin to hang the bundle from a line, rack, or other structure in a dry, dark location. The best flowers include astilbe, delphinium, globe thistle, lady's mantle, and yarrow.

Stop pinching fall-blooming perennials, including asters, goldenrod, and chrysanthemums, by July 15 (or the first of the month in Zones 7 and 8).

If blue fescue goes dormant in summer, cut it back to the crown. It will regrow when the weather cools.

ROSES

If the weather is scorching hot, make a tent of lightweight, white, polyspun fabric to lessen the transplant shock for new plantings. Don't pin it to the ground; raise it up so air can move between the plants.

Prune climbers, which bloom on old wood (the previous year's growth), as soon as the first flush of bloom has finished. Prune to keep it in bounds or train the canes. Remove any weak canes, cutting them all the way down to the base of the plant. Allow the sturdiest two or three canes to continue growing as they are, and do light cosmetic pruning only.

Keep up with deadheading miniatures, grandifloras, hybrid teas, and shrub roses. To extend the beauty of floribundas, which bloom in a cluster, remove the largest, central flower while it is still in bud and let the surrounding blooms show their profusion.

■ *Use hand pruners or loppers to maintain shrubs' shape and remove any spent flowers. You may get a second flush of blooms.*

TREES & SHRUBS

Lightly prune hedges and sheared shrubs to keep their shape, remove faded flowers, and encourage rebloom. Repeat pruning if the plant reblooms;

you may be rewarded with a third flush of flowers (generally sparser but still colorful). The top of a hedge should be narrower than the bottom so sunlight can penetrate everywhere.

■ *Prune out branches that cross the center of the tree (the black branch in this drawing).*

Prune to repair trees and deciduous shrubs this month. Cut out branches that cross, are damaged, or are diseased. See Appendix (page 192) for detailed instructions. Know your limits—how high you can safely reach with a pole saw or with a ladder. Call a professional arborist to do the big jobs; refer to June Plan (page 101) for information on choosing one.

Prune junipers in mid-July. Remove dead and damaged branches back to a healthy stem deep in the plant to hide cuts. Disinfect tools with a solution of 1 part bleach to 9 parts water. Remove overly long branches back to shorter side shoots to control size.

Prune yews and arborvitae once new growth flushes out. To limit growth, prune back to a healthy bud or side shoot. See Appendix (page 193) for details on pruning evergreens.

VINES & GROUNDCOVERS

Shear goutweed (a.k.a. bishop's weed) down to 6 inches several times during the growing season. This prevents flowers, reduces reseeding (which prevents it from becoming a thug), and keeps the foliage fresh. Or cut back *once* to 6 inches when

foliage starts to turn brown at the edges and wait for new and improved growth.

Deadhead summer-blooming sedum to encourage repeat bloom.

Prune overgrown stems on vines and groundcovers back to a healthy bud or side shoot. Cutting a little shorter than the rest of the plant hides the pruning job.

WATER

ALL

As the temperature climbs, long slow watering is ideal as it allows the water to be drawn deeper into the soil, encouraging plants to grow deeper roots. That, in turn, keeps plants from wilting as soon as they would with shallower roots.

When the temperature is in the 90s or above, a midday spritz from a sprinkler or a good misting from a hose helps to cool plants down. As perspiration helps us to keep our bodies cool through evaporation, the evaporation of water from a plant's leaves cools it down.

■ *A raised rain gauge is easier to read and empty than one that is at ground level.*

The measurements in a rain gauge may be misleading. An inch or more of rain might fall during a severe weather event, such as a thunderstorm or hail. However, it falls so fast and furious that none of the water is absorbed into the soil; it all runs off. When in doubt, stick your index finger in the soil to feel the moisture—or lack thereof.

In the heat of summer, a container can easily dry out despite daily watering. If it does dry out, water it with a solution made of three drops of Ivory dish liquid in a quart of tepid (not ice-cold) water. If you can, put the container in a pan of the liquid so it can hydrate from top and bottom. Slowly water the soil with the soap solution over a period of a few days. The soap allows the water to stick to the soil rather than running through it.

ANNUALS & BIENNIALS
Water established plantings when the top few inches of soil are slightly dry. Follow the watering regimen in June Water (page 106).

BULBS
Keep caladiums, cannas, calla lilies, tuberoses, and peacock orchids lightly moist. Don't let them dry out.

Refrain from watering crown imperials until bulb planting time.

Keep watering hyacinths until their foliage dries out and turns yellow or brown.

EDIBLES
Keep vegetables and herbs (except Mediterranean herbs) well watered.

LAWNS
As the weather get hotter and drier, it's time to decide whether to let your lawn go dormant or continue watering so it stays green. Dormancy is the normal reaction that cool-weather grasses like fine fescues, Kentucky bluegrasses, and perennial ryegrasses have to the heat and dryness of summer. As the weather gets cooler and wetter, they naturally revive. A straw-colored or brown lawn may not be attractive, but it is environmentally friendly. But in a prolonged drought, even dormant lawns benefit from ¼ inch of water every three weeks.

If you choose to keep your lawn green, provide 1 inch of water a week. If you have clay soil, water once a week. In loam or sandy soil, divide it into two waterings, and give the lawn ½ to ¾ inch twice a week.

PERENNIALS & ORNAMENTAL GRASSES
Check new transplants several times a week. Water thoroughly anytime the top few inches start to dry. Established plants need less frequent watering.

Most ornamental grasses need no water. Japanese grass sedge and tufted hair grass need regular watering. Keep the soil uniformly lightly moist; don't let them dry out.

■ *Japanese sedge grass (pictured) and Japanese forest grass are among the few ornamental grasses that require regular watering through summer.*

■ *A large expanse of dormant lawn looks stark. Break it up with beds of drought-tolerant ornamental grasses and native perennials.*

ROSES

Even with a good layer of mulch, roses will need more water than the standard 1 inch a week if the temperature nears or tops the triple-digit mark. Take extra care with new plantings.

TREES & SHRUBS

During extended periods of drought—and if water is rationed—prioritize your use of water.

- Check trees and shrubs in planters daily; water when the top 3 to 6 inches is dry (depending on size of the planter).
- Check new plantings in sandy soil twice a week; those in clay soil every five to seven days. Water thoroughly when the top few inches begin to dry.
- Established trees and shrubs can go the longest time without supplemental water. During long dry periods, water them slowly and thoroughly until the top 8 to 12 inches are moist.

VINES & GROUNDCOVERS

Continue the watering regimen from June. See June Water (page 108).

FERTILIZE

ALL

When using any fertilizer, always follow all package instructions for proper application, frequency, concentration, and mixing/dilution.

Don't foliar feed if the temperature is over 80 degrees Fahrenheit or if rain threatens. Feed early in the day so that leaves can dry; you don't want to be setting the plant up for fungal problems.

ANNUALS & BIENNIALS

Do not fertilize plants if you used a slow-release fertilizer; it is still providing your plants with the nutrients they need.

Foliar feed any other plants with a solution of fish emulsion or kelp every two weeks.

Do not fertilize cosmos and nasturtiums; too much nitrogen prevents blooming (you want to have nasturtium flowers to eat) and results in floppy growth.

BULBS

Foliar feed caladiums, calla lilies, and cannas once with a solution of kelp or fish emulsion.

When gladiolus flower spikes reach one-third of their height, apply a high potash (potassium—K—the middle number on a fertilizer package) fertilizer every 10 days until they finish flowering. See April Fertilize (page 75) for an explanation of N-P-K.

Feed lilies monthly until the plants stop blooming.

■ *Sidedressing with granular fertilizer is a good way to give heavy feeders such as tomatoes a much-needed boost of nutrition anytime.*

EDIBLES

Skip the foliar feeding for Mediterranean herbs this month. Foliar feed all other herbs and vegetables.

Some plants need a lot of energy to keep growing and fruiting, so foliar feeding by itself is not enough. Sidedress the plants by spreading 2 to 3 inches of compost, earthworm castings, or humus around the base of the plant. Avoid smothering the stem by keeping the compost/mulch an inch away from it. Tomatoes, squashes, melons, peppers, eggplants, and cucumbers benefit from a nutritional boost. Unlike many commercial fertilizers, which give the plant a big meal all at once, compost enriches the soil, so a plant receives a constant supply of nutrients.

PERENNIALS & ORNAMENTAL GRASSES

Avoid overfertilizing. Most perennials and ornamental grasses get all the nutrients they need from the soil. Give stunted, less vigorous plants a boost with a foliar feeding.

Consider fertilizing heavy feeders and those cut back for rebloom. Use a low-nitrogen, slow-release fertilizer to avoid burning the plant.

Foliar feed Japanese grass sedge once in early July with a half-strength solution of liquid kelp or fish emulsion.

ROSES

Foliar feed established roses once a month with a solution of fish emulsion or seaweed.

Start monthly foliar feeding on roses planted in spring.

If using traditional fertilizer, give plants their final feeding now, after they have finished their first bloom. If you haven't mulched, just sprinkle granular fertilizer around the base of the plant and water it in well. If you did mulch, remove the mulch from around the plant, sprinkle the fertilizer evenly around the plant, water well, and replace the mulch. Or you can sprinkle it on top of the mulch and water and rake it through the mulch. Add more mulch if it has broken down into compost and there is less than 3 inches left. If using liquid fertilizer, no need to remove the mulch, just pour the diluted fertilizer around the plant.

TREES & SHRUBS

Continue the fertilizing regimen from June (see June Fertilize on page 108).

VINES & GROUNDCOVERS

Continue the fertilizing regimen from June (see June Fertilize on page 109).

PROBLEM-SOLVE

ALL

This is usually peak pest time. The hot weather of July (and August) helps insect populations quickly multiply. Monitor your plantings for problems. Some plants seem to struggle every year no matter what you do. These may be good candidates for replacement. Make notes in your journal on plants that should be replaced or what should be done to minimize future pest problems.

The inconsistency of our weather can wreak havoc in the garden—and create the ideal conditions for some pests. Keep an eye out for aphids, which are small insects (green, black, brown, or orange in color) that suck the juice out of buds, stems, and leaves. Before you do anything, be sure that you know what you have. Once identified, try hosing them off the plant(s) with a strong stream of water. Repeat every other day for a week. If they persist, spray them with insecticidal soap or Neem oil. For directions on making your own insecticidal soap, see January Problem-Solve (page 33).

■ *Japanese beetles can skeletonize leaves. Early in the day they are lethargic so you can shake them into a plastic bag.*

Japanese beetles are now in all states on our region. Lacy leaves are often the first clue that these small, shiny, metallic-looking beetles are present. Remove and destroy the beetles. Insecticides can be used, but they are harmful to beneficial insects. Do not use commercially available traps. These tend to lure more Japanese beetles into your garden. Japanese beetles are not early risers, so in the morning you can shake the insects off the flower or leaf into a zippered plastic bag. Read about other Japanese beetle controls in April Problem-Solve (page 78).

Check and follow all label instructions before mixing and applying any pesticide, insecticide, herbicide, or any other chemical.

Some plants can be killed by Neem oil, especially if it's applied heavily. Before spraying the entire area, test a few leaves and wait 24 hours to see if the leaf has any damage. Apply Neem oil only in indirect light or in the evening to avoid burning foliage and allow time for the preparation to seep into the plant.

Sanitation is usually sufficient to keep flower diseases under control. Pick off spotted leaves as soon as they appear. Deadhead flowers during rainy periods to reduce the risk of botrytis blight.

Continue pulling and cultivating weeds. Mulched gardens need much less attention.

Keep applying repellents to discourage troublesome deer, rabbits, and woodchucks. Make sure fencing is secure and still doing its job.

■ *Learn to recognize leafhoppers, which carry aster yellows disease, infecting asters, coneflowers, daisies, phlox, and hundreds more plants. They average ½ inch in length.*

SUCCESSFUL GARDENING; MANAGING PESTS & DISEASES NATURALLY

Nature is the best pest and disease manager. Birds and predatory insects help keep pest populations under control. The weather can exacerbate disease problems, can also help control them. The time comes for us to get involved when nature's controls are insufficient or the damage is more than we can tolerate. Try these natural pest management tips:

- **Patience.** Give nature time to take care of the problem. Ladybugs will not move into an area if there is no food. So let the aphids graze and wait for the predators to move in.
- **Sanitation** is an environmentally friendly way to reduce pest and disease problems. Remove weeds to reduce the source for insects and disease. Remove infected leaves and stems as soon as you see them. This provides immediate relief while reducing future problems.
- **Handpick or trap** insects whenever you see them. Have a bug hunt with your family or neighborhood children. Offer a prize or a treat for the best hunter in the group. Insects may give *you* the creeps, but they are a great way to get kids into the garden.
- **Environmentally friendly products**, including insecticidal soaps, Bt (*Bacillus thuringiensis*), Neem oil, and baking soda, are very effective at reducing pest and disease problems. However, they do not differentiate between "good bugs" and "bad bugs."

ANNUALS & BIENNIALS

Does the garden have hot spots where your favorite annuals wilt in the heat? Choose heat- and drought-tolerant plants, including zinnias, moss rose, gazanias, dusty miller, sunflowers, and cleome, for these areas.

Check plantings for signs of leafhoppers. These wedge-shaped insects hop off plants when disturbed.

SUCCESSFUL GARDENING: TESTING FOR INSECT PESTS IN YOUR LAWN

Insects don't generally pose a threat to lawns, but there are some exceptions. Before reaching for the pesticide, make sure that insects are really the problem. Conduct these easy tests to determine if insects are damaging your lawn:

- **Flotation Test (for chinch bugs):** Remove both ends of a coffee can or similar container. Sink the can in the grass at the edge of the dead area. Fill the can with water and agitate the grass. Chinch bugs will float to the surface. Test several areas. Treatment is needed if you find two or three of these insects per test.
- **Irritation Test (for sod webworm larvae):** Mix 1 tablespoon dishwashing detergent into 1 gallon water. Sprinkle the soapy water over 1 square yard of lawn. Conduct the test in several areas—damaged spots and areas adjacent to the damaged grass. Check the treated areas several times over the next 10 minutes. Treat if one or more sod webworm larva is present.
- **Turf Removal (for grubs):** Cut out and remove 1 square foot of lawn. Check the top 4 to 6 inches of soil for white grub larvae. Replace the sample and keep the soil moist until it reroots. Treat if three or four grubs are found.

■ *The flotation test can determine if there are chinch bugs in your lawn.*

Their feeding can cause stunting and tip burn on the leaves. Leafhoppers also carry the aster yellows disease that causes a sudden wilting, yellowing, and death of asters and other susceptible plants. Prevent the spread of this disease by controlling the leafhoppers. Treat them with insecticidal soap (see recipe for homemade soap in January Problem-Solve on page 33) or Neem oil. Several applications may be needed.

Thin out plantings infected with powdery mildew. Increased air circulation and light penetration help slow the spread of the disease. Treat the problem by spraying with a baking soda solution (see recipe in May Problem-Solve on page 96) or Neem oil.

BULBS

Check cannas for any sign of fungal leaf spot. Cut off and destroy any suspect leaves.

If grape hyacinths become congested, dig them up in summer when the plants are dormant. Gently tease the bulbs and roots apart. Replant at the original depth and spacing. Use the extra bulbs to start a new area, or share with friends.

EDIBLES

If you covered some plants with floating row covers earlier in the season to prevent insects from eating plants or laying their eggs, remove them. At this time of year, it can get too hot under the cover. Put them away until you need it again in fall.

If you don't have a cold frame, you can make a very simple one with bales of hay or straw (or whatever is available and inexpensive) stacked up two or three high. Make sure that you and anyone who might be helping can easily lean into the cold frame, touch the bottom, and reach to the back without having to lean so hard against the front bales that they could get knocked into the frame. The top of the frame needs to be

■ *Billbug larvae eat the roots of grass, preferring Kentucky bluegrass. If they are a problem, consider overseeding with different grasses.*

clear—glass or some type of plastic. Set the top on the bales; for strength, it should rest on the outsides of the bales. Old windows or glass doors make excellent tops.

LAWNS
Billbug larvae cause small (2- to 4-inch-wide) areas of dead grass. Check the grass leaves for the larvae before treating. Billbugs thrive in lawns with heavy thatch. Core aerating and dethatching can help

■ *Grubs are the larval stage of Japanese and other beetles. Living underground, they feed on lawn and other plant roots.*

avoid future problems. Apply insecticidal soap or Neem oil to control the larvae.

Check for grub damage, evidenced by uniformly thin, droughty-appearing, or even dying lawn. See "Successful Gardening: Testing for Insect Pests in Your Lawn" on page 125. Treat in spring or late summer if you find three or four grubs per 1 square foot of lawn. See April Problem-Solve on page 78 for details on treating grubs with milky spore.

The most common disease is fusarium blight (also known as summer patch), which is evidenced by graying or brown patches of dying or dead grass. It is most prevalent in summer when the temperature is above 85 degrees Fahrenheit. Minimize damage by overseeding with resistant grass. This fungus can often be avoided by mowing the lawn high (3 to 3½ inches) and keeping it evenly moist during hot, dry spells.

Warmer weather seems to bring out the weeds in force. Unfortunately, the quick fix of weedkillers (herbicides) is not an option in summer as they can damage the lawn when applied in hot, dry weather. Go back to the tried-and-true method of digging up weeds. Be sure to get all of the roots. Don't want to dig? At least remove any flowers so the weeds can't produce seeds. Maybe you can convince a child or grandchild to "unplug" and dig weeds for a price. Mowing high helps prevent weed seeds from germinating (page 119).

PERENNIALS & ORNAMENTAL GRASSES
Continue the regimen from June Problem-Solve (page 110).

Remove and destroy insect-infested, diseased, or declining foliage. This reduces the source of future problems.

ROSES
If blackspot persists, remove and replace the mulch; spores may have lodged in it. Spray the entire plant, including leaves and canes, every seven to ten days with baking soda solution (see page 96, May Problem-Solve for the recipe).

Remove affected leaves. If you end up with a leafless scarecrow, you have two choices: if blackspot has been a persistent problem (more than one year), dig up the rose and toss it in the garbage. Otherwise, you can plan on doing the spray routine every year. Get rid of the soil as well, since it is probably contaminated. Never add diseased plants to the compost pile. If it's a new plant, an existing plant that never had blackspot before, or an heirloom or rare rose that you feel you must save, give it a severe pruning. Cut it back to 12 to 16 inches to an outward-facing bud or five- to seven-leaflet leaf. This takes advantage of the fact that each bud can produce three sets of leaves or branches over time.

TREES & SHRUBS

Gypsy moths are now in the cocoon stage. Look for the pupal cases in crevices in the bark and protected areas of the tree trunk. Destroy them.

Borers can cause the stems of shrubs to wilt. Look for holes and sawdust at the base of the stem. Cut off and destroy the branches. Renewal pruning usually controls these pests.

Distorted, spotted, and discolored leaves may indicate an insect or disease problem. See April Problem-Solve (page 79) for tips on controlling Eastern tent caterpillars, emerald ash borer, aphids, and mites. Control aphids and mites with a strong blast of water from the hose. Lady beetle (ladybug) larvae feed on aphids.

Continue to prune out dead or cankered branches. Disinfect tools with rubbing alcohol or a solution of 1 part bleach to 9 parts water between cuts.

Apple scab is a fungal disease that can cause brown spotting on leaves, leaf drop, and eventually defoliate crabapples and apples. Raking and destroying leaves as they fall reduces the source of disease next season. Consider replacing infected trees with newer scab-resistant cultivars.

Anthracnose is another fungal disease that can cause spotting and eventually leaf drop on oaks, maples, ashes, black walnuts, and sycamores. Otherwise healthy trees survive despite the

■ *Powdery mildew, seen here on squash leaves, is unsightly but rarely kills plants. However, it does stress them. Look for resistant varieties.*

damage. Rake and destroy fallen leaves to reduce the source of infection for next year.

Powdery mildew, which appears as a white powder on leaves of lilacs and other shrubs (or other plants), is more of a cosmetic problem than one that will damage a plant. Prune for better air circulation and light. Spraying with Neem oil or baking soda solution (see page 96, May Problem-Solve for the recipe) can help treat it and prevent the fungal disease from spreading.

Check for disease-induced galls (swellings) at the base of euonymus, spirea, and viburnums. They can girdle and kill the stem. Cut down infected stems below the gall. Disinfect tools between cuts with rubbing alcohol or a solution of 1 part bleach to 9 parts water.

VINES & GROUNDCOVERS

Continue the regimen from June Problem-Solve (page 111).

August

The August doldrums or "dog days of summer" is a period of ten days to two weeks when the weather is so hot that you take an unplanned vacation from gardening. It doesn't start intentionally, it just happens. You ignore the garden, except for watering in a drought (consider an automatic watering system for next year). This is a dirty little secret that gardeners guiltily hide. Our inner clocks may not all be in sync, but you know that feeling when comes over you. Have a hammock ready in shady nook, and you can enjoy being in the garden. We won't tell.

Put out a comfortable chair or bench in or facing the garden so you can experience the garden at night. It can take up to 15 minutes for your eyes to adjust to the darkness on a moonless night. As you sit, be aware of the sights, aromas, and sounds of evening. White flowers, such as roses, cosmos, calla lilies, and mums, appear to float in midair. You don't see dark colors at night, so green stems and leaves seem to vanish. Pale colors, such as pink cleome, dahlias, and Endless Summer hydrangeas, stand out well. Some, like moonflowers, angel's trumpet, and four o'clocks, don't even open until the sun starts to set. Ornamental grasses swish in the breeze. You might hear the whirr of a sphinx moth or catch a glimpse of the elusive, exquisite Luna moth. Consider creating an evening garden to enjoy all season long.

When it's not too hot, walk around your neighborhood and note how other gardens are faring. Talk to your neighbors; everyone has a wealth of information—whether they realize it or not—from the experiences they've had with their gardens. Consider organizing a simple progressive tasting party for a few people to go from garden to garden and sample the edibles (a couple of easy recipes) in each. You'll come away with ideas for your garden and ways to use the produce you harvest.

PLAN

ALL

Keep up with your journal. Note problems, solutions, successes, failures, and what is just acceptable. Take photos and videos to help you remember specifics. Consider changes you want to make. Look for ways to cut down on maintenance and increase your success with plants. Start a to-do list of tasks like lawn repair, pruning, creating new beds and digging and storing summer-blooming bulbs.

Continue making plant wish lists. Some people like to have a master list, others one for each garden area. Do whatever works best for you. Include the plant name, variety, bloom time, and other features that caught your attention (color, fragrance, size, shape). The list is designed to change as you find new plants to add, and delete ones you decide you don't want.

Keep visiting botanical and public gardens and participate in their educational events and garden tours. This is a great way to find out if the plants that seed companies, nurseries, and garden bloggers rave about do well in our area.

Visit your local nursery, garden center, or home-improvement store with an eye for sale plants.

BULBS

Color and time of bloom are two of the most important elements to consider when planning your bulb and garden planting. It's helpful to sketch your garden before planting. Consider which bulbs to plant and where based upon height, sunlight requirement, color, and bloom time. Remember: the bulbs you are planting now are hardy and can remain undisturbed for years.

If your roses or other flowers aren't as perky as they were earlier in the season, you can add some pizzazz in the form of autumn-blooming bulbs. Order autumn crocus (*Colchicum autumnale*) bulbs now and plant them as soon as they arrive. They'll add a bright color accent near ground level. Mark their spots so you don't plant over them. In spring, the leaves emerge rich green, broad, and grow about a foot high. Even the leaves are ephemeral;

they'll disappear within six weeks. There will be no sign of the plant until the leafless flowers arise in late summer.

EDIBLES

Go to your state or county fair and head for the horticulture competition. You'll see some new varieties of amazing-looking fruits and vegetables. Unfortunately, you can't taste these beauties, but the variety name is on the entry card. When you come across something to add to your wish list, contact the entrant and garner as much information as possible before ordering seeds. I saw one gorgeous beefsteak-type tomato that looked mouth-wateringly flavorful. However, the grower said it was watery and mealy inside. Yet it was a blue-ribbon winner for many years for its looks—*caveat emptor*.

Think ahead to spring and start planning with edibility in mind—edible flowers. Order some tulip bulbs. The petals of yellow, orange, and red tulips taste the best: they have a pea- or beanlike flavor and a nice crunch at the base of the petal.

Grow dandelions on purpose? Yes! There are some wonderful French and European varieties that were bred for the flavors of the leaves and young flowers. Favorites include 'Garnet Stem',

■ *Autumn crocus are beautiful, late-summer-blooming bulbs. Plant them now among low-growing groundcovers or at the edge of a bed.*

SUCCESSFUL GARDENING: SUMMER-BLOOMING BULBS— KEEPERS OR NOT?

This is a perfect time to take an inventory of the tender bulbs in your garden. Mull it over for a few days, picturing each in your mind's eye, and then decide whether you want to make the effort to dig them all up in fall and store them for winter. Review journal entries and photos of them in the garden. As you go through this process, list everything and then cross out plants as you consider the following and make your decisions:

■ *A hanging basket of caladiums can be brought indoors as is and overwintered in a sunny, warm space.*

- Do you like the plant? If not, offer it to a friend. Dig it early and pot it up or let the lucky recipient dig it up at the right time. This is the first cut; it may take a lot of bulbs out of the running or you may like them all.
- Is it hardy? If you are lucky enough to live in Zone 8 or have a nice warm microclimate in Zone 6 or 7, you might get away with leaving some in the ground and covering the soil with a 3- to 6-inch layer of mulch as the ground freezes. Try it with a few different bulbs and see what works. Amaryllis, caladium, tuberose, and tuberous begonia definitely will *not* survive outside in winter—even in Zone 8.
- Was the bulb expensive? Peacock orchids, for example, are very inexpensive, so it's easier to treat them as annuals than a costly exotic canna.
- How many bulbs do you have of that particular plant? If you have a lot, consider digging up some to overwinter and leaving the rest in the ground and see how they fare.
- Do you have ample space to store all the bulbs indoors (basement or garage)?
- Do you have neighbors, friends, or relatives who might want to share the work and the bulbs?
- How much time and energy do you realistically think you'll have when it's time to dig up the bulbs?

Tip: Going through this survey when you are exhausted allows you to see your capabilities in their true light.

with bright burgundy stems; white-flowered 'French', an heirloom Italian variety; and 'Thick-Leaved French'.

Most daylily flowers are delicious. 'Stella de Oro' is outstanding for its smaller flowers and constant bloom through summer. In spring, cut the leaf shoots (do this only once or you risk weakening or killing the plant) when they are less than 8 inches high to add to salads or stir-fries. Dried daylily flowerbuds, known as golden needles, are a standard ingredient in Chinese hot and sour soup. The flower petals are a low-carb solution to chips with dips. Place a whole flower (pistils and anthers removed) in a wineglass and set a scoop of ice cream or sorbet in the flower. Top with some chopped petals. It's a simple, yet elegant dessert that is sure to wow your guests.

LAWNS

If any area of lawn is more than 50 percent unacceptable weeds, plan to replace it, repair bare areas, or overseed thin ones. Mid-August through mid-September is the prime time for this.

PERENNIALS & ORNAMENTAL GRASSES

Check the garden for holes that need to be filled in with new plants, or for spaces in which to create new beds.

TREES & SHRUBS

Keep an eye out for places that summer-blooming shrubs could enhance. Consider a dwarf conifer that would provide four-season interest. Remember that the term "dwarf" is relative. A dwarf of a 90-foot tree may grow 30 feet or more. Do some research before adding any to your wish list.

VINES & GROUNDCOVERS

Consider what areas would benefit from the addition of vines to provide vertical interest or act as a screen. As you imagine different vines, think about the support they require. Annual vines may require only some string or a lightweight trellis, but some perennial vines demand a very sturdy structure. Maybe you want a DIY project for winter—build a pergola to support the wisteria you've always wanted.

■ *Shade-loving groundcovers such as pachysandra, coral bells, hosta, and deadnettle can thrive at the base of a tree where grass won't grow.*

Groundcovers can be the solution for problem areas. They grow under trees where surface roots make mowing a challenge. On a larger scale, use them to prevent erosion on a hillside. Or line a shady walkway with variegated plants to highlight it.

PLANT

ALL

Continue to follow the strategies for planting and transplanting in summer outlined in July Plant.

HERE'S HOW

TO OVERWINTER ANNUALS AS CUTTINGS

■ *It's easy to root cuttings from favorite annuals from your garden. Be aware that it's illegal to propagate patented plants.*

Start taking cuttings from annuals you want to overwinter indoors, including impatiens, geraniums, begonias, browallia, fuchsias, coleus, annual vinca, and herbs. Garden plants are healthier and will root faster now than they will later in the season as they start to decline.

1. Cut 4 to 6 inches off the tip of a healthy stem. Remove any flowers and the lowest two sets of leaves.
2. Dip the cut end, including the areas where leaves were, in a rooting hormone to encourage rooting and discourage rot. Place the cutting in moist vermiculite, perlite, or sterile seed-starting mix.
3. Place in a bright location away from direct sun. Keep the rooting mix lightly moist.
4. Plant the rooted cutting—usually ready in two weeks—in a small container filled with potting mix. Water with transplant solution. Move to a sunny window and care for it as you do your other houseplants.

ANNUALS & BIENNIALS

Swap out tired annuals for fall bloomers to perk up the garden. Include snapdragons, calendula, pansies, and other cool-weather annuals. Unless you started them from seed, planting may have to wait until transplants are available later this month.

Plant some ornamental kale; it's beautiful *and* edible. There are a number of varieties, some with fringed leaves, others with curled leaves, and some that look like an open cabbage—in mixtures of green and white or rose and green. Ornamental cabbage is lovely too, but it's too fibrous to eat.

BULBS

As soon as you get autumn crocus bulbs (also called magic crocus), plant them in rich, deep, well-drained soil with the bulb's top 4 inches below the soil surface. Cluster seven or more bulbs 2 to 3 inches apart for an impressive show. Water well and they will bloom within a few weeks. To prove their magic, place one or two on a sunny windowsill. Watch them send up their goblet-shaped, 2- to 3-inch, lavender-pink flowers, and then plant them outside.

Plant fall- and spring-blooming crocus corms soon after you get them; otherwise they could dry out.

Start planting all other bulbs. Work a bulb booster formula (follow package instructions) and plenty of compost or organic matter into the soil before planting. A good rule of thumb is that planting depth should be three times the height of the bulb. Cover small bulbs with 1 to 2 inches of soil; plant large bulbs 6 to 8 inches deep. In Zone 8, plant large bulbs 2 inches shallower than the normal recommendations. Space bulbs two times their width apart—from the center of one bulb to the center of the next (sometimes called center-to-center). Cover with soil, and water in well with transplant solution. Mulch with 1 to 2 inches of shredded leaves. When planting, avoid soldierly rows. The most effective planting technique is to plant most bulbs in clusters or groups. Space bulbs according to color with the softer colors in the front and the more vibrant in the background. For a long-lasting show of color, group bulbs according to height and in sequential bloom pattern.

Plant lilies as soon as they arrive. Take care not to break off any stalks or growth that may be on the bulb. Choose a sunny spot, with light, porous, sandy soil enriched with compost or other organic matter. The ideal site is one where the plants get full sun at the tops and are shaded at the soil level to keep the ground moist. Plant 6 to 8 inches deep and 6 inches apart.

SUCCESSFUL GARDENING: BULBS DOS & DON'TS

- *Do*, always, plant bulbs in beds with good drainage.
- *Don't* use any strong commercial fertilizer or fresh manure when planting bulbs.
- *Do*, always, label bulbs as you plant them. Use labels that are long enough so that 2 to 3 inches of the label is below soil level. Shorter labels can heave out of the soil during winter freezing and thawing. Labeling prevents you from accidentally digging up bulbs out of season. Don't rely on your memory alone; labeling is much safer.
- *Don't* grow tulip bulbs year after year in the same place. Sooner or later they may be attacked with a fungus disease called fire blight, which affects both foliage and flowers. Either change the soil or the location; in other words, follow the principle of crop rotation.
- *Don't* dry bulbs for winter storage in the sun; instead, dry them in the shade in a well-ventilated area.
- *Do*, always, store bulbs in a dry, well-ventilated area to prevent mold or mildew.

EDIBLES

Although you can direct-seed fall edibles, germination may not be good in warm soil. In Zones 5 to 8, start them indoors or outside the first two weeks of this month. Outdoors, start them in flats or containers in full shade; once the seeds germinate, move them to dappled shade. Refer to the Planting Chart in January Plan (page 23).

HERE'S HOW

TO GROW SEEDS WHEN IT'S HOT AND DRY

Sowing seeds successfully when it is hot and dry can be a challenge. The moist environment burlap provides is the key to good germination.

1. Make a narrow, 2-inch-deep furrow and water it until the soil is saturated but not muddy.

2. Scatter the seeds in the bottom of the furrow.

3. Cover the furrow with burlap and anchor the cloth to the ground.

4. Sprinkle the burlap with water twice a day until the seeds germinate. Remove the burlap.

5. Water daily until the seedlings have six leaves. After that, water as needed.

■ *When the weather is hot and dry, the best way to start seeds is in a furrow, which is then covered with damp burlap.*

Start transplanting cool-weather vegetables you've started indoors into the garden starting in mid-August. They may need a few days of partial shade to adjust to the sun's brightness.

Sow seeds for lettuces, chard, kale, spinach, mizuna, and other greens to enjoy throughout fall by the second week of the month. With some protection, they might keep going through winter as well. Sow the seeds in the garden or in a cold frame.

■ *Use a spreader to overseed the lawn. Follow the seed package directions for proper application settings for your spreader.*

LAWNS

When the weather starts to cool in mid- to late-August, start seeding lawns. See May Plant for detailed instructions.

Install sod now. Cooler temperatures mean less watering than for lawns sodded in July. See April Plant (page 72) for details.

■ *Nurseries, garden centers, and home-improvement stores carry lawn patch kits, which make fixing small bare areas simple to do.*

Repair bare areas. Start by removing dead grass. Amend the soil as needed, and roughen the soil surface. Use a lawn patch kit or make one yourself. Mix one handful of a quality lawn seed mix into a bucket of topsoil. Sprinkle this over the soil, rake smooth, and mulch. Keep the soil surface moist.

Overseed thin lawns between mid-August and mid-September. See May Plant (page 85) for details.

HERE'S HOW

TO PLANT GARLIC

■ *Grow several different varieties of garlic. Here, cloves are set on the soil, ready to be pushed down into the ground.*

Plant garlic four to six weeks before the ground freezes. Garlic prefers full sun and well-drained soil amended with plenty of organic matter. Get cloves from a local farmer, nursery or garden center, or online and mail-order sources. Garlic from the supermarket may not be hardy, and there are better varieties to grow.

1. Several days before planting, carefully break the bulb into individual cloves. Take care to leave the papery skin on each clove.
2. Plant cloves pointed end up 4 inches apart and 2 inches deep. Gently tamp down the soil with your palms.
3. Water well with transplant solution.
4. After the ground freezes, add a 3- to 5-inch layer of straw as a winter mulch.

PERENNIALS & ORNAMENTAL GRASSES

Continue to plant if you have space. Label plants and add them to your journal and landscape plan.

Dig and divide overgrown iris, poppies, and other spring-blooming perennials.

ROSES

Even though nurseries and plant growers tout "Fall is for Planting," August is the cut-off for planting container-grown roses. (Bare-root roses are available in late winter and early spring when the plants are dormant.) Many nurseries, garden centers, and home-improvement stores have sales now. If you find a "must-have" rose that's a bargain price, get it—unless there is any sign of pests or disease (check under leaves and on stems). Although it is probably stressed, an overnight soak in transplant solution before planting should re-energize it. Loosen any packed roots. Remember that the bud union needs to be under at least 2 inches of soil (except in Zone 8, where you should plant the rose at the same level as it was growing in the container.).

TREES & SHRUBS

This is a good time to plant trees and shrubs; the cooler temperatures as we head to fall are ideal for root growth and getting them established. Many retailers have sales on trees and shrubs, as they don't want to have to carry the plants through winter. Good nurseries and garden centers have religiously watered and maintained their planting stock throughout summer. Those are the ones to buy—not plants that are obviously stressed. A stressed plant isn't likely thrive, even with time and effort.

VINES & GROUNDCOVERS

Keep planting groundcovers and vines. There is still time for the plants to get established.

Plant some autumn crocus in with low-growing groundcovers for an unexpected burst of mauve. They bloom within weeks of planting. See this month's Plant for details on planting them.

See "Here's How To Plant Groundcovers Under a Tree with Surface Roots" on page 136.

TO PLANT GROUNDCOVERS UNDER A TREE WITH SURFACE ROOTS

It's important to select plants suited to the growing conditions. They won't out-compete the trees for water and nutrients.

1. Kill any grass by covering it with newspaper and mulch. This may take six to eight weeks.
2. Space the plants throughout the areas.
3. Dig a hole slightly larger than the root system of the groundcover.
4. Amend the planting holes with peat moss, compost, or other organic matter.
5. Plant the groundcover so it is at the same level as it was growing in the pot.
6. Fill the hole with soil and gently firm it. Water-in with transplant solution.
7. Add a 1- to 2-inch layer of mulch. Keep mulch 1 inch away from the stem and do not cover the crown.

Weed control is critical for the first few years. Once the groundcovers fill in, weeding will be minimal.

CARE

ALL

The heat usually continues and often peaks this month. Protect your plants and yourself from heat stress. Continue the strategies outlined in July Care (page 117).

ANNUALS & BIENNIALS

Mulch annuals to keep their roots cool and moist. Place a 1-inch layer of shredded leaves, compost, well-rotted manure, or other organic material on exposed soil around the plants. Keep mulch 1 inch away from stems.

Some annuals experience heat stall during hot weather and stop blooming. These include French marigolds, garden pinks, lobelia, purple alyssum, and snapdragons. When the weather cools, they'll perk up and bloom again. If this is a recurring problem in your garden, grow the susceptible plants in a cooler area. More heat-tolerant plants include celosia, flowering tobacco, Mexican sunflower, moss rose (portulaca), and zinnias.

Look around the base of biennials, such as hollyhocks and foxgloves, for small plants that have recently sprouted from seed. Mark the area so that they aren't disturbed. Once they have several sets of leaves, thin them to the proper space for them to grow into mature plants next year. Move the thinnings to another area—think cottage garden. Or pot them up and share them.

Deadhead faded flowers. Cut leggy plants one-quarter to halfway back, cutting just above a bud or set of healthy leaves. This will refresh the plant and result in more flowers.

■ *Strawflowers are extremely long lasting. To use as dried flowers, cut them when they just start to open.*

Continue to cut flowers for indoor enjoyment and drying as described in July Care (page 117). Cut strawflowers when the blossoms are less than half open. Remove foliage, tie in a bundle, and hang the flowers upside down to dry.

BULBS

Spray caladium leaves with water frequently during hot, dry weather. Cut off any faded leaves.

After lilies finish flowering, remove only the blooms, not the stems or leaves. Allow the foliage to die back naturally. Carefully cut back the stalks when the foliage has died back completely.

Deadhead cannas to encourage new blooms.

EDIBLES

August is often the most bountiful month in the garden. Graze through the garden, eating tomatoes still warm from the sun. Even when you go through the "August doldrums," take time from the break to harvest whatever is ripe and mature.

Don't pick peppers when they are green. Let sweet and hot peppers ripen to their mature color and they will be more flavorful. Ripe sweet peppers don't cause indigestion like green ones do.

Harvest garlic when the tops begin to yellow and fall over, but before they are completely dry. Carefully lift the bulbs with a spade or garden fork. Gently brush off the soil, and let them cure in a dry, shady spot with good air circulation for

HERE'S HOW TO

FORCE AMARYLLIS TO BLOOM

Potted amaryllis that have spent the summer outdoors need to enter dormancy before you can successfully force them into bloom.

1. Give the potted amaryllis a strong spray of water to dislodge any critters that might have made it their new home.
2. Put the pot on a sunny windowsill for a few days or until the soil dries out.
3. Move the pot to a cool, dry, dark location. Lay it on its side to encourage dormancy.
4. After six to eight weeks, the plant is ready to be forced. If it is still green, that's okay; it is still dormant.
5. If you want to repot it, remember that amaryllis likes to fit tightly in a container, with no more than an inch between the bulb and the side of the pot.
6. Topdress with compost and cut any leaves off ½-inch above the top of the bulb.
7. Water well and set on a sunny windowsill.
8. Let soil dry between waterings.

SUCCESSFUL GARDENING: SHARE THE BOUNTY

If your harvest seems overwhelming, you're not alone. Many gardeners grow more than they have time to eat fresh. Some folks can, freeze, or dry some of it; but the time and energy for doing all that quickly wanes. You've given some veggies to neighbors, friends, and relatives and you still have more.

Share your bounty with those who truly need it. The statistics are shocking: One in six people (one in five in households with children) in the United States face hunger. Donate fresh produce to your local homeless shelter, food bank, or soup kitchen. They are always glad to have fresh food, rather than just canned.

You might want to become part of the nationwide Plant a Row for the Hungry (PAR) campaign sponsored by the Garden Writers Association. Through PAR, people across the country have raised millions of pounds of food. Every two thousand pounds of food translates into 8 million meals. Call the PAR Hotline (877-492-2727) to find out if there's a program near you. It's not necessary to plant an entire row—even one zucchini or other summer squash plant produces enough food to make a difference.

■ *Unless you plan to use garlic right away, hang it in a shady, well-ventilated place to cure and dry.*

about two weeks. The bulbs are cured when the wrappers are dry and papery and the roots are dry.

LAWNS

Mow the grass 3 to 3½ inches tall. Taller grass is more drought tolerant and shades out potential weeds. Mow no more than one-third of the total height with each cutting. As soon as they are well rooted, begin to mow newly sodded lawns.

PERENNIALS & ORNAMENTAL GRASSES

Mulch any new gardens or plantings with a 1- to 2-inch layer of compost, leaf mold, well-rotted manure, twice-shredded bark, shredded leaves, or other organic matter to keep perennial roots cool and moist. Check existing beds and plantings and add more mulch if needed.

Some ornamental grasses, including blue fescue, little bluestem, *Miscanthus* (eulalia grass), and switchgrass, prefer it on the drier side with soil that is not as rich. Use gravel, pebbles, or turkey grit around them as mulch. It will protect the plant and prevent weeds, but unlike organic mulch, will *not* break down and nourish the soil.

If blue fescue goes dormant in summer, cut it back to the crown, and it will regrow when the weather cools.

If winds make the tufted hair grass flower panicles look ragged, cut them down. Otherwise, just enjoy their beauty now and throughout winter.

Cut flowers for indoor enjoyment and drying as described in July Care (page 119).

Cut back and destroy any foliage that is insect-infested, diseased, or declining. This reduces the source of future problems.

Deadhead to encourage rebloom and prevent reseeding. Leave the last set of flowers intact on plants like coneflowers, sedums, and black-eyed Susans. The seedhead is attractive through winter and birds feed on the seeds.

Do not cut Russian sage back. As you enjoy its long flowering display and attractive seed set for winter, the plant will start to harden off naturally. Pruning encourages new growth that would die in winter.

ROSES

For a spectacular cut-flower finale, disbud some of the hybrid tea and grandiflora roses. Remove all but one (the biggest and sturdiest-looking) flower bud on each stem soon after the buds appear. Instead of expending energy on multiple flowers, the plants' resources are channeled into a single flower. The result is a larger, more robust blossom. Try floating fresh flowers (wide-open ones like floribundas and miniatures work best) in a shallow bowl of water.

Last call for pruning this year. August 8 is the cutoff date in Zones 3 and 4 (August 15 in Zones 5 and 6 and August 22 for Zones 7 and 8). Remember to factor in your microclimates, colder or warmer, for the most accurate gauge of time. Don't even cut back faded flowers. After a flower dies, you can remove just the flower if it is unsightly, but don't cut the stem. That means no cutting flowers for bouquets, either. If you cut back the stem, any new growth will not have time to mature and harden off enough to endure the cold of winter. The result—not seen until the following spring—is heavy dieback, even lower than the original cut. Use the petals for potpourri. Let the spent flowers develop into the bright orange fruit (rose hips). Enjoy the bloom on the plant.

TREES & SHRUBS

Do a walk-though inspection of your landscape. If mulch is up against the tree or shrub, pull it back an inch or two. If you don't, it provides a direct entryway for insects and burrowing pests like voles. If the mulch isn't 2 to 3 inches deep, add more. Look closely at the trunks or main stems for any damage. Note it and determine the cause. Look for any twine, wires, or labels left behind on new plantings; remove them. Left on the plant, they can girdle and kill it.

Prune only for damage repair from storms or other causes. Even trees and shrubs need to harden off for winter. Pruning now or later in the season encourages tender new growth that can die back in winter.

HERE'S HOW

TO CREATE A PLANTING BED AROUND TREES & SHRUBS

Reduce maintenance and improve plant health by creating large planting beds around trees and shrubs. The larger bed eliminates competition from grass and damage caused by mowers and weed whackers that get too close to the plants. Decide on the size and shape of bed that complements your design. You can always add more shrubs, perennials, and other plants to fill in the voids.

Use a garden hose to lay out the shape of the bed, and then cut it with a sharp shovel or edger.

1. Lay out a garden hose to mark the area. Use a shovel or edger to create the outline of your new planting bed.
2. Remove the existing grass. Peel it off with a sod cutter and use this grass to repair problem areas. Or cut the grass short and cover with six sheets of moist newspapers and several inches of woodchips. The grass and woodchips will eventually decompose. Do this in fall for a spring planting.
3. After planting, use a 2- to 3-inch layer of woodchips or twice-shredded bark to help reduce future weed problems. Do not put plastic or weed barriers under wood mulch. As the mulch decomposes, it creates the perfect environment for weeds. Weed seeds blow in, nearby turf spreads in, and soon the garden is full of plants that are growing through the weed barrier.

Use weed barriers under rocks to keep the rock from working into the soil. This reduces the need to replenish the settled mulch and makes it easier for you to make changes to the area. Do not use plastic weed barriers that prevent water and nutrients from reaching the roots.

VINES & GROUNDCOVERS

Shear goutweed (a.k.a. bishop's weed) down when foliage starts to turn brown at the edges. This prevents flowers, reduces reseeding (helping prevent it from becoming a thug), and keeps the foliage fresh.

Prune overgrown stems on vines and groundcovers back to a healthy bud or side shoot. Cutting a little shorter than the rest of the plant hides the pruning job.

Check mulch on new and existing plantings. Maintain a 1- to 2-inch layer of woodchips, pine needles, cocoa hulls, shredded leaves or other organic matter. Do not bury the crown of the plants or the base of the stems.

See "Here's How To Renovate Groundcover Plantings" on page 140.

HERE'S HOW

TO RENOVATE GROUNDCOVER PLANTINGS

Renovate overgrown and weed-infested groundcover plantings. Starting over can be easier than trying to fix the existing planting.

1. Dig out the healthy plants. Dig a trench for the groundcovers in an unplanted area of the landscape and heel in the plants. Or place them in pots for temporary storage. Water often enough to keep the roots moist.
2. Edge the bed with a shovel or edger. Spray the area with a total vegetation killer. Avoid contacting trees, shrubs, and other desirable plants. Wait two weeks.
3. Spade or till 2 to 4 inches of the organic matter and fertilizer into the top 6 to 12 inches of soil. Rake smooth and allow to the soil to settle.
4. Divide healthy groundcover plants that were heeled in or potted up. Discard dead and less vigorous portions of the plant. Set plants at proper spacing with the crowns (the point where the stem joins the roots) even with the soil surface.
5. Water thoroughly with transplant solution, wetting the top 6 inches of soil. Mulch the soil with twice-shredded bark, shredded leaves, or other organic matter. Keep mulch at least 1 inch away from the stem; don't smother the crown.
6. Keep the roots lightly moist for the first few weeks. Then water when the top 2 to 3 inches of soil start to dry.

■ *Lay out the plants, allowing ample room between each for them to fill in and make a groundcover carpet.*

WATER

ALL

Continue to follow the watering strategies described in July Water (page 120).

Water early in the morning to reduce the risk of spreading disease and of water loss to evaporation. Use a soaker hose or watering wand to water the soil and roots where it is needed.

Plants in the shade and those that are well mulched need less frequent watering. Check plantings several times a week during extremely hot, dry weather.

Check and empty the rain gauge weekly. Adjust the amount you water according to the amount nature

■ *Vegetables, such as the peppers shown here, benefit from the consistent moisture that a soaker hose provides.*

■ *When using an oscillating sprinkler to water the lawn, make sure all areas are getting even coverage.*

provides. Be aware that when the soil is very dry, the water from a sudden, heavy rain may run off and not get absorbed into the soil.

ANNUALS & BIENNIALS
Check plants growing in containers daily.

Water established plantings when the top few inches of soil are slightly dry. Follow the watering regimen in June Water (page 106).

BULBS
Keep caladiums, cannas, calla lilies, tuberoses, and peacock orchids lightly moist. Don't let them dry out.

Refrain from watering crown imperial.

Keep crocus and other newly planted bulbs lightly moist until the ground freezes.

EDIBLES
Keep vegetables and herbs (except Mediterranean herbs) well watered. Check Mediterranean herbs (thyme, rosemary, oregano, sage) weekly.

Check containers daily. A layer of mulch can help retain moisture in containers too.

LAWNS
Apply 1 inch of water to established lawns when they show signs of wilting. Water if grass blades lose their vibrant color and become dull and blue-gray, the blades begin to roll, or when you leave a footprint when you step on the lawn. Less frequent but more thorough watering encourages deeper roots. If you have clay soil, water once a week. In loam or sandy soil, give the lawn ½ to ¾ inch twice a week.

Give grub-infested, disease-damaged, or stressed lawns at least 1 inch of water weekly. Watering helps the lawn renew itself.

If you let your lawn go dormant, apply ¼ inch of water during a drought lasting more than three weeks. This will keep the grass alive and still dormant; more water will bring out of dormancy.

Water newly sodded and seeded lawns often enough to keep the soil surface moist.

Reduce watering frequency once the sod has rooted into the soil and the grass seed begins to grow.

PERENNIALS & ORNAMENTAL GRASSES

Check new plantings several times a week. Water when the top few inches of soil start to dry. Apply enough water to wet the roots and surrounding soil. New plantings need about 1 inch of water per week. If you have clay soil, water once a week. In loam or sandy soil, divide it, and give the lawn ½ to ¾ inch twice a week.

Check established and mulched plantings weekly. Water thoroughly when the top few inches start to dry. Most perennials may not need water for several weeks. Spot water moisture-loving plants, such as big bluestem, cardinal flower, goatsbeard, hardy hibiscus, Japanese painted fern, and willow blue star, with a watering wand. Most ornamental grasses can last longer.

Japanese grass sedge and tufted hair grass need regular watering. Keep soil uniformly lightly moist; don't let them dry out.

ROSES

Even with a good layer of mulch, roses will need more water than the standard 1 inch a week if the temperature nears or tops the triple-digit mark. Take extra care with new plantings.

TREES & SHRUBS

Continue to follow the watering strategies described in June Water (page 107).

VINES & GROUNDCOVERS

Check container plantings daily. When the top 2 inches of soil starts to dry, water until the excess runs out the bottom.

Water new plantings often enough to keep the soil around the roots slightly moist. Check plants growing in clay soil weekly and those in sandy soil twice a week. When the top 2 to 3 inches of soil start to dry, soak the top 6 to 8 inches of soil. Gradually decrease watering frequency.

Established plants need less frequent watering. Check during extended dry periods. When the top 3 or 4 inches are dry, water enough to wet the top 6 to 8 inches of soil.

FERTILIZE

ANNUALS & BIENNIALS

Do not fertilize plants if you used a slow-release fertilizer; it is still providing the plants with the nutrients they need.

Foliar feed any other plants with a solution of fish emulsion or kelp every two weeks. Feed them early in the morning and never apply fertilizer if the temperature is over 80 degrees Fahrenheit, or you risk burning the leaves.

BULBS

Continue the fertilizing regime described in July Fertilize (page 122).

EDIBLES

Foliar feed young transplants weekly with a solution of fish emulsion or kelp. Foliar feed all other plants once this month.

ROSES

Round out the traditional feeding in early August with a last dose of all-purpose rose food or give roses their last monthly foliar feeding. Don't spray if the temperature is over 80 degrees Fahrenheit or if rain threatens. Fertilize roses planted in May. Roses planted after May don't need any supplemental feeding until next spring.

VINES & GROUNDCOVERS

Continue fertilizing annual and tropical vines grown in containers. Use a half-strength solution of any flowering fertilizer. Stop fertilizing any perennial vines in containers that spend their winter outdoors.

PROBLEM-SOLVE

ALL

Continue the strategies described in July Problem-Solve (page 123).

Pull weeds as they appear. It is much easier to keep up with a few weeds than it is to reclaim an entire garden gone bad. Pull and destroy quackgrass, creeping Charlie, crabgrass, and other perennial weeds; do not compost them. Remove the entire root system or rhizome of a weed, but be careful not to uproot neighboring plants. Use a weeding tool to get leverage if needed.

Distorted, spotted, and discolored leaves may indicate you have an insecte problem. See April Problem-Solve (page 79) for tips on controlling Eastern tent caterpillars and emerald ash borer. Control aphids and mites with a strong blast of water from the hose. Lady beetle (ladybug) larvae feed on aphids.

Remove spotted, blotchy, or discolored leaves, which can be caused by fungal disease, as soon as you see them. Discard or destroy leaves; do not compost. Sanitation is the best way to control and reduce the spread of disease.

Use a flashlight to look for nighttime marauders. Slugs, snails, and earwigs feed at night, eating holes in leaves and flowers. Hostas are a delicacy. Treat by applying snail bait granules around affected plants. Making a ½- to 1-inch-wide ring of diatomaceous earth or wood ashes also works by scratching the tender underbelly of slug and snails.

Now is your last chance to capture and destroy Japanese beetles before they go underground to lay their eggs. The grubs (larvae) will start eating grass

■ *Use weeding tools that reach deep in the soil for weeds, such as dandelions, that grow back unless the taproot is removed completely.*

roots. This is the best time to apply milky spore disease, while the soil is warm and grubs are about to start feeding. See April Problem-Solve (page 78) or more information on milky spore and directions for applying it.

ANNUALS & BIENNIALS

Check zinnias, begonias, and other annuals for powdery mildew. This fungal disease looks as if someone has sprinkled baby powder on the leaves. Proper spacing for improved air circulation and ample sunlight help reduce the risk of this disease. Spray with baking soda solution (see May Problem-Solve, page 96, for the recipe) or Neem oil solution. Do not spray if the temperature is over 80 degrees Fahrenheit.

BULBS

Check cannas for any sign of fungal leaf spot. Cut off and destroy any suspect leaves.

EDIBLES

Do you have tomatoes with black spots on the bottoms? That's blossom end rot, which is caused by a deficiency of calcium and magnesium in your soil. Scratch ½ cup of pelletized lime around each plant and then water them well. Water tomatoes monthly with a solution of ½ cup of Epsom salts diluted in a gallon of water. Give each plant a full gallon drink.

■ *Blossom end rot is more common in container-grown tomatoes, where plants may suffer inconsistent soil moisture compared to those in the ground.*

LAWNS

Continue monitoring for grubs, billbugs, sod webworms, and greenbugs. Make sure the insects are present and the damage is severe enough to warrant treatment. Check with your local Cooperative Extension Service for recommended treatments. See July Problem-Solve (page 125) for detailed information on testing for lawn pests.

Grubs and other larvae attract skunks, raccoons, and moles. They will dig in the lawn to get these tasty morsels (moles will tunnel through the lawn). Treat your lawn with milky spore disease to kill the grubs, and the four-legged pests will go away.

Rust and powdery mildew, both fungal diseases, often appear on newly seeded lawns. If the grass turns yellow, orange, or brown, you have rust. Powdery mildew looks like a whitish coating on the grass blades. Both diseases are more cosmetic problems and don't require treatment.

■ *If fusarium blight is a recurring problem in your lawn, consider overseeding with a blight-resistant grass mix.*

Fusarium blight (also known as summer patch) is evidenced by graying or brown patches of dying or dead grass with reddish rot at the base of the grass blades. See July Problem-Solve for more information and control.

■ *Powdery mildew (shown here on phlox) can be a problem on many different plants. Look for mildew-resistant varieties when replacing plants.*

PERENNIALS & ORNAMENTAL GRASSES

Check beebalm, garden phlox, and other perennials for signs of powdery mildew. Look for a white, powdery substance on the leaves. This fungal disease causes leaves to eventually yellow and brown. Consider moving infected plants into an area with full sun and good air circulation. If the problem is persistent, plant mildew resistant varieties. Keep plants that are mildew-susceptible (including black-eyed Susan, blanket flower, coreopsis, and Shasta daisy) away from each other so they don't spread the fungus. Spray with baking soda solution (see May Problem-Solve, page 96, for detailed information and directions for making it) or Neem oil solution. Do not spray if the temperature is over 80 degrees Fahrenheit.

ROSES

Continue the regimen described in July Problem-Solve (page 126).

TREES & SHRUBS

Surface roots are those that grow slightly above the soil and dull your mower blades as you cut the grass or interfere with the grass growing under your trees. Do not get out the axe. Those roots are important to the support and well being of your tree. Consider mulching under the tree canopy. A 2- to 3-inch layer of mulch provides a good environment for the tree and keeps the surface roots under cover. See this month's Plant, Vines & Groundcovers for details on planting groundcovers in this challenging area.

Keep an eye on the foliage. If it starts to turn its autumn color early, that's a sign that the plant is stressed. This is common in an extended drought. A few thorough, deep waterings may relieve the stress (but the color will continue to turn). Other causes can be girdling roots, trunk damage from mowers or weed whackers, and root rot. Call a professional (a certified arborist) for help with any of those issues. See June Plan for information on finding one.

Prune out dead or cankered branches. Disinfect tools with rubbing alcohol or a solution of 1 part bleach to 9 parts water between cuts.

Watch for female gypsy moths on tree trunks. The 2-inch moths with white to cream-colored wings cannot fly. They crawl up the tree (usually less than 6 feet up) to mate and lay eggs. Use gypsy moth pheromone traps to lure the males. Handpick and destroy the females and scrape off the egg masses. Squashing a female who hasn't laid her eggs forces the eggs out.

■ *Female gypsy moths do not fly, so in years of heavy infestations, you can find many of them on tree trunks waiting to lay their eggs.*

VINES & GROUNDCOVERS

Brown leaf edges can be a sign of scorch, especially in shade-loving plants like hostas growing in sun. Water is not always the solution. Often the plants are unable to take the water up fast enough to replace what they lose during extreme heat. Mulch the soil, water properly by moistening the top 6 inches whenever the top 3 to 4 inches start to dry, and consider moving plants to a more suitable location in the future.

September

September officially ushers in fall. Yet the official first frost date is at the beginning of this month in Zone 3 North Dakota, but not until October 21 in Zone 8 Oklahoma. Like so much else in our region, nature's timing is unpredictable. The first year I moved to Zone 5 Des Moines, I cut roses from the garden to decorate my Christmas table. Had I not pulled out the tomatoes at the end of September (in preparation for frost that was overdue), I might have had vine-ripened tomatoes too. Instead, I enjoyed ones I had brought in green and ripened inside.

It's not too early to start thinking about holiday gifts as you start getting ready to put your garden to bed. If a friend or relative really admired an annual or herb in your garden, pot it up in a nice container or take a cutting, bring it inside, and grow it until the holidays (by which time the cutting will have grown into a small plant).

Another great gift is forced bulbs—spring bloomers like daffodils, crocus, and hyacinths—or tender bulbs, including paperwhite narcissus and amaryllis. I used to try to time them so the flowers would be in full bloom for the holidays, but I was setting myself up for failure. Often they had already finished blooming. One year I was forced to give bulbs that had gone through the chill period, but had not grown much—I had no alternative gift. Months later I got an enthusiastic thank you from the recipient, saying how much he had enjoyed watching the plant grow day-by-day and finally bloom. From then on, my gifts were easier to prepare.

Save money by sharing. A group of neighbors can jointly own pieces of more expensive garden equipment—shredder, snow blower, tiller, sometimes even mulching mowers. It is rare that two people want to use the machinery at the same time. Or instead of joint ownership, each person could own a single piece of equipment with an agreement to share with everyone else.

PLAN

Consider preparing a new area for planting. Follow the directions in April Plant (page 67). This is the best time to kill the existing vegetation by covering with black plastic instead of using chemicals or digging the bed. If you do choose one of the other methods, add a 2- to 4-inch layer of shredded leaves on the bed and till it in. The bed will be ready for spring planting.

■ *Cover an area with black plastic to kill any plant material through heat and lack of light, moisture, and air.*

ANNUALS & BIENNIALS

Did you take cuttings for annuals you want to overwinter inside last month? You can always dig up the plants and bring them indoors. Remember that it is a commitment of time, energy, and space that will continue until planting time next spring. Sometimes an early, unexpected frost makes the decision for you.

BULBS

If you didn't order bulbs for forcing indoors, get them locally at nurseries, garden centers, and home-improvement stores. The best hardy bulbs for forcing include crocus, daffodils, grape hyacinths, hyacinths, squills, and tulips. Tender bulbs include paperwhite narcissus and amaryllis.

EDIBLES

Spend some time doing research now that will benefit next year's garden. Go to the grocery store and note which vegetables and fruits are your favorites, paying special attention to the prices. Then take a realistic look at your garden and budget. It's smarter to grow more costly raspberries or asparagus (up to five dollars a pound) than zucchini, which is inexpensive. Besides, one zucchini is pretty much like the rest. But with carrots, tomatoes, lettuces, cucumbers, and more, the range of varieties seems limitless. Shapes, sizes, colors, and flavors can vary greatly from one variety to another.

LAWNS

Lawn care activity ramps up this month as rain becomes more regular and the temperature moderates. Look carefully at all areas of your lawn and note if any need repair, renewal, or replacement. This is the time to do it.

PERENNIALS & ORNAMENTAL GRASSES

As summer eases into fall, look at the garden and consider what you want to add—more fall-blooming perennials for their vibrant colors (asters, goldenrod, Joe-pye weed, sedums, and sneezeweed); perennials that start blooming in summer and keep going (black-eyed Susan, purple coneflower, phlox, and Russian sage); and/or ornamental grasses, which are outstanding in the fall and winter garden.

Note any new and semi-hardy plantings that will need winter protection. Look for sources of straw, evergreen branches, or other winter mulch materials.

ROSES

Consider creating a new garden just for cut flowers—with roses centerstage. There are other flowers you may want to include as well, such as dahlias, cosmos, and zinnias. In preparation for spring planting, take advantage of the long, cold winter to do much of the work for you and make a no-dig bed.

TO MAKE A NO-DIG BED

1. Mark out the garden in chalk or flour (if it's on existing lawn). Water well.
2. Put down three layers of cardboard over the entire garden, thoroughly wetting each piece as you lay it down.
3. Add about 2 inches of black-and-white newspaper, wetting it thoroughly too.
4. Cover that with a 2- to 3-inch layer of peat moss; water it.
5. Continue watering as you add each subsequent 2- to 3-inch layer: compost (raw or finished); grass clippings, shredded leaves, or shredded paper (junk mail or black-and-white computer printouts); and peat moss. If you have any red wiggler worms, put them in between layers of clippings and peat moss (don't water the worms). Continue adding layers in that order—compost, leaves, and peat moss until you have repeated the sequence at least three times.
6. To keep it from blowing and hasten decomposition, throw a black plastic tarp over the whole thing. By spring, this will have shrunk drastically in height, but what remains is a thick layer of rich soil—perfect for roses.

TREES & SHRUBS

Start watching for colorful signs of fall. The bright red sumac growing along the highway is a good wakeup call. Visit local botanical gardens or take a walk in the woods to get ideas of the trees and shrubs (and combinations with other plants) to include for a spectacular fall show in your garden.

VINES & GROUNDCOVERS

Decide which tender vines, such as mandevilla, passionflower, and black-eyed Susan vine, you will overwinter indoors. They'll need a sunny location or lights to thrive. Perennial vines growing in containers need protection (except in Zone 8); the choice is whether to plant them in the ground, store the container in an unheated garage, or give them extra protection where they are.

What vines and groundcovers do you want to add to the garden? Many provide fruit, flowers, and colorful foliage as a grand finale to the growing season. The fragrance of sweet autumn clematis as it climbs over an arbor or trellis fills the air while its delicate white flowers brighten the landscape.

Watch for fall color; Boston ivy and Virginia creeper are two of the first. They turn a beautiful red that stands out against a house, garage, trellis, or arbor providing support. Some hostas turn brilliant yellow, echoing the yellow of ginkgo and other trees and shrubs in the landscape. Check out Kamtschatica sedum as the leaves turn a lovely bronze to gold. This can add a little fall surprise at ground level in the landscape.

ALL

It's time to get back into the garden and start planting. Warm soil and cooler air temperatures are ideal for establishing new plants.

Use a transplant solution at planting to get plants off to a good start, encouraging strong root growth. Follow mixing directions on the label.

■ *Virginia creeper is eye catching in fall as its leaves turn a brilliant shade of red. Its dark blue berries attract birds.*

ANNUALS & BIENNIALS

Look for pansies at your local nurseries, garden centers, or home-improvement stores. Although they are touting "new fall varieties," any pansy will do. Cut off any flowers and plant them in a place that you can easily see them. They will put out more blooms this fall (edible, with a slight wintergreen flavor) and continue into winter. Let the snow and ice come, and when it melts there will be cheery pansy faces to greet you. They will start growing again in early spring. Ironically, these cold-weather pansies can stand the heat better than ones you plant in spring and may last well into summer.

■ *Fall-planted pansies brighten the garden now and can survive winter, lasting well into next summer.*

Look for ornamental cabbage, kale, chrysanthemums, and other fall annuals and add them to the garden for a colorful autumnal display.

Move self-sown biennials like foxgloves and hollyhocks to their desired location. Transplant early in the month so the seedlings will have time to re-establish before winter.

BULBS

Plant Siberian squill, glory-of-the-snow, crocus, and snowdrops once you get the bulbs. They grow happily in rich, well-drained loam in full sun or partial shade. Space bulbs 3 to 4 inches

SUCCESSFUL GARDENING: GROWING TULIPS

■ *Plant tulips and other bulbs in natural-looking drifts, which are so much more attractive than soldierly rows.*

Many people think of tulips as annuals as they haven't had success getting them to come back year after year. Or they tried digging the bulbs up in early summer when the tulips went dormant and replanting them in fall—also without success. Follow these guidelines and in all but the coldest regions (Zones 3 and 4), tulips will come back each year.

- Tulips need humus-rich, sandy, well-drained soil and at least five or six hours a day; full sun is preferable.
- Dig the soil to a depth of 10 to 12 inches and work in bulb-booster-type food. If your soil is very clayey, dig 1 inch deeper and add an inch of builder's sand.
- Set the bulbs 10 to 12 inches deep and 4 to 8 inches apart, depending on size and variety. Cover with soil, firm it, and water well.
- After flowering, remove the head of the tulip but allow the stem and foliage to die back naturally.

*Early-flowering species tulips come back year after year planted at a depth of 6 to 8 inches.

apart and 3 inches deep in clumps of seven to eleven. Leave the bulbs undisturbed, and they will soon naturalize.

Plant hyacinths in an area with full sun to light shade that has fast-draining, rich soil. Plant clusters

HERE'S HOW

TO INTERPLANT SPRING BULBS

Interplant spring-blooming bulbs with one another for a riot of spring color and continuous bloom. In addition to the color, subsequent flowers and leaves hide the ripening foliage of the earlier bulbs. Although you can plant the bulbs individually, the trick to a breathtaking display is planting one large area in layers.

1. Dig a large hole to the planting depth of the largest bulb. Don't make a circular or rectangular hole; give it a naturalistic shape.
2. Place the large bulbs first; feel free to put those of the same size in clusters at the same level within the hole (hyacinths, lilies, and large daffodils). Don't plant them in soldierly rows.
3. Place plant markers in with the bulbs that reach well above soil level.
4. Cover the bulbs with 1 or 2 inches of soil.
5. Plant another layer with the next largest bulbs, such as tulips and species daffodils. Don't plant them directly on top of the bulbs in the layer below. Place plant markers as in step 3.
6. Add more soil and plant smaller bulbs (crocus, snowdrops, squill, and others) so that each bulb is at its proper depth. Place plant markers as in step 3.
7. After planting, cover bulbs with soil, water well, and mulch with shredded leaves.

If you start out with large lilies, you may have four layers of bulbs.

■ *Always plant bulbs with the pointed end up, root side down. If there's no obvious difference, plant them sideways.*

of three to five bulbs 4 to 6 inches deep and 4 to 8 inches apart. Water deeply.

Spring snowflake (*Leucojum aestivum*) shows off best when planted in drifts of 11 or more. Interplant it with its smaller, earlier-blooming relative, snowdrops—and its later cousin, summer snowflake (*L. vernum*).

You will know when crown imperial bulbs arrive by their scent, alternatively described as skunky or foxlike. That should be enough impetus to get them in the ground quickly. Plant the bulbs 5 to 6 inches deep and 8 inches apart in well-drained, alkaline, deep, sandy loam enriched with organic matter in a lightly shaded, sheltered area. The leaves have the same aroma as the bulbs, so you might not want to put crown imperial next to the bedroom window or adjacent to an outdoor dining area. It does repel deer (for more information, see April Problem-Solve, page 77). Crown imperial does not take well to being moved, so choose its location carefully before planting. Water them deeply after planting; keep the soil lightly moist until the ground freezes.

Plant a companion with your bulbs. Garlic will help keep the squirrels from digging up newly planted bulbs and storing them for a midwinter snack. Break the garlic bulb apart. With the pointed end up, push the clove into the ground so the top is at least an inch below soil level. Plant the cloves at least 6 inches apart. Water well.

EDIBLES

There's still a little time to sow fall vegetables (greens and radishes) in a cold frame. Or make a hoop house with a floating row cover. Although that does not provide ample protection for the big chill, it will give you a few weeks more harvest.

■ *Growing hardy greens and brassicas in a small hoop house extends the harvest well after first frost kills off tender edibles.*

A few weeks before your first fall frost date, sow seeds of some of the hardier greens, such as escarole, radicchio, spinach, and kale, in a raised bed (or any other area that you won't disturb during winter or spring). These greens are for a very early spring harvest. Even though they are small going into late fall and winter, most of them will just stop growing once the mercury plummets only to start growing again as the weather warms.

Plant garlic until four to six weeks before the ground freezes. See August Plant, (page 135) for directions.

LAWNS

Early to mid-September is ideal for planting grass seed. Germination is very good in warm soils, and grass grows better in cooler air than in the summer.

Learn how to start a new lawn in May Plant. There is still time to patch bare lawn areas. For directions, see April Plant (page 69).

Do not seed after September 20 (September 10 in Zone 8). The grass won't have time enough to develop good roots before the ground freezes.

You still have time to put down sod. The good growing conditions speed up the root development of newly laid sod. See April Plant (page 72) for complete instructions.

PERENNIALS & ORNAMENTAL GRASSES

Keep adding perennials and ornamental grasses to your garden and landscape.

Mum's the word. If there is one perennial that says "fall," it's the chrysanthemum. Include mums in every area of the landscape for the range of colors (all except for blue and black), flower sizes, and shapes (giant football mums to tiny button varieties). Include a few mums when you plant bulbs for instant color. Follow the directions for interplanting bulbs in this month's Plant, Bulbs, but leave room to set the mum so it is planted at the same depth it was growing in the pot. Come spring, the mum will help hide the fading bulb foliage.

Grow prairie dropseed from seed sown directly on well-raked soil. Water gently to avoid disturbing the seeds. Keep the soil lightly moist until seedlings are established. Use a polyspun floating row cover to protect seeds from birds while preventing the

■ *Unroll the sod carefully, pressing it down as you go, so it makes good contact with the soil below.*

sun from drying out the soil. Have patience; prairie dropseed is slow to grow but worth the wait.

Change out the plantings in sunken nursery pots under your tree (See April Plant, page 67, for directions on creating the planting area) and put in mums.

Transplant iris until September 15 (first week in Zone 8). This allows them to establish before winter.

ROSES

Although the time for planting roses has passed, consider adding some companions, especially minor spring-blooming bulbs such as glory-of- the-snow, Siberian squill, crocus, grape hyacinths, miniature daffodils, and snowdrops. These will add color interest before the roses leaf out and bloom. More important, they will not take away necessary nutrients.

TREES & SHRUBS

Nurseries, garden centers, home-improvement stores, and the horticulture industry all proclaim, "Fall is for Planting!" Plants get established better in the cooler weather and are less stressed overall. Plant container-grown and balled-and-burlapped trees and shrubs now and right up until the ground freezes. See April Plant (page 70) for detailed planting instructions.

Plant evergreens only until the end of the month.

This is the second-best time to transplant trees and shrubs. Wait until the leaves drop and the plants are dormant. See March (page 56) for detailed transplanting instructions.

VINES & GROUNDCOVERS

Continue the planting regime described in August Plant.

CARE

ALL

Start the fall cleanup and get ready to protect plants from the weather.

Rake leaves out of beds and off the lawn. (Remove and destroy leaves around any pest- or disease-

infected plants.) Don't send healthy leaves to the landfill or even to the municipal compost facility. Use them yourself. Run over them with a mower (oak and other large, tough leaves may require several passes). Use them to mulch new bulb plantings. Mix them into the soil for new beds. Include them when making a no-dig bed (see this month's Plan for more information). Add them to the compost pile for "brown" matter. If you still have any left, start a leaf-mold pile. Rake up the leaves into a pile (3 feet square is ideal), moisten, and let them slowly decompose. By spring or summer, you'll have rich organic matter that's an excellent soil amendment and mulch.

■ Large leaves can smother a lawn over winter. Rake them up, run them over with a mower, and use them as mulch.

ANNUALS & BIENNIALS

Get out the floating row covers (season-extending fabrics), light blankets, sheets, and other frost protection. Light frost in September is common in the colder parts of our region. If you protect plants from the first frosty days, there's more warm weather ahead. Intermittent light frosts can extend a month or more before a killing frost takes everything down. Any extra days with flowers are a gift.

Apply frost protection in late afternoon when the danger of frost is forecast. Remove protection in the morning once the temperature is warm. Cover the plants again each afternoon when there is a danger of nighttime frost.

HERE'S HOW

TO OVERWINTER ANNUAL PLANTS

This works for garden-grown annuals or container plantings of annuals. Dig up the annual from the garden and transplant it into a container with potting mix. You may want to repot the container planting at this time.

■ *Plants, such as these window box geraniums, can be brought indoors and grown throughout the winter on a sunny windowsill or under lights.*

1. Give the plants a good shower of water before bringing them into the garage, screened-in porch, or indoor room—away from your houseplants—to clean them off and remove any pests. If they are in the garage, give them light.
2. Isolate them for several weeks. Check for insects. Use insecticidal soap to treat any mites and aphids you discover. Handpick and destroy larger caterpillars, slugs, earwigs, and beetles.
3. Water thoroughly whenever the top few inches of soil start to dry.
4. Move the plants indoors to a warm, sunny location. A south-facing window, sunroom, or atrium works fine. Or add an artificial light to improve the poor lighting conditions in most homes.
5. Do not fertilize until the plant adjusts to its new location and shows signs of growth.
6. Prune only enough to fit the plant into its winter location. Don't worry about any falling leaves. The plant will replace them as soon as it adjusts to its new location.
7. Continue to watch for pests and water as needed. Enjoy the added greenery and occasional flowers.
8. Prune overgrown plants in late February.

Move containers into the house, porch, or garage when there is a danger of frost. Move them back outdoors during the day.

Move tropical plants indoors if there is any danger of frost. Place them in a south-facing window or under artificial lights.

Dig up your geraniums and store them in the basement in a cool, dark area.

BULBS

Carefully cut back lily stalks when the foliage has died back completely.

After the first frost, carefully dig caladium tubers. Place them on a screen in a warm, dry, airy place for about a week to dry. Store them on a shallow tray in a warm, dry place.

After frost kills dahlia foliage, carefully dig the tubers. Cut the stalks approximately 6 inches above the tubers. Place them on a screen in a dry, airy place for about a week to dry thoroughly. Pack them carefully in dry sand, peat moss, or sawdust, making sure tubers do not touch. Store in a cool (40 to 45 degrees Fahrenheit), dark, dry place.

EDIBLES

Pot up rosemary to bring indoors for winter. Choose a pot that's about as wide as the width of the lowest branches. Rosemary grows best in "lean" soil you can blend at home by mixing equal parts potting mix and cactus soil (available anywhere you buy plants). Dig the plant up—digging down about a foot and around the plant at the tips of the branches. Shake most of the soil off the roots, untwine any ensnarled roots, and cut off overly long roots. Give it a quick shower

HERE'S HOW

TO DIG AND STORE CANNAS

After frost blackens canna leaves, (1) cut off the stems and leaves, and (2) carefully dig up the rhizomes. Shake off loose soil, and (3) let the rhizomes dry. Label and store in barely moist peat moss in a cool (above freezing), dark place for winter.

in water that is slightly cool to the touch and then repot it and move it to a sunny spot or under lights indoors.

If you have the time, put up vegetables—today that ranges from old-fashioned canning to freezing,

HERE'S HOW

TO OVERWINTER SUMMER-FLOWERING BULBS

Most summer-flowering bulbs are tender and cannot withstand temperatures below freezing. Bulbs must be dried before storing or they will rot. Follow the separate directions for caladiums, cannas, and dahlias.

1. Dig the bulbs when the foliage has turned brown due to a light frost.
2. Set bulbs on a screen (raised up from the table or floor so air can circulate all around the bulbs) in a dry, well-ventilated area. Air dry for a week.
3. Remove all soil from the bulbs. If you have had a problem with rotting in past years, consider dusting the bulbs with sulfur before storing for winter.
4. Put the bulbs in dry peat moss or wood shavings in a brown paper bag, open crate, netted bag, or pantyhose. Store in a cool (40 to 45 degrees Fahrenheit), dark, dry place.

making dishes ahead of time, or drying. When you look at a small jar of dried basil for several dollars, you realize that you can make dozens of jars yourself with much better flavor and at a minimal cost.

Continue picking and harvesting vegetables and herbs. Do not harvest all of the stems on the Mediterranean herbs as most will come back next year.

Wait until after the first frost to pick Brussels sprouts; the cold enhances their flavor. Starting at the base of the plant, twist off only as many sprouts as you need at a time. The garden provides free refrigeration for the rest. Most of us don't have enough refrigerator space for even one stalk of sprouts, much less more.

Kale also benefits from a frost. Extend the kale harvest (you can eat ornamental kale if it wasn't sprayed before you bought it) into winter by picking only as many outer leaves as you need at a time. As long as the temperature is at least in the 40s, it will keep producing more leaves at the center of the plant.

If you have green tomatoes still on the vine, bring them indoors to ripen. Pick them off the vine and set them in a cool place where they won't get any direct or indirect sun. Lay them in a shallow box on the dining room buffet making sure that none are touching each other. Some folks bring in the entire vine and hang it upside down in the basement or attic to let the tomatoes ripen.

LAWNS

September is ideal for renovating lawns, including those that have many bare areas, are thin, or are very weedy. It is well worth hiring a professional who has the equipment—a vertical mower and core aerator—to do it properly. Or, replace the lawn area and start fresh.

Check for thatch. See May Problem-Solve for details and treatment.

■ *Core aerating pulls out plugs of lawn, allowing the grass roots to expand into the space and giving them room to breathe.*

PERENNIALS & ORNAMENTAL GRASSES

Dig and divide perennials and ornamental grasses in Zones 3 to 5 until September 15, all others until the end of the month. See May (page 91) for detailed instructions. Wait until spring to divide Siberian iris, astilbe, delphinium, or other slow-to-establish, less-hardy perennials.

You can dig and divide peonies until their foliage is killed by frost. When dividing, leave at least three to five eyes per division. Plant with the eyes no more than 1 inch below soil level.

Keep deadheading to prevent reseeding. Leave the last set of flowers intact on plants like coneflowers, sedums, and black-eyed Susans. The seedheads are attractive through winter, and birds feed on the seeds.

Leave most ornamental grasses for their colorful foliage, form, and seedheads for winter interest. Birds will flock to little bluestem, switch grass, and tufted hair grass.

Cut Northern sea oat seedheads now for drying or using in arrangements,. It readily self-sows, so cutting the seedheads prevents it from spreading.

If winds make the tufted hair grass flower panicles look ragged, cut them down. Otherwise, let them be and enjoy their beauty throughout winter.

ROSES

Unless you are growing only the hardy floribunda, species, and shrub roses—especially any Griffith Buck hybrids or roses in the Canadian Explorer and Brownell Subzero series, it's time to think about winter protection. After the first *light frost*, mound 4 to 6 inches of light soil around established hybrid tea and grandiflora roses. After the first *hard frost* and that layer has frozen, add another few inches of soil. Continue adding soil, allowing each layer

HERE'S HOW

TO MAKE ROSE HIP JELLY

If the birds have not gotten to them, pick the large colorful hips (the fruit) from species roses like *Rosa rugosa* and its cultivars. You can make rose hip jelly simply by boiling the hips in fresh apple cider for about an hour. Process the mixture in a blender or food processor. Strain it through a sieve. Follow your favorite jelly recipe, using the strained "hip juice," but cut the sugar at least by half. You'll need less pectin, as the cider is a good source. Start your day with a slice of toast slathered with rose hip jelly for more vitamin C than in a glass of orange juice.

to freeze before adding another. Top off at about 12 inches. You'll see a broad cone of soil with rose canes sticking up from that. In Zone 4 and below (and for any success with hybrid teas), cover the frozen mound with leaves. Cover any new plant or the extreme cold will kill the tender canes.

If you prefer to use the Styrofoam or plastic "cones" around your roses, be sure to use ones that with a removable top or no top. This allows you to vent the roses on warm days. When the night is chilly, recover the cone. If you cannot vent the cone, the roses can easily roast when the mercury climbs for several days. If you can mound dry, shredded leaves all around the rose and place the cone over it, the leaves will help stabilize the temperature inside. If you are still considering the cone, look at its height. To fit a rose inside, you would have to give it a major pruning—not a good idea at this time of year. Not only would pruning stimulate new growth, so would the warmth inside the cone. There is no room for new growth.

TREES & SHRUBS

Rake leaves as they accumulate. See this month's Care, All, for ways to use them.

Once the leaves have dropped, you can see the trees' structure. This makes pruning much easier. See Appendix, Pruning for details on pruning.

Call a certified arborist to prune large trees. The arborist can offer advice on training young trees. See June Care for information on finding one.

VINES & GROUNDCOVERS

Move tender vines, including passionflower, mandevilla, and bougainvillea, indoors for winter as the temperatures cool but before the first killing frost.

Hardy vines in containers can be wintered outdoors. Sink the pot in the ground to insulate the roots from cold winter temperatures. Or store the planters in an unheated garage, placed in a protected corner away from the door. Use packing peanuts or other material to help insulate the roots. As a last resort, move the container to a protected location near the house. Insulate the roots by surrounding the pot with bales of straw or hay.

WATER

ALL

Water as needed. As the temperatures cool, you will need to water less frequently.

Check plantings growing in containers daily.

ANNUALS & BIENNIALS

Water established plantings when the top few inches of soil are slightly dry.

BULBS

Keep caladiums, cannas, and peacock orchids lightly moist. Don't let them dry out.

Keep newly planted crocus lightly moist until the ground freezes.

EDIBLES

Water weekly if the plants need it.

LAWNS

Water newly sodded and seeded lawns often enough to keep the soil surface moist. Reduce watering frequency once the sod has rooted into the soil and the grass seed begins to grow.

PERENNIALS & ORNAMENTAL GRASSES

Check new plantings several times a week. Keep the top 4 to 6 inches lightly moist.

New gardens need about 1 inch of water every seven to ten days. Water established plantings when the top few inches of soil are dry.

ROSES

Even though many garden tasks are done, do not neglect watering. Roses need 1 inch of water a week.

TREES & SHRUBS

Continue watering new plantings throughout fall. Check the top 6 inches of soil and water thoroughly as it begins to dry.

Established plants benefit from supplemental watering during a dry fall. Check the soil and water thoroughly when the top 6 inches are dry.

SEPTEMBER

Water aboveground planters thoroughly anytime the top few inches of soil begin to dry. Continue to water planters until the soil in the planter freezes.

Make sure all new plantings and evergreens receive a thorough watering before the ground freezes.

VINES & GROUNDCOVERS
Water outdoor containers thoroughly whenever the top 2 to 3 inches of soil begin to dry until water runs out the bottom of the pot.

Keep soil moist around recently planted vines and groundcovers. Allow the top 3 to 4 inches of soil to start to dry before watering plants that have been in the ground for several weeks.

Check established plants during long dry periods. Water when the top 4 inches of soil are dry.

FERTILIZE

ALL
No fertilizing is needed for most in-ground plantings. Feeding only stimulates tender new growth that is more likely to be damaged by freezing weather.

When using any fertilizer, always follow all package instructions for proper application, frequency, concentration, and mixing/dilution.

Take a soil test if your plants show signs of nutrient deficiencies.

ANNUALS & BIENNIALS
Continue foliar feeding container plants as needed with a solution of fish emulsion or kelp.

LAWNS
Fertilize the soil, following soil test recommendations, before seeding or sodding a new lawn.

ROSES
If you eat bananas, which are high in potassium, bury the peels around your roses. Over time they break down and turn into rich organic matter. The added potassium strengthens rose canes. Dig in banana peels anytime the ground isn't frozen. To keep from planting the bananas in the same place

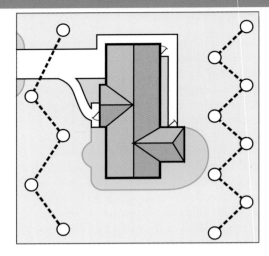

■ *Take soil samples from various areas of the lawn, as results can vary from one area to another.*

twice, start with one rose. Bury up to six peels, staggering them to make a circle at least 1 foot out from the base of the rose. Then move on to the next rose. By the time you bury the last peel by the last bush, those around the first will be well composted, and you can start all over again.

TREES & SHRUBS
Fertilize established trees after they go dormant, following the recommendations from the soil test.

Fertilizer can be sprinkled over and raked through mulch. Water to move the fertilizer into the soil. For trees growing in lawn areas, remove small cores of soil 6 inches deep and 2 to 3 feet apart, starting several feet away from the trunk and continuing several feet beyond the drip line of the tree. Divide recommended fertilizer evenly between the holes. Water until the top 12 inches of soil are moist.

Wait a year to fertilize new tree plantings. They have been well tended in the nursery and fertilizer may harm new developing roots.

Do not fertilize aboveground planters. Fall fertilization stimulates growth and reduces winter survival.

PROBLEM-SOLVE

ALL
If Japanese beetles have been a problem during this growing season, attack them where they overwinter.

■ *Kill individual weeds by putting a 1-gallon plastic jug over it (bottom cut out) and spraying weed killer.*

Apply milky spore to lawn and garden areas—about 1 teaspoon every 4 feet, creating a grid pattern. Water it in. As the beetle grubs eat, they ingest some of the bacteria, which will kill them and only them. One application can last 20 to 30 years. But there's a catch: chemical herbicides and pesticides kill all bacteria, which is another reason to go organic.

Follow the regimes for weeds and dealing with insect-infested plants as described in August Problem-Solve (page 143).

Powdery mildew can be worst in fall. Make a note in your journal to use mildew-resistant plants and to correct growing conditions next year. Proper spacing for improved air circulation and ample sunlight help reduce the risk of this disease. Use baking soda spray to prevent its spread. Do not spray if the temperature is above 80 degrees Fahrenheit. See May Problem-Solve (page 96) for directions on making the solution.

BULBS

Inspect daffodil, tulip, and hyacinth bulbs for fungal infections—soft, greenish blue or black areas. Throw out any suspicious bulbs.

LAWNS

Consider replacing lawns that contain more than 50 percent weeds. Starting over gives you quicker and more effective results. Reclaiming a weed-infested lawn often requires more pesticides and gives poor results over a long period. See May Plant, Lawns for details on starting a lawn.

Squirrels stash their nuts and bulbs (dug from your plantings) in the lawn for safekeeping. Tamp down any disturbed areas. Enjoy the surprises that appear in the lawn next spring.

Grubs and other larvae attract skunks, raccoons, and moles. They will dig in the lawn to get these tasty morsels (moles will tunnel through the lawn). Treat your lawn with milky spore disease to kill the grubs. When there's no more food, the moles will go away

ROSES

Control blackspot by spraying the entire plant, including leaves and canes, every seven to ten days with baking soda solution. This should be the last month of spraying.

Clean up leaves as they fall. Oak leaves in particular mat together when wet and don't allow water to pass through. Shred dry leaves and use them for winter mulch, add them to the compost pile, or make a leaf mold pile (leaves will disintegrate in about a year).

TREES & SHRUBS

Gypsy moth egg masses appear like fuzzy, beige blotches on tree trunks. Scrape them into a plastic bag and throw it in the garbage.

Watch for the last few pests of the season. Cooler temperatures usually mean fewer aphids and mites.

Contact a certified arborist if your landscape suffered *severe* feeding damage from Japanese beetles, scale, and other pests. Professionals can use a soil-applied systemic insecticide in fall. Ask to see the label instructions. Improper use of systemics can contaminate groundwater and can cause an increase in other pests.

■ *When a lawn looks this bad after using a weed killer, it's time to dig it up and start over—sod or seed.*

October

October is the last hurrah for the garden. If you haven't had a frost, annuals are still showy. Late perennials are colorful, with mums dotted throughout the landscape. Ornamental grasses are hitting their stride— putting on a show that in many cases will last into or through winter. As trees and shrubs prepare for winter, chlorophyll recedes from the leaves, revealing the colors that were masked all season. They go out in a flame of glory before they drop their foliage. Container gardens, if protected, continue to bestow their beauty on us all.

As we begin to prepare for winter—overwintering some plants and letting nature run its course with others—it's only too easy to overlook the containers that hold everything that isn't growing in the ground. Like plants, some containers are hardy and can survive winter outdoors. Wood, concrete, metal, and resin pots with drainage holes are fine outside. Others, including terracotta and glazed pots, easily break if water gets in a crack and freezes. Empty *all* containers (put the potting mix in the compost pile; start fresh next year) and wash them out. Turn those that are staying outside upside down. Move the others to the basement or garage.

Plant labels are often overlooked too. As plants are completely harvested or pulled out, collect the labels. Make any last-minute notes on each label as you pull it out of the ground. Otherwise, it's likely that you won't remember the information. I learned my lesson after throwing all the markers in a plastic bag and taking them into the house. A week later, I jotted notes on the labels. When I finally had time to scrutinize them, I found that I had written information for the wrong cultivar, and in two instances—the wrong plant entirely.

Do not remove markers from any plants that are still in the ground—annuals and edibles that are still growing, as well as all the perennial and woody plants. Check those labels; if they're getting hard to read, rewrite them.

Take time from your fall chores to revel in the splendor of the garden's last hurrah.

OCTOBER

PLAN

Make a final review of the garden's performance. Take a few minutes to record what worked and what needs improvement for next season. Mark next year's calendar (based on this year's problems) for potential times of peak pest activity. Catching the problems early makes control easier and more successful.

Review your wish list. Add some outstanding fall bloomers and evaluate some of the early bloomers on your list.

As you finish your last few growing chores, it's time to start preparing for winter. Make a list of plants you protect from cold, snow, and animals. Check your journal to see if there were plants that had damage that should have been protected. Gather materials now so that you won't need to scramble for them as the first flakes of snow fall.

Start gathering winter protection materials— burlap for windscreens and salt barriers, hardware cloth for tree wraps, fencing for snow loads, and animal barriers.

Get a jumpstart on creating new garden beds by letting nature kill the existing grass and weeds over the winter. See April Plant (page 67) for complete directions. Start a bed in fall so it will be ready for spring planting. Your effort will pay off with less work during the remainder of the season.

Winter snow and ice *are* on their way. The nasty weather can start this month, depending on how the jet stream dips. Plan now for how to deal with it. Salt and deicers spread on drives, sidewalks, and walkways get on adjacent lawns and plantings and can harm them. Reduce the amount of salt/deicer you use by first shoveling driveways, sidewalks, and other surfaces to remove as much snow and ice as possible. A non-salt deicer like magnesium chloride or calcium acetate causes less damage to lawns and plantings. For traction only, non-clumping kitty litter, sand, or turkey grit works well.

EDIBLES
Nothing improves plant growth in clay soil better than a raised bed. The soil warms up earlier, and you can start planting—and harvesting—earlier. Plan to build one this fall or winter. You'll finally be able to grow root crops successfully.

ROSES
Stockpile shredded leaves for winterizing roses.

PLANT

EDIBLES
If you don't have an evergreen and a deciduous shrub growing in or near the vegetables, take advantage of fall sales to buy one now and plant it ASAP. It will give winter and wind protection to early and late season plantings. Use transplant solution to encourage new roots so the plants can get established before winter comes blowing in.

LAWNS
Continue to lay sod if you haven't had a killing frost.

PERENNIALS & ORNAMENTAL GRASSES
Continue planting until the middle of the month (end of the month in Zone 8) to give plants ample time to get established before it gets cold.

Collect and sow seeds of black-eyed Susan, coneflowers, and other late summer- and fall-blooming perennials. Spread the seeds outdoors on well-prepared soil.

Continue to dig and divide peonies until a hard frost. See May Care for detailed instructions on dividing perennials. Leave at least three to five eyes per division. Plant the eyes no more than 1 inch below soil level.

TREES & SHRUBS
Fall is a great time to plant most trees and shrubs. The soil is warm, air temperatures are cool (good for the plant and the person planting), and trees are in place and ready to start growing as soon as spring arrives. Continue planting as long as the ground is workable. See April Plant for detailed instructions.

SUCCESSFUL GARDENING: LET NATURE PLANT YOUR GARDEN— SELF-SOWING PLANTS

■ *Calendula (pot marigolds or poor man's saffron) petals give the rich golden color and flavor of saffron when cooked.*

Self-sowing (self-seeding) annuals and biennials are favorites among many gardeners. Once planted, they seem perennial as they come back year after year with little to no effort on your part. When you deadhead or pinch the plants back in summer, let a few stems (or a single plant) go to seed. Leave bare soil beneath a plant onto which the seeds can fall and germinate in spring. If you mulch, collect seeds when they are ripe. Pull back the mulch and sow the seed. Do *not* replace mulch. Store extra seeds in a clean envelope to share. *Note:* When cultivated hybrids self-sow, the resulting plants won't be the same as the original ones. It's fun to see the variations that pop up the following year, though.

Bachelor's buttons	Flowering tobacco	Johnny jump-up	Plains coreopsis
Black-eyed Susan	Four o'clocks	Love-in-a-mist	Rose mallow
Cleome	*Foxglove	Morning glory	*Sweet William
Cosmos	Golden marguerite	Moss rose	
Dame's rocket	*Hollyhock		(* denotes biennials)

Local nurseries, garden centers, and home-improvement stores may still have balled-and-burlapped and container-grown plants for sale. Only buy those that are healthy and free from signs of pests, disease, and stress. Scorched (brown edges), tattered, and discolored leaves are clues that a plant is struggling. That bargain tree may not be such a deal if it needs replacing in several years.

Do not plant trees now that are slow to root, including black gum, cherry, crabapple, birch, hawthorn, honey locust, linden, magnolia, oak, poplar, red maple, tulip tree, and willow. Wait until spring to plant them.

Ttransplant small trees and shrubs after the leaves drop and the plants are dormant. See March Plant (page 56) for detailed transplanting instructions.

VINES & GROUNDCOVERS

Plant groundcovers and vines up to the middle of the month (end of the month for Zone 8). This still gives the plants time to establish roots before winter sets in.

CARE

ALL

Continue fall cleanup as described in September Care (page 153). Another use for those shredded leaves is to mix them into the soil once you have cleaned out annual beds.

Clean up, remove, and destroy or discard any diseased or insect-infested leaves, stems, and flowers.

ANNUALS & BIENNIALS

Hopefully the weather has been mild and your gardens are still in their glory. If frost threatens, follow the guidelines in September Care (page 153).

If you have had a hard frost, most annuals are dead. Pull them up, shake the soil from the roots and add

HERE'S HOW

TO FORCE SPRING-BLOOMING BULBS INDOORS FOR WINTER BLOOM

Get a breath of spring by forcing bulbs indoors. The best bulbs for forcing include crocus, daffodils, grape hyacinths, hyacinths, squills, and tulips.

1. Fill a pot three-quarters full with potting soil. Look for bulb-forcing pans, which are shallower than normal pots (about 6 inches high).
2. Place the bulbs ½ inch apart with pointed ends up. Gently press them into the soil so that the tips are level with the rim of the pot.
3. Once the bulbs are positioned, fill the pots with soil to within ¼ to ½ inch of the rim, leaving the tips exposed.
4. Water gently until soil is evenly moist.

5. Put the bulbs in a cool (between 35 to 45 degrees Fahrenheit), dark place to grow roots for a minimum of eight weeks, averaging 12 to 15 weeks. The best places for the big chill are the refrigerator (not the crisper drawer) or outdoors. There can be no apples in the fridge; they give off ethylene gas that prevents bulbs from flowering. Heat interferes with the forcing process, so any outdoor storage space has to stay between below 50 degrees Fahrenheit. (Dig a 2-foot trench and line it with 6 inches of mulch or hay. Set the pots in the trench and cover them with 6 to 8 inches of chopped leaves, mulch, or hay. Top it with 3 to 4 inches of soil.)
6. Don't let the pots dry out.

7. Check the pots after eight weeks. If the bulbs stay in place when you try to wiggle them and shoots have begun to emerge from the bulb, gradually move the pots into the warmth and light. (If they bulbs wiggle, check them again it two weeks).
8. Start with a cool room and indirect sunlight. After a week, move the pots into full sun at 60 to 65 degrees Fahrenheit. Keep the soil lightly moist; within a month you'll be enjoying flowers.

Once the bulbs are in full bud, you can slow down or speed up the process by controlling the temperature: warmer temperatures make the flowers open faster, cooler temperature will make them last longer.

■ *When cleaning out mixed flowerbeds, be sure that the plants you pull out are annuals—not perennials.*

them to your compost pile. Do not add any that had pests or diseases (powdery mildew); destroy or discard them. Pansies should still be green; leave them and any other plants that are still alive.

Remove faded flowers as well as dried-up leaves and stems on plants moved inside for winter. Allow them to adjust to their new location before cutting back severely, if that's what you want to do. That's your choice; leave them as full-sized plants if you have the space.

BULBS

Continue to dig and store tender bulbs after the first frost. See September Care for detailed instructions.

In Zones 7 and 8 when the leaves of potted caladium begin to droop, take the pots inside. Water sparingly until the leaves fall off. Store the pots in a warm place (about 55 to 65 degrees Fahrenheit).

Mulch lilies and hyacinths with 3 inches of organic matter (leaf mold, chopped leaves, compost, well-rotted manure) as soon as the ground freezes.

After the ground freezes, mulch tulips with straw.

EDIBLES

Check the tomatoes you brought indoors to ripen every couple of days. Remove any bad or overripe ones immediately. If you need ripe tomatoes soon, put a few in a brown paper bag with an apple. Close the bag, and lay it on its side so the fruits don't touch. The ethylene gas that the apple gives off encourages fast ripening. You may have noticed that when you have apples in the refrigerator, other fruits and vegetables will spoil faster than normal.

After the ground freezes, add a 3- to 5-inch layer of straw as a winter mulch over garlic plantings.

LAWNS

Fall has arrived, and you may be tired of raking all those leaves. And, of course, there is that Norway maple that just will not let go of its leaves. Once most of the leaves have fallen from the trees, don't worry about raking the rest that fall or get blown onto the lawn. Just shred them when you mow. Some leaves may require another pass to cut them small enough to leave on the lawn (so you can see the blades of grass). The leaves will break down and nourish the lawn over winter.

Many plants are shutting down for the season, but your lawn is not. Fall is when lawns use their energy to spread and develop deeper root systems instead of top growth. Keep cutting the grass as long as it keeps growing. Remove no more than one-third of the total height at each cutting.

Make the last mowing of the season short—1½ to 2 inches—just before hard frost.

PERENNIALS & ORNAMENTAL GRASSES

Continue digging and dividing peonies until the foliage is killed by frost. When dividing, leave at least three to five eyes per division. Plant with the eyes no more than 1 inch below soil level.

Overwinter plants, such as salvia and mums, without removing their dead stems; they seem to perform better the next year.

■ *Goldfinches and other birds feed on the seedheads of purple coneflowers throughout autumn—or as long as seeds last.*

Leave the seedheads of coneflowers, sedums (stonecrop), and black-eyed Susans. They provide visual relief for the otherwise bleak winter garden, but they also attract birds, which feast on the seeds.

If winds make the tufted hair grass flower panicles look ragged, cut them down. Otherwise, let them be and enjoy their beauty throughout winter.

Many ornamental grasses are hitting their stride with colorful foliage, form, and seedheads that will provide interest well into winter. Birds will flock to little bluestem, switch grass, and tufted hair grass for the seeds. If you must cut little bluestem back in fall, use the leaves in bunches to add softness and color in dried arrangements or twist them into holiday wreaths.

ROSES
Continue with the winter protection detailed on page 156 in September Care.

TREES & SHRUBS
Apply winter protection to shrubs before the heavy snows arrive. Wrap evergreens loosely with burlap.

Continue pruning trees (except evergreens). See Appendix (page 192) for details. Do not prune evergreens; wait until early spring.

Although you can prune shrubs now, some gardeners prefer to wait until late winter. Plants recover quicker from pruning then. Plus the stems, fruits, and dried flowers remain intact for winter interest. Low-input (*not* lazy) gardeners do all their chores at one time. Late winter pruning allows us to repair winter and animal damage while shaping the shrubs—one time spent pruning versus two.

Do not prune spring-blooming shrubs like forsythia and lilacs (except to remove damaged branches); you'll cut off the flower buds. See Appendix (page 194) for detailed pruning directions.

Move aboveground planters to an enclosed porch or unheated garage for winter. If they are too heavy to move, insulate the plants by surrounding them with bales of hay.

VINES & GROUNDCOVERS
Continue preparations for winter discussed in September Care (page 157).

■ *Ornamental grasses add such a variety of color, texture, size, and shape to the fall and winter garden.*

HERE'S HOW

TO WINTERIZE DRIP IRRIGATION

If you had any sort of drip or leaky hose irrigation system and the layout worked well, follow these steps to save time and aggravation next spring. Pull back the mulch so you can see the system; photograph or make a rough sketch of the placement. You will need two boxes large enough to hold all of the many pieces of the drip irrigation (so you don't risk accidentally leaving some attachment or emitter on the ground); masking or art tape; and a permanent (waterproof) marker.

1. Blow the water from the pipes and hoses.
2. Start at one end of the drip system and remove sections (as large as can easily fit into the box) one at a time. Wrap a piece of tape around each section and loop it over itself so it makes a tab label that won't come off the plastic while it's in winter storage. Use the marker to number each section sequentially.
3. Continue removing and labeling sections until you reach the end. Move mulch back into place. Once you and the box are back in the house, get the second box. Place the sections in it, keeping them in order (going from the last number to the first). Include the map or photo of the layout. Store indoors in a cool, dry place.

■ *Everywhere, except Zone 8, pull up drip irrigation lines and store indoors. Otherwise, freezing water can expand and break the lines.*

In spring, tube or pipe number 1 is on the top, covered by the map of the layout, and you are ready to go.

WATER

ALL

It is almost time to pack away the garden hose and water wand. Wait until the ground has frozen and the lawn stops growing.

Continue to thoroughly water all outdoor plantings until the ground freezes. See September Water (page 157) for specifics.

ANNUALS & BIENNIALS

Water annuals overwintering indoors thoroughly when the top 2 inches of soil begin to dry.

BULBS

Keep crocus and other newly planted bulbs lightly moist until the ground freezes.

Keep the refrigerated potted bulbs you are forcing lightly moist. Do not overwater or mildew can form on the cold soil.

LAWNS

Make sure new plantings are watered. Keep the soil surface moist under newly laid sod. Continue to water thoroughly, but less frequently, once the sod is rooted into the soil below.

Water established lawns if they show signs of wilting. See August Water (page 141).

VINES & GROUNDCOVERS

Water plants overwintering indoors thoroughly until the excess runs out the bottom. Pour out any water that collects in the saucer. Wait until the top few inches of soil are dry before watering again.

FERTILIZE

Take a soil test of all your gardens if you have not already done so. Send the sample in now so that you will have the results back in time for winter planning and spring soil preparation.

■ *Adjust the settings on your spreader to the rate specified on the fertilizer package.*

■ *Before fertilizing, do a test run (with sand) to determine how fast to walk and the uniformity of the spread pattern.*

LAWNS

If you only fertilize the lawn once a year, this is *the* time to do it. Fall feeding will strengthen your lawn's roots, giving them a strong base on which to thrive next spring. In Zones 3 and 4, fertilize during the first half of the month, Zones 5 and 6 during the second half. Zones 7 and 8 can even wait until November.

Plan to fertilize just before the forecast calls for a day of light, steady rain. Apply 1 to 1½ pounds of actual nitrogen per 1,000 square feet. (2.2 pounds of sulfur-coated urea [45-0-0] or 6¼ to 8 pounds of a 16-percent nitrogen fertilizer). Use a slow-release fertilizer. Any unused nitrogen remains in the soil for the grass to use when the ground thaws.

TREES & SHRUBS

Follow the recommendations from September Fertilize (page 158). Most trees get sufficient nutrients from decomposing mulch, lawn fertilizers, and grass clippings left on the lawn.

PROBLEM-SOLVE

ALL

Continue weeding. Fall is the time many weeds set seed for next season's crop. Don't give weeds the chance to go to seed. Be sure to get out all the roots to prevent the weed from growing back. Spot spray with herbicide, if necessary.

Fall cleanup is one of the most important pest- and disease-management tools. Removing all insect- and disease-infested plant material now reduces the potential for problems next year. Destroy or discard any affected leaves on permanent plantings and the entire plant on others. Do not compost or send to recycling. You don't want to bring diseases and pests into the garden when you get free compost or mulch. Instead, throw the tainted material in a large black plastic bag and add it to your trash.

BULBS

Monitor tender bulbs in storage. Remove and discard or destroy any soft, discolored, or rotting bulbs.

Check on the chilling bulbs that you are forcing. Keep an eye out for mold or mildew on the soil. Often letting the soil dry a bit or moving the pot

■ *Squirrels and chipmunks love digging up and eating newly planted bulbs—but not when spiced with cayenne or other hot pepper.*

Squirrels are still stashing their nuts and bulbs in the lawn for safekeeping. Tamp down any disturbed areas. Enjoy all the surprises that appear in the lawn next spring.

ROSES

If you haven't already, remove and discard all mulch and fallen leaves within a 2- to 3-foot radius of any diseased rose. Pick any remaining leaves off the plant and destroy them as well as the old mulch.

TREES & SHRUBS

Monitor for cankerworm and apply sticky bands if needed. Leave them on until December. See March Problem-Solve (page 61) for detailed information.

Continue monitoring for gypsy moth egg masses, which appear like fuzzy, beige blotches on tree trunks. Scrape them into a plastic bag and throw it in the garbage.

■ *It's worth the time and effort to put hardware cloth around young trees and shrubs to ward off hungry winter pests.*

to another shelf of the refrigerator (humidity seems to vary) can clear up the problem.

Squirrels and chipmunks seem to appear from nowhere as soon as the bulbs go into the ground. Cayenne pepper or other repellents may provide some relief. Or plant bulbs in cages.

EDIBLES

Check every plant you bring indoors for any sign of pests. It's the ideal time to pot or repot herbs and other plants. Shake off most of the soil from the roots and then give them a quick shower in tepid water (slightly cool to the touch). Repot and separate them from houseplants for about three weeks. After that, if they are still clean, let them join the other plants.

LAWNS

If not otherwise controlled, creeping Charlie and other invasive weeds respond well to broadleaf herbicides applied after a hard frost. Spot treat to keep the use of chemicals to a minimum.

Start installing animal fencing around new plantings, fruit trees, euonymus, and other animal favorites. Place a 4-foot-tall cylinder of hardware cloth (reinforced wire screen) around these trees. Sink it several inches into the soil to keep voles and rabbits away from tree trunks.

Visit your favorite garden center and stock up on repellents if animals have been a problem in the past. Early applications, before feeding starts, appear to be more effective. Reapply repellents after harsh weather and as recommended on the label.

We talk about concepts like "before the first frost," "before a hard frost," and "after the ground has frozen." Local meteorologists keep you up to date on the first two—their predictions are quite accurate. But how do you know when the ground is frozen? Do you try to jab an ice pick into the soil—to what depth? The ground is considered frozen after a week of freezing temperatures. That's when the garden is officially asleep.

Does your rain gauge have the capacity for measuring snow? Consider getting a snow gauge; some are highly decorative. Put it on your holiday wish list. Or give one to a member of your household for everyone to enjoy. On a budget? Simplify and use an old-fashioned yardstick to measure snow depth.

If your winter landscape is dull and monochromatic, consider adding some colorful yard art. But that can be expensive (again, holiday wish list). An inexpensive alternative is to spray paint—bold and bright, pale and subdued, or holiday silver and gold—a few of the seedheads left standing. In future, let giant allium heads dry and leave them as winter decoration (painted or plain). They look like fireworks.

Keep the Japanese handsaw, loppers, and pruners sharp. Put them in a basket, bucket, or other container with sturdy gloves and twine so you don't have to hunt them down to do any winter pruning or retying necessary after storms, strong winds, snow, or ice break branches.

Be prepared. That seems to be the recurring theme for gardeners, especially in our region where the weather conditions can fluctuate wildly—from drought to flood, record-setting high temperatures to bone-chilling lows—seemingly overnight. The media feeds on these extremes and potential disasters (decimation from rose rosette disease and emerald ash borer). Because we were prepared, we thwarted potential problems large and small, often without realizing it.

As you get ready to give thanks this month, be aware of all that you accomplished and give yourself a pat on the back. When you sit down to your holiday meal, give thanks for the beauty and the bounty your garden bestowed on you.

PLAN

It is never too early to begin planning for next season. Take inventory of all your tools, seeds, and gardening equipment as you pack them away for winter storage. Start a list of replacements and what you'll need for next year. Do not forget to include those items you have always wanted but keep forgetting to buy. Remember, gift-giving (and receiving) season is coming.

Finish journal entries for this growing season. Once the snow flies and holidays arrive, it will be hard to remember the details of the past summer. Take a good look at each area of your garden as you finish putting it to bed. Note any changes and improvements you want to make. Amend your wish lists.

Be prepared for the first snow. Have your shovel and deicers at the ready. Consider investing in a snow blower if the snow regularly gets too deep to shovel. Or share the task with a neighbor who has one. An alternative is to hire a reliable person for snow removal. Be clear about when snow will be removed; many professionals will not come out if less than 2 inches of snow falls. Small snowfalls add up quickly and can be hazardous.

BULBS

Make a list of the people to whom you want to give forced bulbs during the holiday season. If you haven't started them, there's still time. See October, page 164, for directions on forcing paper white narcissus and spring-blooming bulbs.

EDIBLES

Start planning your garden for next year based on what you grew this year and where you grew it.

LAWNS

The work is about done, even though the grass keeps growing until the ground freezes. Though we do not see much happening, there is a lot growing underground. Take one last look at the lawn and evaluate its overall performance.

PERENNIALS & ORNAMENTAL GRASSES

You have spent the season enjoying the beauty of your garden. Continue doing this through winter, but think about the amount of time and effort you had to spend to keep the garden looking good. Decide if you want to cut back on parts of the garden, consolidate, or eliminate them.

ROSES

Review your master list and think about next year's garden. As life gets more hectic with the approaching end-of-year celebrations, take a moment to bring your new garden scheme to mind. Don't write it down yet; just visualize it as it will be with additions, subtractions, multiplications, and divisions. Roughly sketch it. Feel free to edit anytime; it's your garden and your fantasy.

TREES & SHRUBS

You can do a lot to maintain the health of your trees, but sometimes it may be necessary to call in a professional. See June Plan for tips on hiring a certified arborist.

PLANT

ALL

Do you still have container-grown hardy plants you haven't had time to get into the ground? This temporary solution will get them through winter. Plant them—pots and all—in a sheltered spot on your property. When spring comes, give them a proper planting in their chosen location.

ANNUALS & BIENNIALS

Store leftover seeds in their original packets. These contain all the plant and planting information you need. Store them in an airtight jar in the refrigerator to help to preserve the seeds' viability.

BULBS

For an instant bulb gift or a beautiful blooming decoration for your house, you can buy a crocus pot already planted with pre-cooled crocus corms. Often the side holes of a crocus pot are planted, yet the top is not. Plant five to seven corms there for an even more spectacular display. The

SUCCESSFUL GARDENING: ROTATING VEGETABLE FAMILIES

Some plants are heavy feeders, while others actually enrich the soil. Also, by rotating the plants growing in one area the first year to a new space the second year, and to yet another place the third year, you will have fewer pests and diseases than if you grew the same vegetables in the same place year after year. Grouping these plants by families makes it easier to know which crops should or shouldn't follow in succession. This is not critical if you are only growing one or two plants in the same family, but when you grow a "patch of tomatoes," be sure to plant something else there the following year. You will find that you will have more success with even a few tomato plants when you move them from year to year. Here's what to do and the reason why.

Here, members of the nightshade family (tomatoes, eggplants, and peppers) are grouped together; next year, pea family (legumes) will grow in that space.

Family Name	Vegetable Crops	Rotation Rationale
Amaryllis Family (*Amaryllidaceae*)	Onions, garlic, leeks, shallots, chives, scallions	Rotate with legumes; *never* plant in soil that contains uncomposted or non-decomposed organic matter
Carrot Family (*Apiaceae*)	Carrots, parsley, dill, fennel, coriander, celery	Moderate feeders; precede with any other plant family; amend soil with compost before planting; follow with heavy mulch or pea family
Gourd Family (*Cucurbitaceae*)	Cucumber, melons, squash, watermelon	Precede with winter rye or winter wheat for improved weed and insect control; follow with pea family
Grass Family (*Poaceae*)	Wheat, oats, rye, corn	Plant to control weeds and improve soil drainage; plant before nightshade or gourd family crops
Mustard Family (*Brassicaceae*)	Broccoli, Brussels sprouts, cabbage, cauliflower, kale, kohlrabi, radish, turnip	Require lots of soil maintenance; heavy feeders; precede with pea family, follow with compost
Nightshade Family (*Solanaceae*)	Eggplant, peppers, tomatoes, potatoes	Heavy feeders; have many fungal diseases and pests; precede with grass family, follow with pea family
Pea Family (*Fabaceae*)	Beans, peas (legumes)	Fixes nitrogen to the soil, adds to soil fertility; beneficial to soil with few pest problems; may be rotated alternately with any and all other garden crops

pre-cooled crocus will be flowering within two to three weeks. Simply water them three times a week. When the flowers start to open, keep the crocus pot in the coolest part of the room away from radiators or direct sun. You can prolong the bloom by moving the pot into a cooler room at night. When the flowers fade, water bulbs only once every two weeks. When the weather warms

SUCCESSFUL GARDENING: CELEBRATE WITH A LIVE CHRISTMAS TREE

Too often a live Christmas tree does not survive the holiday season. Follow these steps for success, and you will enjoy a beautiful new evergreen in your garden for years to come.

1. Start looking now for a local nursery or Christmas tree farm that sells living Christmas trees.
2. Find out if it is balled and burlapped or container grown. Balled-and-burlapped trees need a large container for indoor display.
3. Purchase a tree that meets both your landscape and holiday needs. Make sure the tree will tolerate the growing conditions and fit in the planting location once it reaches mature size.
4. Dig a hole big enough for the rootball. Roughen the sides with a shovel. Scrape the bottom to prevent glazing. Cover the hole with a board or fill it with woodchips. Store the soil from the hole under a tarp where it won't freeze.

Even a container-grown Christmas tree will not thrive indoors. Have a planting hole ready to move it into right after the holiday.

5. Keep the tree in a cool, protected area outdoors. Water often enough to keep the roots moist.
6. Move the tree inside to a cool location just before your holiday celebration. Place a container-grown tree on a large saucer and a balled-and-burlapped tree in a large tub. Keep the roots moist.
7. After a week to 10 days, move the tree to a screened-in porch or unheated garage for several weeks to allow it to adjust gradually to the colder outdoor temperatures. Any longer inside and the tree may break bud and begin growing. If the tree does start to grow, you will have an indoor evergreen tree to decorate for Valentine's Day, Easter, and May Day.
8. Plant, water, mulch, and shield from winter wind and sun. And keep your fingers crossed.

in spring, remove the bulbs from the pot and plant outside. They will lie dormant during summer and winter, and then bloom again in the garden for your enjoyment the following spring.

EDIBLES

Begin your winter break early—at least from outdoor planting.

If you want to grow lettuces and other salad greens in time for the holidays, start around the middle of the month. To have Thanksgiving greens, start on the first of the month, although that's cutting it close if Thanksgiving occurs earlier rather than later. Refer to January Plant (page 27) for complete directions on growing a salad garden indoors.

LAWNS

If you haven't already had a killing frost, you can still lay sod, providing you can find fresh-cut sod. See April Plant for instructions. Keep it well watered.

TREES & SHRUBS

Plant any remaining deciduous container-grown or balled-and-burlapped trees and shrubs as soon as possible so they can get established before the ground freezes.

SUCCESSFUL GARDENING: DON'T FIGHT THE SHADE

Hostas are versatile, shade-tolerant perennials ranging in leaf size from 2 inches to 2 feet with solid-colored and variegated leaves in hues of gold, green, and cream.

Are you tired of watching grass die in the shade of your house or Norway maple? Grow one of the many shade-tolerant groundcovers instead. They provide an attractive solution to this problem. Consider plants with variegated leaves, which brighten up the shade and provide color all season long. Deadnettle grows well in the dry shade found under many large shade trees. Use one or more of the many colorful hostas to liven up the shade.

Canadian ginger thrives under spruce and pine trees. It tolerates the heavy shade and grows right through the evergreen needle mulch. The attractive leaves provide texture throughout the season.

Do not forget the flowers. Vinca (periwinkle), moneywort, deadnettle, and epimedium flower in shade. This seasonal flash of color is something your languishing lawn could never provide.

Sometimes an area is just too densely shaded for even these groundcovers grow. It's okay to quit fighting the shade and give in to nature. Use woodchips or twice-shredded bark around trees. Or strategically place flagstone steppers in heavily shaded areas. Allow moss to grow and call it a moss garden.

CARE

ALL

Finish soil preparation as the last few leaves drop and before the ground freezes.

Finish the fall cleanup and protect plants from the coming winter weather.

Finish raking leaves out of beds and off the lawn. Norway maples and Callery pears are reluctant to give in to winter. Some oaks hold onto their leaves and don't shed them until spring. Don't send the leaves to the landfill or even to the municipal compost facility. Use them! Run over them with a mower (oak and other large, tough leaves may require several passes). After the ground freezes, use them to mulch new bulb plantings. Mix them into the soil for new beds. Include them when making a no-dig bed (see September Plan page 149 for more information). Add them to the compost pile for brown matter. If you still have any left, start a leaf-mold pile. Rake up the leaves into a pile (3 feet square is ideal), moisten, and let them slowly decompose. By spring or summer, you'll have rich organic matter that's an excellent soil amendment and mulch.

When you have an overabundance of fall leaves, make a bin of chicken wire and pile them in. They'll slowly decompose into rich, composted leaf mold.

Remove and destroy leaves around any pest- or disease-infected plant.

Clean and sharpen garden tools before storing them for winter. See January Care for details.

Gather fertilizers, herbicides, and pesticides from sheds and unheated garages. Inventory and store them in a secure, dark, dry, frost-free location away from pets and children.

ANNUALS & BIENNIALS

If you have had a hard frost, most annuals are dead. Pull them up, shake the soil from their roots, and add them to your compost pile. Do not add any that had pests or diseases (powdery mildew). Destroy or discard those. Pansies should still be green; leave them and any other plants that are still alive.

Check on geraniums and other annuals in dormant storage. Move plants to a cooler, darker location if they begin to grow. If growth continues, pot them up and move them to a sunny window or under artificial lights.

BULBS

Continue to dig and store tender bulbs including cannas, caladiums, dahlias, calla lilies, and gladiolus after the first frost. See September Care for detailed instructions.

Put a 2- to 4-inch layer of mulch (evergreen branches or straw) over fall-planted bulbs after the ground has frozen. The mulch helps maintain a consistent soil temperature and keeps bulbs from heaving out of the ground during winter's alternate spells of freezing and thawing.

HERE'S HOW

TO FORCE PAPERWHITE NARCISSUS

These tender *Narcissus* are not hardy outdoors (except Zone 8) and do not need a chilling period to bloom. There are two way of forcing them—in soil and without it. You can simply plant the bulbs in potting soil with the top just above the surface. Water well and keep the soil evenly moist. Place the pot in a sunny window. Flowers appear within four to six weeks. Or grow them in the traditional way—in gravel, stone, sand, marbles, or other material that anchors the roots.

■ *The fragrance of this elegant centerpiece— paperwhites forced in a shallow bowl—can be overwhelming. Move them away at mealtimes.*

1. Use a shallow, decorative container *without* a drainage hole.
2. Place the bulbs so that the lower third of the bulb is covered with gravel or whatever material you are using.
3. Add water to a level of the base of the bulb. Place the pot in a sunny window. Give the pot a quarter turn daily to keep stems from leaning toward the light.
4. Check the bulbs twice a day. Add enough water to keep the base of the bulb and roots submerged. As the roots grow, if they push the bulb up out of the anchor material, add more gravel to surround the roots and hold them firm.
5. When flower buds appear, you can speed up or slow down the blooming process by moving the pot to a warmer or cooler area. To prolong bloom once the flowers have opened, keep them in a cool room when they aren't on display.
6. Once they have finished blooming, add them to the compost pile. All their energy has been spent.
7. For gift-giving, tie a pretty ribbon around the stems when they are at least 3 inches high, and attach a care card.

Mulch lilies and hyacinths with 3 inches of organic matter (leaf mold, chopped leaves, compost, or well-rotted manure) as soon as the ground freezes.

■ *No need to give a pre-planted crocus pot in full bloom. The recipient will get weeks to enjoy the bulbs starting to grow and then flower.*

EDIBLES

Cut any vegetables and herbs that are still left. Cut leaves of perennial herbs, such as sage, thyme, and oregano, to dry or freeze for winter use. Continue to clean up your garden as neighbors' leaves blow into it.

Wait until after the first frost to pick Brussels sprouts; cold enhances their flavor. Starting at the base of the plant, twist or cut off only as many sprouts as you need at a time. The garden provides free refrigeration for the rest. And, most of us don't have enough refrigerator space for even one stalk of sprouts, much less several.

Kale also benefits from a frost. Extend the harvest by picking only as many outer leaves as you need at a time. As long as the temperature is around 40 degrees Fahrenheit, it will keep producing more leaves at the center of the plant. Even when the mercury

HERE'S HOW

■ *Even if you can't easily take apart your hand pruners, they— and your plants—will benefit from a good sharpening.*

TO SHARPEN HAND PRUNERS

Hand pruners need a little more TLC than hoes or shovels.

1. Take the pruners apart for easier sharpening.
2. Replace nicked, damaged, or old blades that can no longer be sharpened. You can get replacement blades for high-quality pruners, while cheaper pruners must be thrown away when damaged. You can find replacement blades through online and mail-order garden supply catalogs as well as some garden centers.
3. Use a three-cornered (tapered) metal file to sharpen the cutting edge of your hand pruners. Sharpen away from the blade for safety or toward the cutting edge. Just be careful.
4. Smooth off any burrs that form along the edge. Make a test cut to check for sharpness.
5. Clean the blades with a lightweight oil. Spray to lubricate the working parts and prevent rust.

falls below freezing, you can still cut kale. It will deteriorate if there are extended rainy periods or when snow intermittently thaws on the leaves.

Pick a few branches from your indoor rosemary plant to flavor your Thanksgiving stuffing. Chop up a few fresh sage and parsley leaves and mix them into the stuffing for an authentic flavor. They taste so much better than dried, powdered spices in a tin or bottle.

Keep checking the tomatoes ripening indoors every couple of days. Remove any bad or overripe ones immediately. To hasten ripening, put a few in a brown paper bag with an apple. Close the bag, and lay it on its side so the fruits don't touch. The ethylene gas that the apple gives off encourages fast ripening. You may have noticed that when you have apples in the refrigerator, other fruits and vegetables will spoil faster than normal.

LAWNS

If the lawn is still growing, keep mowing.

Shred leaves with the mower the next time you cut the grass. You may need to make several passes with the mower to chop up thick layers of large leaves like Norway maple and oak. As long as you can see the grass blades, the lawn will be fine. In fact, the leaves add nutrients and organic matter to the soil. This is a great way to improve the soil while reducing time spent on lawn care.

Make the last mowing of the season short—1½ to 2 inches—just before a hard frost.

PERENNIALS & ORNAMENTAL GRASSES

Every three to four years, topdress perennials with 2 to 3 inches of organic matter (compost, leaf mold, shredded leaves, and humus).

After the ground has frozen, add a layer of mulch (or use evergreen boughs) over shallow-rooted plants to prevent them from heaving out of the ground during thawing and refreezing.

Finish cleanup and enjoy the winter interest that ornamental grasses add to the garden.

ROSES

Top off soil mounds around roses at about a foot. It may look strange—a broad cone of soil with rose canes sticking up. In Zone 4 and below (and for any success with hybrid teas), cover the frozen mound with leaves. Cover any new plant completely or the extreme cold will kill the tender canes. If you live in an area with little winter snow cover,

HERE'S HOW

TO WINTERIZE YOUR LAWNMOWER

Once mowing is done for the year, winterizing the mower is the last task you need to perform for your lawn. Come spring, fill it with gas and it'll be ready to go.

■ *Safety comes first when working near the lawnmower blade—wear heavy-duty gloves.*

1. Add fuel stabilizer to the tank. Run the mower for several minutes to distribute it through the system. Turn the mower off and let the engine cool. Siphon the gas into a clean gas can for winter storage. Start the mower and run it until it stops; repeat until the engine no longer starts.
2. Disconnect the spark plug.
3. Detach the blade. Wear thick gloves when handling the blade to avoid injury.
4. If the mower has a four-cycle engine, drain the oil. This isn't necessary in two-cycle engines where oil is mixed with the gas.
5. Scrape off the grass and mud caked on the mower deck with a putty knife and brush.
6. Sharpen the blade and reattach it.
7. Fill the oil tank with fresh SAE 30 or 30-weight oil.
8. Change the air filter.
9. Remove and replace the spark plug.
10. Store the mower in the garage for winter.

add 6 inches of mulch (shredded leaves are good) around the roses to reduce the freeze/heave cycle that can damage the plants. It doesn't hurt to mulch hardy roses, such as the Canadian Explorer and Griffith Buck roses, in Zones 4 and colder if you have relatively dry winters.

In case of a heavy, wet snow, use a soft broom to gently brush the snow off exposed branches and canes, especially on climbers and any tall roses. Get out and brush it before too much accumulates, or you risk both broken canes and supports. However, don't try to remove *frozen* snow; this could cause greater damage.

TREES & SHRUBS

If you haven't already, move aboveground planters to an enclosed porch or unheated garage for winter. If they are too heavy to move, insulate the plants by surrounding the pots with bales of straw.

Apply winter protection to shrubs before heavy snows arrive. Give special attention to rhododendrons, boxwood, and other broadleaf evergreens. These plants are susceptible to sunburn from reflected snow. Use a screen of burlap to cut the winter winds and shade the plants from the winter sun. Or circle the plants with a cylinder of hardware cloth several feet tall and sunk several inches into the ground. Fill with straw or evergreen branches to protect the plants.

■ *When winterizing roses, continue to add several inches of soil to the mound as the layer below freezes. Top off at about 12 inches.*

Upright junipers and arborvitae are easily damaged by heavy snow. Wrap the plants by loosely tying the stems up with strips of cloth or old stockings.

There are anti-desiccant products that protect plants against winterkill, windburn, drought, and transplant shock. They help broadleaf (and other) evergreens retain moisture and keep them from drying out from winter's bitter cold, dryness, and harsh wind. Spray it on the leaves following the package instructions.

Continue to prune trees and shrubs now or wait until late winter for structural and major pruning. Prune only for damage repair. See Appendix for detailed information on pruning.

VINES & GROUNDCOVERS

Gently rake or blow the last of the fall leaves off groundcover plantings. Maple, oak, and other large leaves trap moisture and block sunlight from reaching groundcovers. This can lead to crown rot and other fungal diseases.

WATER

ALL

Continue to water all outdoor plantings thoroughly if the ground is not frozen. Before the ground freezes, give them all a soaking to wet the top 6 to 8 inches of soil.

Shut off the valves to outside water spigots. You can put a Styrofoam form around the spigot and knob to protect it from freezing—a good idea if you water during winter.

Drain water from all hoses and loosely coil them after the final watering. Move them to a cool (above freezing), dry storage space.

ANNUALS & BIENNIALS

Water overwintering indoor annuals thoroughly when the top 2 inches of soil begin to dry.

BULBS

Keep crocus and other fall-planted bulbs lightly moist until the ground freezes. Check moisture and water levels on all the bulbs you are forcing.

EDIBLES

Take care not to overwater the indoor plants. Don't let them sit in a saucer of water.

LAWNS

If the ground has not yet frozen, keep the soil surface moist under newly laid sod. Continue to water thoroughly, but less frequently, once the sod is rooted into the soil below.

Water established lawns if they show signs of wilting (see page 141, August Water for a full description).

VINES & GROUNDCOVERS

Water pots stored outdoors and in the garage whenever the soil is thawed and dry.

Check indoor plants several times a week. When the top 2 to 3 inches start to dry, water thoroughly until the excess runs out the bottom. Pour out any water that collects in the saucer.

FERTILIZE

ALL

Take a soil test now if you did not get around to it last month. Test soil every three to five years, or whenever soil conditions change or plant problems develop.

Store fertilizers in a cool (above freezing), dark, dry place. Consider storing them with chemicals in an area that is safe from children and pets.

ANNUALS & BIENNIALS

Overwintering plants do not need any fertilizer until they adjust to their new location and are actively growing. Use a dilute solution only if plants show signs of nutrient deficiency.

BULBS

When the amaryllis starts to bloom, feed it with half-strength liquid fertilizer.

EDIBLES

There's nothing to feed this month except you at Thanksgiving.

LAWNS

Didn't apply fertilizer in October? There is still time if the ground hasn't frozen. Fertilize just before the forecast calls for a day of light, steady rain. Apply 1 to 1½ pounds of actual nitrogen per 1,000 square feet (2.2 pounds of sulfur-coated urea [45-0-0], or 6¼ to 8 pounds of a 16-percent nitrogen fertilizer). Use a slow-release fertilizer. Any unused nitrogen remains in the soil for the grass to use when the ground thaws.

VINES & GROUNDCOVERS

Like the annuals overwintering indoors, tender vines being overwintered need to adjust to their new location and light. Once they are actively growing, feed any stunted vines with a dilute solution of fertilizer for flowering houseplants.

PROBLEM-SOLVE

ALL

Look for signs of animal damage. Droppings, tracks, and feeding damage are clues you need to address the problem. Use repellents to keep deer and rabbits away. Reapply after bad weather or as recommended by the label directions.

Watch for voles. These small rodents are active all winter. They scurry across the turf and under the snow in search of seeds, bark, and roots to eat. Protect trees and shrubs from these critters. Lawn damage can be repaired in the spring.

ANNUALS & BIENNIALS

Check plants for fungus gnats, mites, aphids, scale, and whiteflies. Fungus gnats do not hurt plants, but are a nuisance, feeding on organic matter in the soil such as dead plant roots and peat moss. Often mistaken for fruit flies, they flit throughout the house. Keeping the soil slightly drier than normal will reduce the population. Use sticky yellow traps to lure fungus gnats and whiteflies.

Aphids, mites, and whiteflies suck plant juices, causing leaves to yellow and brown. Signs of infestation are poor growth and a clear sticky substance (honeydew) on the leaves. Several minutes in a strong shower (cover the soil with aluminum foil) in water that is slightly cool to the touch can wash off the offenders. For good measure, repot the plant in a clean pot and new soil just in case any insects were in the soil.

Control aphids and mites with insecticidal soap. Check the label before mixing and applying this or any other chemical. See January Problem-Solve (page 33) for directions for making your own soap solution. Spray the upper and lower surfaces of leaves and stems. Repeat weekly until these pests are under control.

Whiteflies can stress and stunt plants. These insects multiply quickly and are much harder to control. Try trapping whiteflies with commercial yellow sticky traps available at hardware stores, garden centers, and home-improvement stores. Or make your own using yellow cardboard and a sticky pine resin commercial product—even cooking or motor oil will work. Whiteflies are attracted by the yellow color, stick there, and die. Although this won't get rid of all whiteflies, it reduces the populations enough to minimize stress to plants. Whiteflies are difficult to control with pesticides. It's safer for you, your children, and pets not to use chemical pesticides indoors.

BULBS
Check stored bulbs for any sign of rot or disease; discard if any are affected.

EDIBLES
Keep an eye on the indoor plants for any signs of pest or disease. See this month's Problem-Solve, Annuals for more information and treatment options.

PERENNIALS & ORNAMENTAL GRASSES
Monitor for animal and rodent damage. Fall cleanup may help reduce the damage.

Chipmunks and squirrels can damage perennials by digging up plants and leaving the roots exposed to cold winter temperatures. There is not much you can do when the plants are buried in the snow. Next year, plan ahead and try to prevent the damage.

ROSES
If a climber breaks free of its support, tie it back with an old pair of pantyhose. It's not the most aesthetically pleasing look, but pantyhose provide more support than a narrow piece of string or a twist-tie. In addition, they give and stretch so you don't have to worry about the cane being girdled.

TREES & SHRUBS
Finish installing animal protection. A 4-foot-high cylinder of hardware cloth around the trunk of new and thin-barked trees will reduce the risk of rabbit and vole damage. To keep the voles out, sink the bottom few inches into the ground before it freezes.

Place snow fencing around desirable plants. A 5-foot fence around a small area will often keep out the deer. Make sure they cannot reach in and feed.

Apply repellents to plantings that are favored by deer and rabbits. All young trees as well as fruit trees, ornamental plums, and euonymus are a few of their favorites. Start before feeding begins. This encourages them to go elsewhere for dinner. Reapply after heavy rains or as specified on label directions.

Use burlap, fencing, or other structures to protect plants from roadway salts. A physical barrier can keep the salt off the plants and reduce damage.

Continue to monitor for cankerworm and apply sticky bands if needed. Leave cankerworm sticky traps in place until December. See March Problem-Solve (page 61) for details.

Monitor for egg masses of gypsy moths and tent caterpillars. Remove and destroy as soon as you find them.

VINES & GROUNDCOVERS
Protect plantings from voles and rabbits. Place a cylinder of hardware cloth around euonymus and other susceptible vines. Sink it several inches into the soil. Make sure it is at least 4 feet tall to discourage rabbits.

Spray susceptible vines and groundcovers, such as cranberry cotoneaster, with a homemade or commercial repellent. Repeat throughout the season.

December

Instead of visions of sugarplums dancing in your head, lull yourself to sleep with visions of gardens. Pull out photos and videos (of your own garden and ones you visited) and look at them before you go to sleep. Google images of famous gardens here and abroad: Chanticleer and Dumbarton Oaks on the East Coast; The Huntington and the myriad gardens of Portland on the West Coast; Denver Botanic Garden, Minnesota Landscape Arboretum, Missouri Botanical Garden, and Chicago Botanic Garden in between. Pop in on Great Dixter and Sissinghurst Castle Garden in England, Villandry in France, The Alhambra Gardens in Spain, and Canada's Butchart Gardens. Sleep on them, and in the following days and weeks, you will find that these gardens provide colorful inspirations for your garden in plant combinations and overall design. Make notes and sketches as you envision changes and new ideas.

Ask Santa for a good insect identification book. Tell him you want a book that shows both the good bugs and the bad bugs in all their life stages. After reading this book during winter, you'll be familiar with the most likely candidates to visit or take up residence in your garden in the upcoming seasons. This will allow you to make informed decisions on if and how you want to deal with them.

You encouraged birds in your garden during the growing year, so don't abandon them now. Birds always need fresh water. Get a heater for the birdbath to keep it from freezing over. Plan on giving them some holiday treats. Tie half a bagel to a string, cover it with peanut butter and hang it nearby. Other "tweet" treats to hang include a pinecone rolled in a mixture of peanut butter and birdseed or suet mixed with birdseed, raisins, or other small pieces of dried fruit. Melt the suet slowly in a saucepan over low heat, add the birdseed, fruit or nuts (or a mixture of all). Stir well. As it cools, form it into whatever shape you want, either freehand or using an ice cream or chocolate mold for form. Wrap it with mesh and hang it outdoors for your fine feathered friends.

PLAN

ALL

Relax, enjoy the holidays, and finish taking notes on the past growing season. Gather photos, videos, plant tags, landscape plans, and your journal. Reflect on the old year and plan for the new one.

Take advantage of the holidays to extend your garden season and share it with others. 'Tis the season for giving: Make bouquets and arrangements with the flowers you have been drying. Add a beautiful ribbon as a finishing touch. Mat and frame your best photos. Friends, neighbors, and relatives appreciate pictures of their own gardens and unique views of plants (think close-ups).

Garden planning often gets lost in the chaos of the holiday preparations. Make your holiday wish list of garden-related things you want—large and small to accommodate everyone's budgets. Suggestions: seeds; harvest basket; new journal; plant labels (copper or metal ones for perennials, trees, and shrubs); tools (good hand pruners, shovel, spade, ergonomic snow shovel); books; memberships to botanic gardens or arboreta; equipment (lawnmower, snow blower, drop-spreader); clothing (long gloves

■ *Even though they aren't hardy (except in Zone 8), dahlias are worth growing for their impressively lively show in late summer.*

to protect your arms in the rose garden, convertible pants that zip off at knee, gardening hat); gift certificate for your favorite (local and online) nurseries, garden centers, and home-improvement stores; and anything else garden related.

SUCCESSFUL GARDENING: ORGANIZING TOOLS

After sharpening your hand pruners and other cutting tools, consider painting the handles a nice bright color. Not only will this help you to see them, it enables you to find the necessary tools easily.

Take this a step further, and paint all the handles in a color code. Group the tools in the way that is most logical to you. For instance, put all the digging tools together, the lawn tools, the hand tools, and so on. A new garden helper can quickly help you if you ask for the purple-handled tools instead of naming and describing each one.

When tools have brightly colored handles, it's unlikely that you'll lose another pair of pruners, a trowel, or hand fork in the garden again. It may cut down on accidents too; you should see the rake's bright handle before you step on the tines, causing the handle to knock you in the head.

■ *Garden tools seem to disappear in the garden. Tools with brightly colored handles stand out so they're easy to spot.*

Consider some of the items on your holiday wish list as gifts for others.

ANNUALS & BIENNIALS

As you review your journal and photos, start your wish list for next year—seeds and plants as well as seed-starting supplies you may need, such as flats, containers, soilless mixes, and lights).

BULBS

Dahlias should be a mainstay for every garden. Once planted, they are easy to grow, especially if you're content with a nice bushy plant and are not trying to grow giant, exhibition-sized dahlias.

Since dahlias come in an array of colors, forms, and sizes, it's easy to find at least one for every garden. They range in size from small mum-like flowers to the 12-inch dinner plate varieties in almost every color of the rainbow (except for the ever-elusive blue) including exquisite bi- and tricolors. With several different kinds of dahlias, you can, depending on the weather, have blooms from July right up to the first frost. Plan to add dahlias to your garden.

EDIBLES

Many longtime organic gardeners and immigrants who bring their gardening traditions with them steadfastly believe that plants are healthier and yields are greater when they are planted in sync with the moon. Although this has not been scientifically proven or disproven, it adds an interesting twist to planning the garden. The premise is based on the great influence that the moon exerts on the earth, as evidenced by the pull of the tides. It's easy to remember; plant annuals that produce their yield (flowers, vegetables, and fruit) above the ground during the increasing light from the new moon to full moon. From full moon to new moon, during the decreasing light, plant biennials, perennials, bulbs, trees, shrubs and annuals which produce their yield (such as potatoes, beets, turnips— the root crops) underground.

■ *Many culinary herbs have colorful edible flowers, such as the purples of Thai basil, anise hyssop, and lavender, accented with yellow dill.*

Consider the colors of herb flowers when you are planning the garden. Although the leaves generally get the attention—in hues of green—the flowers add interest and a range of colors:

- Blue to purple: borage, lavender, rosemary, and sage
- Pink to lavender: anise hyssop, chives, marjoram, mint, oregano, and thyme
- Red: beebalm, nasturtium, and pineapple sage
- White: basil, chamomile, garlic chives, sweet woodruff, and thyme
- Yellow to orange: calendula, dill, fennel, mustard, nasturtium, and safflower

PERENNIALS & ORNAMENTAL GRASSES

How does the garden look as it transitions into winter? Look for perennials like yucca, with its spiky leaves, that have year-round architectural form. Consider adding more ornamental grasses for winter interest at varying heights.

TREES & SHRUBS

Look out your windows and take a look at your trees and shrubs. Do they provide nice scenery as you gaze outside? Growth habit, bark color, and fruit can all add color and interest to the winter landscape. To some, Harry Lauder's walking stick and Japanese maples are more eye-catching when their branches are bare, revealing their form. Note areas in the garden that are large enough to accommodate a tree or shrub and need some winter interest.

PLANT

BULBS

Continue to plant paperwhites and amaryllis. See November Plant for detailed instructions for growing paperwhites. They are perfect last-minute hostess and holiday gifts to have on hand.

To avoid the inevitable post-holiday letdown, plant some paperwhites for yourself.

It seems that people either love or hate paperwhites. Their fragrance is intense; 'Ziva' has the mildest

scent. Avoid putting blooming plants in the kitchen or dining room, as their perfume can overwhelm the wonderful cooking aromas.

EDIBLES

Unless you want more salad greens, take a holiday from planting.

ROSES

Although it's too late in the season to plant roses, it's the perfect time plant the *idea* by giving roses as gifts to friends and family. Order a miniature rose (usually packaged in a cute container) for immediate pleasure, or give a gift certificate to a nursery, mail-order, or online rose company. Make the certificate "good for one rose" rather than a dollar amount, if you can. If there is a special rose that you know the person wants or that you want him/her to have, make the certificate specific "good for one 'Prairie Princess' rose," for example.

An alternative is fresh or dried roses. As elegant as fresh roses can be, they won't last long. Consider an arrangement of dried roses in a special container, a dried wreath with roses to hang indoors, or a pot or hanging sachet of dried rose buds. If you're creative and handy with a glue gun, you can make them yourself. Otherwise, you will find rose gifts in many of the plant and garden online sites or the catalogs that are filling your mailbox.

TREES & SHRUBS

Plant your live Christmas tree as soon after the holidays as possible. Make sure you dig the planting hole before the ground freezes. See November Plan.

CARE

ALL

Make sure all liquid, granular, and powdered chemicals (fertilizer, pesticides, and herbicides) are stored in a secure, cool (above freezing), dark, dry location away from pets and children.

Collect the old products you no longer use. Store the unwanted materials together safely and plan to dispose of them at the household hazardous waste site nearest you next spring. Some municipalities

■ *The first big snow is magical, transforming the drab gray-and-brown garden into a sparkling fantasy, highlighting Japanese maple's form.*

have spring cleanup days when they provide convenient drop-off sites in neighborhoods.

Snow is nature's mulch. So if you have not yet mulched any outdoor areas that need it (plants that are semi-hardy, newly planted bulbs, shallow-rooted perennials that may heave during periods of thawing and refreezing), relax and let the snow be your mulch. When (if) it starts to melt, add evergreen boughs or mulch (compost, chopped leaves, shredded bark, or other organic matter).

ANNUALS & BIENNIALS
Check on geraniums and other annuals in dormant storage. Move plants to a cooler, darker location if they begin to grow. If growth continues, pot them up and move them to a sunny window or under artificial lights.

BULBS
Tie a colorful ribbon around the stems or foliage of all gift plants. It gives them a professional appearance and supports the foliage.

Tidy up any gift plants. If there is very loose skin on paperwhites, remove it. Clean the outsides and rims of pots.

If the ground had not yet frozen and you did not mulch fall-planted outdoor bulbs last month, apply a 2- to 4-inch layer of mulch (evergreen branches or straw) after the ground has frozen. The mulch helps maintain a consistent soil temperature and keeps bulbs from heaving out of the ground when it thaws and refreezes.

Mulch lilies and hyacinths with 3 inches of organic matter (leaf mold, chopped leaves, compost, or well-rotted manure) as soon as the ground freezes.

EDIBLES
Continue to harvest kale, Brussels sprouts, and any other vegetables and herbs still in the garden. See November Care for details.

SUCCESSFUL GARDENING: USING INDOOR HERBS

Make use of the herbs you're growing indoors:

- Add chopped herbs to marinades for meat, poultry, or fish.
- Cut up some chives and toss them into a salad.
- Pretend it's summer. Buy some fresh mozzarella cheese. Cut slices of several of the tomatoes you have been ripening inside. Make a white, red, and green ring (Caprese salad) by overlapping a slice of cheese with a slice of tomato, and then a large basil leaf. Repeat until you have a ring of the desired size. Drizzle with extra virgin olive oil and balsamic vinegar. What a festive start for a holiday meal!
- Stuff a sprig or two of rosemary (or thyme) under the skin when roasting a chicken.
- Make herbal bath salts by infusing lavender, basil, or even rosemary (use whole branches rather than just the leaves) in a mixture of 2 parts sea salt, 1 part dried milk powder, and 3 tablespoons of Epsom salts. Place the stems in a glass jar, and pour in the salt mixture. Cover tightly and store it in a dark place for about a month. Open the jar, remove the herbs and sniff; you don't want to be overwhelmed with fragrance, you want a lilt of perfume. If the scent is too strong, add proportional amounts of dried milk powder and salt until you get just the right fragrance for you. Add 1 or 2 tablespoons under the faucet when running your bath. Bath salts make a wonderful holiday gift; put them in a fancy bottle or jar with a big bow.

■ *Use the basil growing on the windowsill and tomatoes ripening inside to make a summery Caprese salad with fresh mozzarella.*

■ *Road sanding wreaks havoc on nearby plants, spraying them with salt and chemical deicers. Make a note to water the plants well in spring to wash the chemicals away.*

LAWNS

Salt and deicers spread on drives, sidewalks, and walkways get on adjacent lawns and harm them. Cut down on the amount of salt/deicer you use by first shoveling the driveway, sidewalk, and other surfaces.

To cut down on potential damage to plants, spread the deicer from the center of the walkway and avoid applying it along the edges.

Consider switching to a non-salt deicer like magnesium chloride or calcium magnesium acetate (CMA), which cause less damage to the lawn and plantings. For traction only, non-clumping kitty litter, sand, or turkey grit works well.

Clean and store your mower if you have not done so already (see details in November Care).

PERENNIALS & ORNAMENTAL GRASSES

Finish garden cleanup.

Once the ground has frozen, add a layer of mulch (or use evergreen boughs) over shallow-rooted plants to prevent them from heaving out of the ground during thawing and refreezing.

ROSES

If you haven't topped off the winter protection, continue as detailed on page 178 in November Care).

If snow or ice damages rose canes, prune them back as soon as you can. If you need to cut back to the main cane, graft, or root, leave about an inch of cane to allow the cut to heal properly.

TREES & SHRUBS

Clean and pack away the tools—another planting season is over. While storing your tools, do a quick inventory. Remember the holidays are coming and gardening tools would make a great gift to give—or receive.

■ *Holiday wreaths and swags are expensive. Make your own with evergreen cuttings, dried berries, and fruit from the garden.*

Finish applying winter protection to shrubs before the heavy snows arrive. See November Care (page 179) for details.

Continue to prune trees and shrubs now or wait until late winter for structural and major pruning. See Appendix for detailed information on pruning.

Do not prune evergreens now; wait until spring.

Cut a few of these for indoor or holiday decorating or wreath making: colorful branches (redleaf rose, red twig and yellow twig dogwoods); evergreen boughs (arborvitae, Austrian or Scotch pine, blue spruce, Canada hemlock, Eastern red cedar, firs, junipers, and yews); and fruiting or berried branches (bittersweet, bayberry, cotoneaster, crabapples, euonymus, hawthorn, snowberry, sumac, viburnum, and winterberry). Gather nuts and seed capsules (acorns, black walnut, hazelnuts, and sweetgum) to glue on for added interest.

Be careful when hanging holiday lights on trees and shrubs outside. Always use lights UL listed for outdoor use.

Loosely attach lights to the tree branches and trunks. Remove lights in spring before growth begins. Tightly wrapped lights can girdle a tree in one season. Use a sturdy ladder and work with a buddy. Or consider hiring a professional. Many landscape companies now install lights and other holiday decor. They have the equipment and training to do the job safely.

Move live Christmas trees inside to a cool location *just before* your holiday celebration. Place a container-grown tree on a large saucer and a balled-and-burlapped one in a large tub. Keep roots moist.

After a week to 10 days, move the tree to a screened-in porch or unheated garage for several weeks to allow it to adjust to the cold outdoor temperatures. Any longer inside and the tree may break bud and begin growing. If the tree does start to grow, you will have an indoor evergreen tree to decorate for Valentine's Day, Easter, and May Day.

VINES & GROUNDCOVERS

After the holidays, recycle your cut tree as a windbreak or to provide shade for tender and evergreen vines that would suffer leaf burn.

Once the ground has frozen, cover European ginger and other semi-hardy groundcovers with evergreen boughs.

VINES & GROUNDCOVERS

Water pots stored outdoors and in the garage whenever the soil is thawed and dry.

Check indoor plants several times a week. When the top 2 to 3 inches start to dry, water thoroughly until the excess runs out the bottom. Pour out any water that collects in the saucer.

WATER

ALL

Outdoor watering is usually not needed—if the ground has frozen. However, if the ground has not yet frozen, before it does freeze, give all beds and plants a soaking to wet the top 6 to 8 inches of soil.

Once the ground freezes, pack away the garden hose. Drain the water from the hose and loosely coil it. Move it to a cool (above freezing), dry storage space.

Turn off the water or insulate outside faucets to prevent freezing.

ANNUALS & BIENNIALS

Water overwintering indoor annuals thoroughly when the top 2 inches of soil begin to dry. Do not allow any water to remain in the saucer.

BULBS

Check all the bulbs you are forcing and water when necessary.

EDIBLES

Don't overwater or let plants sit in a saucer of water.

LAWNS

If the ground has not frozen, following the watering regime described in November Water, (page 180).

TREES & SHRUBS

Check the soil moisture in aboveground planters. Water planters anytime the soil thaws and dries.

FERTILIZE

ALL

Review soil tests and make a list of fertilizer and soil amendment needs. Make a note on next year's calendar so that you will not forget to implement your soil improvement plans.

ANNUALS & BIENNIALS

Foliar feed with fish emulsion or kelp (following package instructions) any plants that are actively growing *and* showing signs of nutrient deficiencies.

LAWNS

Do not fertilize frozen lawns. Winter rains and melting snow can wash the fertilizer off the frozen soil surfaces and into our waterways.

PROBLEM-SOLVE

ANNUALS & BIENNIALS

Monitor plants for fungus gnats, mites, aphids, scale, and whiteflies. See January Problem-Solve (page 32) for detailed description and controls.

BULBS

Check summer-blooming bulbs in storage for any sign of rot. If you do find rot in bulbs stored in sawdust or other material, examine all the bulbs carefully and feel for any soft spots. Throw out any bad bulbs. Discard the storage medium and replace it with fresh material.

EDIBLES

Keep a watchful eye out for intruders on your indoor plants; often a strong shower of tepid—not cold or hot—water will do the trick. See January Problem-Solve (page 32) for detailed description of pests and controls.

■ *Gypsy moth egg masses (seen below the female moth) persist on tree trunks though the winter. Scrape them off and destroy them.*

PERENNIALS & ORNAMENTAL GRASSES

Continue to monitor for animal and rodent damage.

TREES & SHRUBS

If not already done, install animal fencing as described in November Problem-Solve, (page 181).

Use repellents for deer, rabbits, squirrels, and other four-legged pests. An early application, before feeding starts, appears to be most effective. Reapply repellents after harsh weather and as recommended on the label.

Continue to monitor for cankerworm and apply sticky bands if needed. See March Problem-Solve (page 61) for detailed information.

Continue to scout and destroy egg masses of tent caterpillars, tussock moths, and gypsy moths.

VINES & GROUNDCOVERS

Finish installing vole and rabbit protection around susceptible plants. See November Problem-Solve (page 181) for details.

SUCCESSFUL GARDENING: TRUMPET VINE AND WISTERIA

Another season ends and once again your trumpet vine or wisteria did not flower. Here are some tips to get it blooming.

- Be patient. Both of these hardy vines need to reach maturity to flower—three to five years old.
- Keep these rampant growers under control. Prune them back to several buds beyond the main framework.
- Check the growing conditions. Make sure the plant is in full sun.
- Avoid high-nitrogen fertilizers that encourage leaf growth and discourage flowers.
- As a last resort, root prune. Use a sharp shovel and slice through a few roots. Do this in one or two locations several feet from the trunk. Do not cut the roots all the way around the plant. This can injure the plant.
- Enjoy the flowers when they come. Be sure these vines have a support that is sturdy enough to hold them. Consider making a pergola—a good winter DIY project.

Pruning

Pruning is intimidating to many, but don't be afraid of killing a plant; it is tough. In fact, pruning is essential to plant health and beauty. Through pruning, you control growth and encourage the best performance (shape, form, flowering, and fruiting) from woody plants—trees, shrubs, roses, and perennial vines. *Note:* Do not paint pruning cuts. Research shows that plants will heal better without these products.

It is important to use the right pruning tool for the size of the stem, branch, or cane. Invest in a good pair of hand pruners (also called pruning shears or secateurs) that are comfortable for *your* hand. High-end pruners come in sizes to fit delicate or burly hands. Bypass pruners cut cleaner than anvil-type pruners. Hand pruners work well on branches up to ½-inch in diameter. For branches up to 1-inch in diameter, use long-handled loppers. A fine-toothed saw like a Japanese handsaw is best for larger branches. Wear gloves to protect your hands.

WHY PRUNE?

To *repair injury*—anytime. For example, jagged stubs from a broken branch can be dangerous to passersby and may provide an entry for disease and insects.

- Make a clean cut near the base of the branch, flush with the branch bark collar. To *remove disease and insect problems*—anytime. If a tree or shrub has a fungal disease (canker, blackspot, and so forth) prune out (and destroy) the infected limb.
- Cut back to within an inch of the base of the limb, flush with the branch bark collar.
- Disinfect tools between cuts with rubbing alcohol or a solution of 1 part bleach to 9 parts water.

The best time to prune trees is when they're dormant. Prune in late winter, and you can repair any winter damage at the same time as you prune to maintain structure.

To *train a young tree* and establish its framework. Wait two to four years before beginning training. Until then

- Only remove damaged or diseased wood.
- Thin crowded branches.
- Eliminate crossed or rubbing branches.
- Cut off a competing branch to establish a single leader if necessary.
- Remove parallel branches.
- Prune out excess branches so remaining ones are well spaced around the trunk and from the top of the tree to the bottom. You want an all-over form with branches that are more horizontal than vertical.
- Once the tree is trained, it will need minimal pruning.

To *maintain the strong, healthy, and attractive structure of an established tree.*

- Remove dead or damaged branches.
- Eliminate crossed branches.
- Remove water sprouts (narrow shoots that grow upright from a branch) at their base.
- Remove multiple branches coming out of the same spot on the trunk.
- Remove suckers (narrow shoots coming up from the base of the tree) at their base.

TREES

HOW TO REMOVE A LARGE LIMB (OVER 2 INCHES IN DIAMETER)
Double cutting a large branch prevents a tear that may strip the bark down onto the trunk when you cut through the limb from above.

1. About 12 inches from the trunk, use a saw to undercut the branch about one-quarter of the way through.
2. Top cut the branch a short way farther out from the trunk. Cut all the way through the branch.
3. Remove the cut portion. Identify the branch collar at the base of the branch.
4. Cut the branch just beyond the collar. The tree will heal on its own.

PRUNING EVERGREENS

Prune evergreens to control size, remove damaged branches, and direct growth. Select the time and method of pruning that is best suited for the plants you are growing. To prevent browning, clip the tips when they are damp.

- **Arborvitae and yews:** Prune in spring before growth begins or in early summer after new growth has expanded. Prune back to a bud or branch. Keep the bottom of formal sheared hedges wider than the tops.
- **Junipers:** Prune in spring or early summer to control growth and keep the plant within bounds. These require little pruning when you select the right size and variety for the location. Cut branches back to sideshoots to cover cuts. Tip prune in summer for additional sizing.

■ *In spring, cut the candles (new growth on pine trees) back by one-half to two-thirds.*

- **Pines:** Prune in spring to control size. Pines send out new growth from stem tips once a year. Remove one-half to two-thirds of the expanding buds (candles). More severe pruning on stems that lack terminal buds will kill the branch.
- **Spruce:** Prune in spring before growth begins. Cut stem tips back to a healthy bud, making cuts at a slight angle just above the bud. Do not leave stubs that create an entryway for insects and disease.

SHRUBS

For shrubs, *when* and *how* you prune are important. A simple rule of thumb: prune spring-flowering shrubs, such as azaleas, rhododendrons, forsythia, and lilacs *right after they finish blooming*. If you prune them earlier, you cut off the flower buds and have fewer blooms. If you wait too long, the shrub will have set its buds for next year and you will cut them off. Prune summer- and fall-blooming shrubs in winter when they are dormant.

The *how* of pruning shrubs is a little trickier than the *when*. Match the type of pruning to the plant and your landscape goals. Some plants, such as cotoneasters and barberries, need very little pruning, while forsythias and lilacs need regular attention.

When pruning a stem, cut just above an outward-facing bud at a slight angle. This encourages an open center, eliminates crossed branches, and provides better air circulation.

REJUVENATION PRUNING

■ *Rejuvenate shrubs that flower on new wood by pruning them nearly to ground level in late winter or early spring.*

Some shrubs that bloom on new wood are marginally hardy. Cut them back to within several inches of the ground in late winter to early spring—before they start to grow. These include bluebeard, butterfly bush, many of the hydrangeas, and Russian sage. Leaving the stems in fall adds winter interest and helps protect the roots.

RENEWAL PRUNING

■ *Renew suckering shrubs (lots of stems at ground level) by cutting one-third of the older stems to ground level after their spring bloom.*

When a suckering shrub (one with many stems that come from the base of the plant such as forsythia, lilacs, and bridal wreath spirea) has become overgrown, and does not perform well, it's time for renewal pruning. In spring after it blooms, cut one-third of the older stems down to ground level. You can also prune back remaining stems by one-third if they are very overgrown. In three years' time, you will have pruned back all of the shrub and have fresh new growth throughout.

HEADING

■ *Control the size of the plant by cutting back individual branches (heading cut).*

This is the most basic pruning—cutting single branches back to control growth. Avoid creating crossed branches by cutting back to just above an out-facing leaf. Stagger cuts to slightly different heights to maintain a natural shape.

SHEARING

This method of pruning transforms shrubs into rectangular hedges or spheres of green (sometimes called meatballs and lollipops for their unnatural shapes that need continuous pruning, which often keeps them from blooming). This is less healthy for shrubs than letting them grow in their natural form. Instead of trying to change the shape of a shrub dramatically, choose a shrub that has the form you want instead, like the conical dwarf Alberta spruce and spherical littleleaf boxwood. Shearing is also done to maintain the shape of hedges. When pruning hedges, make sure that the top is narrower than the bottom. This allows sun to get to all plant parts.

THINNING

■ *Thin shrubs that have become overgrown by cutting individual branches down to a crotch.*

Thinning helps to control the size of the shrub, opening it up while keeping its natural shape. Unlike renewal pruning, do not cut down to the base of the plant. Instead, cut branches down to a crotch. Again, you can remove one-third of the branches each year over a three-year period.

WHEN TO PRUNE COMMON SHRUBS

- **Barberry:** Prune in spring before growth begins. Slow growing; remove only damaged and diseased stems to ground level.
- **Bluebeard:** Prune in late winter. Cut back to several inches above the ground.

- **Burning bush:** Prune when dormant. Requires minimal pruning; selectively remove vigorous growth to major side branches to maintain the desired size and shape. Do not use renewal or rejuvenation pruning on this shrub.
- **Butterfly bush:** Prune in late winter or early spring before growth begins. Cut back to 3 to 4 inches above ground level.
- **Cotoneaster:** Prune in spring before growth begins. Slow growing; remove only damaged and diseased stems to ground level.
- **Dogwood:** Prune when dormant. Cut old and discolored stems of the suckering type to ground level.
- **Forsythia:** Prune after flowering. Finish pruning by early June so it has time to set flower buds.
- **Honeysuckle:** Prune when dormant. Renewal prune to encourage new growth at the base of the plant. These tough shrubs will tolerate rejuvenation pruning back to several inches above ground level. Consider removing invasive species (including Japanese honeysuckle) from the landscape.
- **Hydrangea:** *Snowball types:* Prune in winter down to ground level. Wait until late winter to enjoy the dried flowers in the winter landscape. *PeeGee hydrangeas:* Prune when dormant. Often trained into small trees or specimen plants. Regular pruning is not needed but improves flowering. Cut back to the first set of healthy buds above this framework.
- **Lilac:** Prune after flowering. Blooms on old wood. Remove old flowers to increase next year's display. Prune one-third of the older branches back to ground level to encourage fuller growth at the base of the plant.
- **Rose-of-Sharon:** Prune in late spring. Remove dead branches and prune out dead tips to healthy buds or sideshoots.
- **Serviceberry:** Prune in late winter or just after spring bloom. Can be trained as multistemmed large shrubs or small trees. Do minimal pruning once the main stems are selected. Prune suckering varieties like forsythias.
- **Spirea:** Prune *spring-flowering* bridal wreath/Vanhouttei spirea right after it blooms. Remove flowering tips to improve next year's flowering. Remove one-quarter of the older stems to ground level on established plants. Older, overgrown plants may be slow to respond to rejuvenation pruning. Prune *summer-flowering* Anthony

Waterer, Japanese, Bumald, and others when dormant. Wait until late winter if you want to enjoy the winter interest provided by the chestnut brown stems and dried flowers.

- **Viburnum:** Remove old, damaged, and unproductive branches to ground level.

ROSES

Without pruning, most roses would become a jungle of tangled stems bearing fewer and smaller flowers—like the wild roses at the edges of woodlands. Cutting off dead or broken stems, removing faded flowers, or snipping long stems with fresh flowers to enjoy indoors are all forms of pruning.

To gain confidence with pruning, practice on a dead branch. Make a 45-degree cut ¼ to ½ inch above an outward-facing bud, leaf, or branchlet. If the practice branch is bare, make some dots on it with an indelible marker; use them as pruning guides.

By pruning, you can remove diseased or dead wood and train a plant to grow so that the crown area is as open as possible, allowing for optimal air circulation. If you are pruning to remove disease (blackspot, powdery mildew), dip the pruners in isopropyl alcohol or a solution of 1 part bleach to 9 parts water between each cut. Wipe your hands and pruners well with alcohol when you have finished working on a diseased plant and are moving on to another—healthy or diseased—to avoid spreading the problem to other plants.

Wait until late winter/early spring—when the plants are still dormant—to do major pruning.

■ *Prune roses by cutting just above an outward-facing bud or five- to seven-leaflet leaf. This opens the center and improves air circulation.*

Floribunda, hybrid tea, grandiflora, and miniature roses respond to a good dormant pruning, rewarding you with a healthier, more floriferous plant. As you prune, look for bud eyes—small nubs on the stems. They can be a bit hard to see in the early part of the season, but once the plant is growing, they are easily found in the crotch between the leaf attachment and the stem. Always prune at a 45-degree angle just above an outfacing bud or leaf; each bud can produce up to three branches. You can cut these roses down as low as 8 to 12 inches, if necessary, when they are dormant. Shrub roses and climbers only need minimal pruning to keep them in shape.

What many folks don't realize is that pruning encourages new growth. When you cut back the faded blooms of many modern roses (wait for the last in the cluster to finish blooming), you are often rewarded with a new flush of flowers. Whether pruning or cutting a bloom, make the cut just above an outward-facing five- to seven-leaflet leaf at a 45-degree angle. This makes the new branch grow *outward* from the shrub, rather than crowding the center.

VINES & GROUNDCOVERS

Unless otherwise noted, after planting, prune to train young stems to climb their support.

- **Bittersweet:** Prune in winter or early spring to control size. Cut overly long shoots back to three to four buds from the main stem. Prune large shoots to 12 to 16 inches above ground level. Do not overprune, which stimulates excess growth that will require additional pruning.
- **Boston ivy:** Prune when dormant to control growth and keep within bounds. Remove or shorten any stems that are growing away from the support. Renovate overgrown plants by pruning them back to 3 feet of the base. Wear a leather glove to rub dried suction pads off the support.
- **Clematis:** Prune to control growth, encourage branching near the base of the plant, and improve flowering. The type of clematis determines the timing and type of pruning it requires. *Spring-blooming clematis*, including 'Frankie', 'Markham's Pink', and 'Rosy O'Grady', bloom on old wood.

Prune right after they finish blooming. *Repeat-blooming clematis*, such as 'Bees Jubilee', 'Henryi', 'Nelly Moser', and 'The President', bloom on old and new growth. Prune dead and weak stems back to a healthy stem or ground level in late winter or early spring before growth begins. Prune the remaining stems back to a pair of strong buds. *Summer and fall-blooming clematis*, including Jackman clematis, 'Niobe', and sweet autumn clematis, bloom on new growth. Prune in late winter or early spring before growth begins. Cut dead stems down to ground level and the remaining stems back to 6 to 12 inches.

- **Climbing hydrangea:** Prune after it flowers. For young plants, limit pruning to broken and damaged branches. These slow-growing plants do not need formative training. For established plants, prune overly long shoots and outward-facing stems. They require little pruning.
- **English ivy (*groundcover*):** Prune in early spring. For established plants, use a mower or hedge shears to control growth (winter often does this chore). In that case, cut off dead tips.
- **English ivy (*vine*):** Prune in late winter or early spring. After planting, pinch back weak stems to encourage new growth. For established plants, remove dead tips and stems killed over winter. This is usually the only pruning that is needed. Cut any wayward growth back to a healthy bud. Prune back within the plant to hide the cut.
- **Five-leaf akebia:** Prune after flowering. Follow the pruning guidelines for hardy kiwi.
- **Hardy kiwi:** Prune in late winter or early spring. After planting, cut back to strong buds about 12 to 16 inches above the ground. Train five to seven strong shoots on the support. Next spring, prune stout sideshoots (laterals) by one-third and weak laterals back to one or two buds. For established plants, shorten growth by one-third to one-half to control its size. Occasionally remove an old stem to ground level. This stimulates new growth at the base of the plant.
- **Honeysuckle:** Prune in early spring. After planting, cut back young plants by two-thirds. This encourages strong shoots to develop at the base of the plant. Next year, select strong shoots to form a framework. Remove other shoots. For established plants, prune out the tips of shoots that have reached the desired height. Cut off

overly long shoots to healthy buds. Renovate overgrown plants by pruning stems back to 2 feet above the ground. Thin the new growth as needed.

- **Trumpet vine:** Prune in late winter or early spring. After planting, prune all stems back to 6 inches above ground level. Remove all but two or three of the strongest shoots. Train these stems to the support. Allow the framework to develop over the next two to three years, or until the plant fills the support. For established plants, prune yearly to control growth. Remove weak and damaged stems to the main framework. Cut the sideshoots back to two or three buds from the main stems forming the framework. Prune out dead main branches to the base. Train the strongest shoot to replace it. Renovate by cutting all growth back to 12 inches off the ground.
- **Virginia creeper:** Prune when dormant to control growth and keep within bounds. Remove or shorten any stems that are growing away from the support. Renovate overgrown plants by pruning them back to 3 feet of the base. Wear a leather glove to rub dried suction pads off the support.
- **Wintercreeper (*groundcover*):** Prune in early spring. Cut established plants back to 4 to 8 inches to encourage vigorous, dense growth. Use a hedge clipper or mower (on its highest setting) for large plantings.
- **Wintercreeper (*vine*):** Prune in mid- to late spring. For young plants, tip prune to encourage fuller growth. For established plants, remove old and dead wood. Train new growth to cover the support.
- **Wisteria:** At planting, cut back the main stem (leader) to a strong bud 30 to 36 inches above ground level. Train two strong sideshoots (laterals) over the fence, trellis, or arbor. Next spring, prune the leader back to 30 inches above the topmost lateral branch. Shorten the laterals by one-third of their total lengths. Select another pair of laterals to grow and help cover the trellis. Next winter, cut the leader back to 30 inches above the uppermost lateral. Then prune all the laterals back by one-third. Repeat each winter until the plant reaches full size. Prune established plants in early summer right after flowering. Cut offshoots (small branches) back to within five or six buds of a main branch.

Glossary

Acid soil: soil with a pH less than 7.0. This is often found in regions with high rainfall. Most garden plants thrive in a slightly acidic soil with a pH between 6.0 and 7.0.

Alkaline soil: soil with a pH greater than 7.0. Sometimes called sweet soil. Limestone (or concrete leaching from a house foundation) can contribute to alkalinity. Much of the prairie and plains region has alkaline soil.

All-purpose fertilizer: powdered, liquid, or granular fertilizer with a balanced proportion of the three key nutrients—nitrogen (N), phosphorus (P), and potassium (K). It is suitable for maintenance nutrition for most plants. 10-10-10 is an all-purpose, balanced fertilizer.

Amend: the addition of organic matter (compost, leaf mold, manure, etc.), minerals, or other matter, such as builder's sand, to improve the soil.

Annual: a plant that lives its entire life in one season. It is genetically determined to germinate, grow, flower, set seed, and die the same year. In our region, there are numerous plants that are perennial in warmer climates that we grow as annuals. Rightfully these should be called "tender perennials."

***Bacillus thuringiensis* (Bt):** a biological insecticide (which can kill good and bad insects) that, when sprayed at the right stage of an insect's growth, can control caterpillars, cabbageworms, and mosquito larvae. Another species *B. papillae*, more commonly known as milky spore disease, is used to treat Japanese beetles and other grubs.

Backfill: the soil that is put back into a planting hole after the plant has been positioned. This soil may be native (as is) or amended.

Balled and burlapped: a tree or shrub grown in the field, dug up, and had its rootball wrapped with protective burlap (cloth or plastic) and twine.

Bare root: a dormant plant that has been packaged without any soil around its roots. (Young shrubs, trees, roses, and sometimes perennials bought online or by mail order arrive with their exposed roots covered with moist peat or sphagnum moss, sawdust, or similar material, and wrapped in plastic.)

Beneficial insects: insects or their larvae that prey on pest organisms and/or their eggs. They may be flying insects, such as ladybugs, parasitic wasps, praying mantis, and soldier bugs, or land dwellers such as spiders and ants.

Bicolor: a flower or leaf which is comprised of two colors; in leaves, this is often called *variegation*.

Biennial: a plant that takes two years to complete its life cycle; it sprouts and grows the first year, flowers, sets seed, and dies the second. Many reseed (foxglove, hollyhock), so seem perennial.

Blackspot: a fungal rose disease that manifests itself as small black spots on the leaves. Leaves turn yellow and fall off. It may also infect the canes or branches.

Bones: the hardscape of a garden; the background that provides the structure; all non-plant material in the garden.

Bt: see *Bacillus thuringiensis*.

Bud: a small swelling or nub on a plant that will develop into a flower, leaf, or stem.

Bud union: the place where the top (tender) variety of a plant was grafted to the hardier rootstock; on roses this "knob" is near the base of the stem. In this region (except Zone 8), plant the bud union 2 inches below soil level.

Cane: a long, pliable stem, such as a grape or raspberry; commonly one of the main stems of a rose.

Canopy: the total overhead area of a tree including the branches and leaves.

Climber: a plant with the ability to wend its way upward, whether by tendrils, rootlets, adhesive pads, or twining stems; needs to be planted near a support.

Cold hardiness: the ability of a perennial plant (including trees, shrubs, and vines) to survive the winter cold in a particular area.

Complete fertilizer: powdered, liquid, or granular fertilizer with a balanced proportion of the three key nutrients: nitrogen (N), phosphorus (P), and potassium (K). 10-10-10 is a complete fertilizer.

Composite: 1. a flower, such as sunflower, black-eyed Susan, and daisy, that is actually composed of many tiny flowers. Typically, there are flat clusters of tiny, tight florets, surrounded by wider-petaled ray florets. Composite flowers are highly attractive to bees and beneficial insects. **2.** a daisylike flower.

Compost: organic matter that has undergone progressive decomposition by microbial and macrobial activity until it is reduced to a spongy, fluffy texture. Added to soil of any type, it aerates the soil and improves drainage and fertility. Every gardener should be making his or her own compost, no matter how small the garden.

Compost tea: liquid fertilizer made by steeping compost in water—several days is ideal; good for general watering or foliar feeding.

Conifer: a tree or shrub with needlelike leaves that forms a cone that holds the seeds. Most (hemlocks, pines, cedars) are evergreen, but a few (larch, dawn redwood, bald cypress) are deciduous.

Container-grown: a plant that has been grown from seed or cutting in a container, usually at a nursery (as opposed to a plant that is dug up from the ground and put into a container with soil).

Corm: the swollen energy-storing structure, analogous to a bulb, under the soil at the base of the stem of plants such as crocus and gladiolus.

Crotch: the place where a major stem or branch of a shrub or tree joins the trunk.

Crown: the base of a plant at, or just beneath, the surface of the soil where the roots meet the stem(s).

Cultivar: a hybrid plant variety (CULTIvated VARiety) that is only reproduced vegetatively (from cuttings) or inbred seed. It was selected for particular desirable qualities. In a plant name, the cultivar name is always denoted within single quotes, such as a specific lilac: *Syringa vulgaris* 'Scentsation'.

Cutting: **1.** a method of propagation in which a portion of the stem is cut from the plant and induced to produce roots, eventually growing into a plant on its own. **2.** the part of a plant cut off from the parent plant that is treated so it produces roots and becomes a plant itself.

Dappled shade: the pattern of light cast by trees with branches open enough to let light pass through their leaves, branches, or needles.

Deadhead: to remove faded flowerheads from plants to improve their appearance, prevent seed

production, and stimulate further flowering. May be done manually or by pruning. Deadheading, however, will remove seeds that some birds and other animals use as a food source.

Deciduous: trees and shrubs that drop their leaves in fall and send out new leaves in spring. Plants may also drop their leaves in order to survive a prolonged drought.

Desiccation: drying out of foliage tissues, usually due to drought or wind.

Dieback: a stem that has died, beginning at its tip and continuing inward, most often caused by cold temperatures; may also be a result of insufficient water, insect attack, nutrient deficiency, or injury.

Dioecious: male or female flowers are on separate plants (holly and kiwi, for example). A plant of each sex is necessary for fruiting.

Disk flower: the center of a composite flower, composed of tightly packed florets. This is the center of a daisy, black-eyed Susan, purple coneflower, and other flowers.

Division: the practice of splitting apart perennial plants to create several smaller-rooted segments. The practice is useful for controlling the plant's size and for creating more plants; it is also essential to the health and continued flowering of certain perennials.

Dormant: the state in which a plant, although alive, is not actively growing. For many plants, especially deciduous ones, this is in winter. A survival method for cold or drought. Spring-blooming bulbs are dormant from summer through winter.

Drip line: the area underneath the farthest-reaching branches of a tree that receives water from rain dripping down from the leaves and branches.

Dwarf: a naturally occurring smaller version of a plant, such as a dwarf conifer. The dwarf is small in relation to the original plant, but is not necessarily diminutive in stature.

Established: the point at which a newly planted tree, shrub, flower, or any type of plant begins to produce new growth—either leaves, flowers, or stems. This indicates that the roots have begun to grow and spread.

Evergreen: perennial plants (woody or herbaceous) that do not lose their foliage every year with the onset of winter. Needled or broadleaf foliage will persist and continue to function on a plant through winter, aging and dropping unobtrusively in cycles of three or four years or more.

Fertilizer: a substance that is used to feed a plant; may be liquid, granular, or powder form.

Firm: to gently press the soil down around a plant with your hands—never feet—after planting in order to eliminate air pockets.

First frost date: the date in fall before which it is *unlikely* that the temperature will drop below 32 degrees Fahrenheit.

Floret: a tiny flower, usually one of many forming a cluster, that comprises a single blossom.

Foliar: of or about leaves.

Foliar feed: spraying the leaves with liquid fertilizer (often kelp or fish emulsion, but may be another liquid fertilizer diluted according to package directions); leaf tissues absorb liquid directly for fast results, and the soil is not affected.

Germinate: to sprout. Germination is a fertile seed's first stage of development.

Graft: the area on a woody plant where a plant with hardy roots was joined with the stem of another plant—often one that is less hardy. Roses are commonly grafted. Some plants, such as members of the apple family, may be grafted onto a different plant, such as an apricot onto a peach. This technique is often used to produce dwarf plants.

Hardscape: the permanent, structural, non-plant part of a landscape, such as the house, wall, shed, garage, pool, patio, arbor, and walkway.

Heel in: temporarily plant bare-root trees, shrubs, or perennials until they can be planted in a permanent location. Set plants at an angle in a shallow trough so their roots are covered with lightly moist soil.

Heirloom: a non-hybrid, open-pollinated plant that has been in cultivation for more than 50 years. These are often vegetables and flowers that have been passed down from generation to generation as seeds and brought to the United States by immigrants.

Herbaceous: plants having fleshy or soft stems that die back with frost; the opposite of woody. Annuals, biennials, most perennials, many herbs and edibles are herbaceous.

Hybrid: a plant that is the result of intentional or natural cross-pollination between two or more plants of the same species, variety, or genus.

Last frost date: the date in spring after which is it *unlikely* that the temperature will go below 32 degrees Fahrenheit.

Leaflet: the leaflike parts that make up a compound leaf, as on a rose, for example.

Mulch: a layer of material put over bare soil to protect it from erosion, slow the evaporation of water, modulate soil temperature, prevent the soil from heaving due to thawing and freezing in winter, and discourage weeds. It may be inorganic (gravel, turkey grit, sand, or fabric) or organic (wood chips, shredded bark, pine needles, chopped leaves, compost, etc.). Mulch is usually put around and between plants.

Naturalize: 1. to plant seeds, bulbs, or plants in a random, informal pattern as they would appear in their natural habitat; 2. to adapt to and spread throughout adopted habitats by self-sowing or other methods (a tendency of some non-native plants; a sought-after trait in bulbs).

Nectar: the sweet fluid produced by glands on flowers that attract pollinators such as honeybees and hummingbirds, for whom it is a source of energy.

Neem oil: derived from the seeds of the Indian neem tree, it can be used as a pesticide, fungicide, and pest repellent. It does not affect bees, pollinators, birds, fish, or wildlife.

Neutral soil: soil with a pH of 7.0. It is neither acid nor alkaline.

Organic material, organic matter: any material or debris that is derived from plants. It is carbon-based material capable of decomposition and decay.

Peat moss: organic matter from peat sedges (United States) or sphagnum mosses (Canada), often used to improve soil texture. The acidity of sphagnum peat moss makes it ideal for boosting or maintaining soil acidity while also improving its drainage. It also helps hold moisture.

Perennial: a flowering plant that lives over two or more seasons. Many die back with frost, but the roots survive winter and generate new stems in the spring.

pH: a measurement of the relative acidity (low pH) or alkalinity (high pH) of soil or water based on a scale of 1 to 14, with 7 being neutral. Individual plants require soil to be within a certain range so dissolved nutrients are available to them.

Pinch: to remove tender stems and/or leaves by pressing them between thumb and forefinger. This pruning technique encourages branching, compactness, and flowering in plants, or it removes aphids clustered at growing tips.

Pollen: the yellow, powdery grains in the center of a flower. A plant's male sex cells that are transferred to the female plant parts by means of wind, insect, or animal pollinators to fertilize them and create seeds.

Potbound: the condition of a plant that has been confined in a container too long, its roots having been forced to wrap around themselves and even swell out of the container. Successful transplanting or repotting requires untangling and trimming away of some of the matted roots.

®: the registered symbol denotes a trademarked or patented plant. It is illegal to propagate these plants.

Ray flower: a flat petal-like floret in a composite or daisylike flower. The ray flowers surround the central disk flower.

Rhizome: a swollen energy-storing stem structure, similar to a bulb, that lies horizontally in the soil, with roots emerging from its lower surface and growth shoots from a growing point at or near its tip, as in bearded iris.

Rootbound: another term for potbound.

Root flare: the transition at the base of a tree trunk where the bark tissue begins to differentiate and roots begin to form just before entering the soil. This area should not be covered with soil when planting a tree.

Self-seeding: the tendency of some plants to drop their seeds—or have the wind scatter them—freely around the garden. These plant, often annuals and biennials, will come back year after year, as in cosmos, hollyhocks, and cleome.

Self-sowing: another term for self-seeding.

Semi-evergreen: a plant that remains evergreen in a mild climate but loses some or all of its leaves in a colder one.

Shearing: a pruning technique whereby plant stems and branches are cut uniformly with long-bladed pruning shears (hedge shears) or hedge trimmers. It is used when creating and maintaining hedges and topiary; also used to cut back the spent flowers and some of the foliage from some annuals and perennials such as dianthus and creeping phlox.

Sidedress: apply fertilizer on the soil near the roots of a plant or between rows of plants. Usually refers to fertilizing edibles.

Slow-acting fertilizer (slow-release fertilizer): fertilizer that is water insoluble and releases its nutrients gradually. Typically granular, it may be organic or synthetic.

Succulent growth: the sometimes undesirable production of fleshy, water-storing leaves or stems that results from over-fertilization.

Sucker: a new growing shoot. Underground plant roots produce suckers to form new stems and spread by means of these suckering roots to form large plantings, or colonies. Some plants produce root suckers or branch suckers as a result of pruning or wounding.

Tamp: when sowing a seed or putting a plant in the ground, the act of gently pressing on the soil with the palms of your hands to make contact of seed and soil, and to help eliminate air pockets.

Tender perennial: a plant that is perennial in warm climates (usually Zones 8 to 11) that cannot survive below-freezing temperatures of winter. These plants are grown as annuals in cold-weather regions.

™: the trademark symbol denotes a patented plant. It is illegal to propagate these plants.

Topdress: apply fertilizer on a lawn or on top of the soil.

Tuber: a type of underground storage structure in a plant stem, analogous to a bulb. It generates roots below and stems above ground (as in dahlias).

Variegated: having various colors or color patterns. The term usually refers to plant foliage that is streaked, edged, blotched, or mottled with a contrasting color, often green with yellow, cream, or white. Usually two different colors, less commonly three or more.

Index

Meet Cathy Wilkinson Barash

Cathy Wilkinson Barash is a lifelong organic gardener. From childhood, Cathy has held a firm belief in economy of space and time in the garden by planting edibles among ornamentals. A garden designer whose designs have been published nationally, Cathy specializes in low-maintenance and edible landscapes.

Cathy is the author of 13 books, and is a successful photographer, nationally acclaimed speaker, and avid cat lover. She is the author of *Edible Flowers: From Garden to Palate*.

Cathy's other books include *Prairie & Plains States Getting Started Garden Guide*; *Edible Flowers: Desserts & Drinks*; *Evening Gardens*; *Choosing Plant Combinations*; *Month-by-Month Gardening in the Prairie Lands*; *Prairie Lands Gardeners' Guide*; *Roses*; *Taylor's Weekend Guide: Kitchen Gardens*; *The Climbing Garden*; *The Cultivated Gardener* (co-authored with Jim Wilson); and *Vines & Climbers*. Her writing and photographs have appeared in hundreds of books, magazines, and newspapers, including *Foodscaping*, *Cooking Light*, *Garden Gate*, *Horticulture*, *Woman's Day*, and the *New York Times*.

Cathy has been active in the Garden Writers Association (a group of more than 1,500 professional garden communicators) since 1988, served as president for two years, and in 2010 was honored as a Fellow.

A lifelong New Yorker (Long Islander), Barash moved to Des Moines in 1997. She is continuing to learn and grow, while in awe of the prairie and plains states weather, plants, gardens, and most of all, the gardeners.

Photo Credits